MY YEAR
WITHOUT
MATCHES

MY YEAR WITHOUT MATCHES

Escaping the city in search of the wild

CLAIRE DUNN

NERO

Published by Nero,
an imprint of Schwartz Publishing Pty Ltd
37–39 Langridge Street
Collingwood VIC 3066 Australia
email: enquiries@blackincbooks.com
http://www.nerobooks.com.au

The National Library of Australia Cataloguing-in-Publication entry:

Dunn, Claire, author.
My year without matches : escaping the city in search of the wild
/ Claire Dunn.
2nd edition.
9781863957212 (pbk)
9781922231534 (ebook)
Dunn, Claire. Rural women – Australia – Biography. Wilderness
survival – Australia. Urban-rural migration – Australia – Biography.
Country life – Australia. Rural conditions – Australia – Biography.
Australia – Rural conditions
920.720994

Dedicated to my parents, Bob and Pauline,
with my deepest gratitude

And to the Earth and all its wild inhabitants

SUMMER

*

Awaken your spirit to adventure;
hold nothing back, learn to find ease in risk.
Soon you will be home in a new rhythm,
for your soul senses the world that awaits you.
JOHN O'DONOHUE

*

THE SACRED ORDER OF SURVIVAL:

*1. **Shelter***
2. Water
3. Fire
4. Food

1.

thought I knew the forest until we moved in together. And then, as is often the case with flatmates, I realised I barely knew it at all. It had been an easy assumption to make. I was a forest campaigner; the forest was my life. All day every day it was what I spoke of, what I thought about, what I loved.

I knew its names and numbers – hectares lost, saved and under contention; species extinct, threatened and rare. I knew its borders and boundaries from luridly coloured harvest plans – straight lines demarcating logging compartments, riparian buffers, clear-fell zones. Computer logarithms revealed its inhabitants' most private figures – the length and breadth of their terrain, the short-falls in habitat needed to maintain viable future populations; their terminal diagnoses ruthlessly spat out in tables and percentages. Timber modelling software had informed me of the forest's weight and density in cubic metres and wood supply quotas. I could tell you the precise number of megalitres of water held back from catchments clogged with thirsty saplings, and list the Latin names of the frogs affected by creek siltation. I could even take you to the place by the harbour where the forest sat behind barbed wire, a mountain of chips waiting to be exported and made into serviettes and printer paper. It was the kind of knowledge that led me to believe I knew the forest intimately.

But now, standing in front of a blank canvas of bushland that is sizzling and spitting at me, contemplating how I might build a shelter with only natural materials that will keep me dry in torrential rain and warm in sub-zero temperatures for a year, I am suddenly aware how very little I know about the forest. I was its spokesperson yet didn't have a clue how to survive in one. I knew how many acres were cleared each week but would struggle to point out more than half a dozen eucalypts by name. I couldn't tell you what the first bird of the morning was, or which direction the storms rolled in from.

What I knew was "The Forest" – revered, magnificent, faraway. The Forest was vulnerable. It needed me. This, however, is the forest. Searingly hot and seemingly repelling me with every prickle it can muster.

"Don't forget to check for dead overhead branches," says Kate.

"And jumping-ant nests," laughs her husband, Sam. He swings one tanned and muscly arm around her waist as she sways from side to side with newborn Bella in a sling. Kate flicks her long brown curls back to smile up at him. They seem pretty chuffed that their long-held dream of offering Australia's first year-long residential wilderness-skills program is actually happening, their six guinea pigs about to be unleashed on the bush block they bought especially for the purpose.

Our mission is to build our own shelters, and gradually to acquire skills such as making fire without matches, hunting and trapping, tanning hides, gathering bush food, weaving baskets, making rope and string, moulding pottery, tracking, increasing sensory awareness, learning bird language and navigating in the bush. Visiting instructors will join Kate and Sam to teach a series of workshops over the first half of the year. Then we will be left to fend for ourselves.

The rules are few. Apart from no booze, we are limited to thirty days out of camp, and thirty days of visitors in. It is essentially to be a Choose Your Own Adventure story, with equal emphasis on experiencing the changing face of the bush and ourselves, over four full seasons. A cross between the reality-TV show *Survivor* and the solo wilderness reverie that American poet and naturalist Henry David Thoreau elucidated in his book *Walden*.

"Simplicity, simplicity, simplicity!" Thoreau had exclaimed in exaltation of his self-styled life as a forest hermit, words I had inscribed on the inside cover of my journal. To qualify for the program, all we had needed to do was study the basics over two week-long courses, and prove that our motivations weren't madness or law evasion.

"Madness" is a word that comes to me, though, as I do a swivelling glance at the hundred acres of baking scrubland that will be my home for the next year. And, by the looks on the faces of my new tribe members, it's a word they might be contemplating too. Even the routinely optimistic Nikki is slightly perturbed, which makes me feel better. She lifts her Akubra to wipe away the sweat gathering under her hatband, releasing a mane of blonde corkscrew curls. If it wasn't for the crow's-feet around her eyes, you wouldn't guess Nikki is the elder of our crew (at the ripe age of thirty-five). I've known Nik for a few years, but not well. She's the ultimate outdoorsy, go-getter gal. She's ridden a bike around Australia and hiked more trails than I could name, so she's a yardstick for me to measure how hardcore, fit and adventurous I am (or am not). She squats back on her lean haunches, quadriceps bulging, and scratches a stick in the dirt.

Chloe, swatting flies from her face, lowers herself down next to Nik. Under an enormous sombrero her pale cheeks are flushed pink, her mouth pursed. The blue cotton of her long-sleeved shirt is marked with dark patches under each armpit. She lifts the rim of her hat and catches my eye. I return her question mark with an eyebrow raise. Chloe was a good friend in the city, although she moved north a year ago. Seeing her again here feels like an odd mix of the familiar and the strange.

Ryan doesn't just look uncomfortable, he looks shell-shocked. This is hardly surprising given that he's just left blizzards at his Colorado mountain home. The baseball cap he wears barely shades his nose, his neck growing pinker by the minute. On his feet are a well-worn pair of Teva sandals, which seem to be part of the uniform for athletic Americans. Ryan's also a mate. We met while I was travelling in the United States a year ago, both taking the same course at a tracking and wilderness school. Knowing that this program needed six people to get off the ground, I had shamelessly head-hunted him. His dry humour and practical mountain skills, I thought, would be a great contribution. He is currently intent on staring at one featureless spot on the ground. Is he avoiding my gaze?

"What about snakes?" asks Dan, scratching a marmalade-coloured goatee. His dog, Jessie, pants laboriously at his feet, looking up at him pleadingly. Dan's right foot is jiggling continually, which is distracting. He folds his arms across a trucker's singlet and sighs. I look down to see "Follow Your Heart" tattooed under his thong strap in large calligraphic lettering. From our brief conversation, I've ascertained that Dan is on an escape mission from Sydney. A public servant for the last decade, he had been balancing boredom with a little too much of the high life in recent years, it sounded like. "I need something to ground me," he said. Dry you out, too, I thought. Well, you can't get much more dry and grounded than this. I'm a bit worried that apart from sharing the same age of thirty-one and a few favourite books, we mightn't find much in common.

"What about them?" snorts Shaun, the other wildcard. Hatless and shirtless, Shaun is either immune to the heat or trying out primitive sun protection. He shifts from foot to foot in a new pair of five-toed wet shoes, with more knives than a chef would use hanging from his belt. I've heard Shaun is only with us for six months before he leaves for the army. He stares out into the scrub, biting his top lip impatiently.

"Good luck," Kate says, giving us a wave in farewell for our shelter location hunt.

Stepping gingerly out of the paltry shade, I wander off in no particular direction, a lump of fear in my throat, in search of a place to call home.

*

I stick to the rutted four-wheel-drive track and follow it downhill to where the canopy of trees greens and thickens, pausing to look for a way in. The brush looks impenetrable on all sides. I sigh, and kneel down to crawl under the spiky bush hedge. The brush clears a little but remains thick. I push vines from my face and penetrate further in. It's cooler here than on the ridge. But there's winter to consider – six months away. My stomach suddenly tightens, as if gripped by a firm handshake. *One whole year.* What am I going to do out here all day? The grip releases a cloud of skittish butterflies.

I hear someone crashing off in the bush across the road, so it's too close. And where would I put a shelter in here, anyway? I'd have to knock down several trees first. I am pinned in by foliage. A wet, slippery sensation alerts me to two large striped leeches sneaking up my ankle. Others are closing in, their heads sniffing me out. I freeze. They freeze too. I'm going to have to make the first move. My decisive flick sends the first racer flying into a nearby bush. The second wraps around my middle finger like a slimy ring. I wave my hand madly in the air. It's no good, this sucker is on tight. Scraping my finger up and down the trunk of a tree, the leech falls with a plop onto the fern below, taking a layer of my skin with it. I scuttle back to the road before the next wave of cavalry descends.

"Simplicity," I mutter. Easy for Thoreau to say. He moved straight into a comfortable hut on the edge of a clear-water lake, only two miles from town, *and* he took his laundry home every week.

Back on the main trail, I trudge uphill until the scrub thins out, rubbing shoulders with stringybarks, dusty red termite mounds and unnamed spiky shrubs. The shrieks of cicadas are so loud my hands involuntarily rise to cover my ears. I try to remember the mud map of the property that Sam drew on the whiteboard. The boundary to the east is bordered by a creek – or river, if Kate had her way, the two of them spending a good ten minutes bantering about how to classify the modest water source. The bridge over it is our exit to the tarred road, highway, beach, civilisation. On the western border Sam sketched another waterway, no challenge this time when he wrote "Snake Creek" in neat letters under the squiggly blue line. Chloe and I shared a glance at that one, knowing well her snake phobia. Sam filled in the white space beyond that boundary with large slashed lines, indicating the sandstone cliffs that I had spied in the distance, and the start of a vast tract of national park. To the north and south are fire trails that demarcate our territory, although the private land beyond is largely uninhabited and, from what I could gather, can be considered part of our larger backyard.

I head in a direction that I think is south. Innumerable tracks criss-cross my path in differing states of degradation, some no more than vague depressions. So much for wilderness. This place has been trashed. It's sure not the kind of bush I imagined for my precious year of nature immersion. Judging by the map, it's the only stretch of bushland in the state where the west extends its jagged arm of dry sandstone down to the coast. I'm struck by a pang of homesickness for the place I had originally pictured: towering old-growth forest gums, clear mountain streams, soft grassy groves.

I know what Dad would say if he were here. He'd take off his wide-brimmed hat, give the top of his balding head a good scratch, screw up his nose and announce with derision, "Green-ant country." It's his euphemism for any land unfit for running cows, or human use of any kind. I smile at the thought of his standing here next to me, looking around with disdain. His sweeping judgment is usually my cue to argue the virtues of the land independent of any European sensibility of beauty or usefulness, but today it's comforting. Poor fella. I've really given him a hard time over the years, and yet he was right there for me a few days ago, wishing me luck on what he thinks is a crazy mission.

I had woken beneath the pink doona of my childhood and rose to watch the dawn sun cast spokes of gold onto the glossy black swans, perhaps offspring of the original swans that came to nest when my parents created the dam, in the year I was born. I packed the last of my things and turned back to wave at the two most familiar and constant figures in my life.

"Keep in touch," Mum called out, and then corrected herself, "I mean, we're here if you need us." Dad had one hand on the collar of the family border collie, who was straining to chase me out the gate. In my rear-vision mirror they looked frozen mid-wave, as if in a photo.

I stop centimetres short of a pebbly mound of giant ants. This isn't just green-ant country, try every-aggressive-and-oversized-ant country. Sweat rolls down my cheek and I wipe at it with the back of my hand, the smallest edge of panic lengthening my stride.

I follow one trail, my eye drawn to a large log in front of a clearing. It's still fairly shade deficient but could maybe make a reasonable home, with a bit of imagination. It'd be nice to have something to sit on. I step closer and something rustles. Something close. Something large. I force myself to look around, and another long rustle comes from inside the log. My heart urges a scramble to safety as I catch sight of the something. It's dark, shiny and tessellated, and emerging from within the hollow. A tongue flicks in and out. "No vacancy," it hisses. "Move on!" I manage to uproot my feet and take a few slow backwards steps before spinning around into a sprint. I crash through the bush, making as much noise as possible, propelled by the image of two black beady eyes chasing me.

Just as the sensible thought arises that maybe I should be taking more notice of the direction I'm heading in, I stumble out into a large disused quarry. I collapse against the single spindly tree in the middle to catch my breath. The sun bounces shards of glare from the quartz into my eyes. Damn, I didn't pack a pair of sunglasses. It's about the only thing I didn't bring. Nerves jangle like keys in my belly. I check back a few times to see if the snake has followed me.

The same nerves have been a constant companion in the last few months, a niggling question mark every time I let myself think about an entire year in the bush. If the goal was simplicity, the preparation was not.

First there was revenue raising. The initial cost of the program was $4000. It hadn't taken too much effort to save the $50 a week

I budgeted for food and essentials ($2600 for the entire year – was this possible?) The more difficult task was untangling the cords that held me to society: cutting some, tying off others, securing some down for the long hiatus. I was like a puppet realising for the first time the full extent of my attachment to the puppeteer. I justified the whirlwind speed and exhausted haze of preparation with a promise to myself that when I got there, *then* I could slow down.

There were trips to dentists, doctors, banks, mechanics, camping shops, shoe repairers and hardware stores. I did endless research on the nuances between brands of tools and equipment, and became the proud owner of my first hand-saw and hatchet. I gathered a selection of knives and sharpening stones, billies and camp ovens. I splashed out on some Merino wool clothes and a second-hand mountain bike. I invested in Australian field guides on everything from frogs to fungus ("field guide porn", I was told, apparently a common habit for budding naturalists), which joined the rapidly growing pile of second-hand books on every subject that I had been planning to educate myself in for years.

As quickly as I was getting rid of whatever belongings wouldn't fit in the few boxes stashed at my parents' place, I was being given bivvy bags full of every possible gizmo and gadget I might possibly need, from eel traps to camouflage army clothing, rehydration fluid to Chupa Chups (emergency sugar?). Apart from no firearms, drugs or alcohol, there were no limits on what to bring. Although I doubted I'd need the camouflage mozzie head-net, the multiple ponchos, the kaleidoscope of topographical maps, the guitar tuner, the waterproof tracking notepad, most of the field guides, the box of ten-year-old army rations, or the solar panel, the solid weight of *stuff* I was amassing helped to dull the creeping fear that nothing, not even three tubes of tinea cream, could prepare me for what lay ahead.

As much as I had always been a nature lover, running wild on the riverbank as a child, running feral in my early twenties for weeks at a time in forest protest camps, I still had no real reference point for what it would mean to spend a year in the bush, full time. Without a comfy couch and DVD to retreat to at the end of whatever muddy adventure I'd been on. Without a washing machine, a hot shower or music. Without matches. While I knew it wasn't going to be a *Man vs Wild*, scorpions-for-dinner affair, the privations were not inconsequential.

Was I going to cope without soft furnishings for a year? Without a kettle? A fridge? Was it naive to think I could go a whole year of lighting fires only with sticks? Perhaps I would be slowly worn down by the small things – no 3pm chai, no Thai take-out, no weekend paper. While still living in the land of cars and phones, it was hard to fathom what it meant for the bush to be home, not some place I went to sometimes for inspiration and dirt-under-my-fingernails fun. The *idea* of it sounded great, but as the moment loomed when idea would collide with reality, waves of doubt started rolling in, usually in the middle of the night.

It wasn't the encouragement of friends but the doubting of naysayers that was most helpful in keeping me to task. Their jokes about "Claire vs Wild" and *Lord of the Flies*, and their not-so-subtle hints that they would see me much sooner than I planned, switched on my stubbornness. I pushed the nerves aside and buried my head in the lists.

After all, I reminded myself, there was no plan B. This was it. Operation Freedom. One bold leap in the direction of peace, stillness, wholeness. If I couldn't find it here, I wouldn't find it anywhere. This had to work.

*

"COOOOOOO-EEEEEEEEEE!" The call to regather echoes off the gravel mounds. I'm too shaken to send the cooee out further, as we were instructed to do. A whole morning gone and not only have I not found anything worth calling home base, I've been told in no uncertain terms that I'm not welcome. I bet any decent spots have been taken now. I head back towards the Gunyah, camp central, eyes on my feet, my heart somewhere in that vicinity.

The Gunyah is a tin roof over a sawdust floor in the middle of a gravel clearing. The only other shelter on the property is the "kitchen" that Kate and Sam use when they run short courses – a smaller tin roof (on the edge of another quarry) that collects drinking water in a tank, and a few benches where we have stacked our bulk dry food and some wilting veggies.

The others are back already, the girls gathered around Sam, leaning in to gurgle over Bella, who has woken up.

"Okay, let's see these shelter sites," says Kate jovially. She's enjoying being on the other side of the equation, having spent a year in the woods a while back, at the tracker school where Ryan and I studied.

"I'm still looking for mine," I say, the only one it seems.

"Oh, really?" Kate looks surprised. "Well, I guess you've got 'til dusk."

Refilling my water bottle, I tag along at the back of the group. Shaun strides ahead, leading us to his site, or rather to his mound, set amongst the youngest, spindliest regrowth on top of the ridge. Shaun excitedly describes his plans to convert this pile of pushed-up quarry gravel into a grand treehouse. He clearly has more imagination than me. "I'm going to use these two trees as poles, sink two more poles in here," he says, jumping to the other side of the mound, "build a floor up here," indicating with a hand pointed way above his head, "maybe an underground storage space too." I can see images spilling out of his brain almost too fast for him to keep up with. I grimace enviously at his youthful confidence. Sam nods, masking a smile, I notice.

"Well, it's a bit bloody close," Dan says, hands on hips. He picks his way further west to what has to be the hottest spot on the property. Forgetting the proximity to his neighbour, Dan sweeps his arms wide to explain his vision of a sprawling homestead. "I'm going to put my kitchen here. I'm thinking a lean-to with bark guttering to collect rainwater, maybe with a detachable reed-matting shade curtain facing south-west to block out the afternoon sun. My fireplace, right here," he says, scratching out a circle in the leaf litter with his thong. Gushing with plans, Dan looks up at Kate and Sam for approval.

"And what about your shelter?" Kate asks, shielding Bella with her hand from the sun.

"Oh, yes," says Dan, "I'm thinking a square log-cabin number over here, you know, kinda *Brokeback Mountain*-style." He peals with laughter. Jessie mirrors his enthusiasm, jumping all over me. I push him away.

Trying to pin Nikki down is like trying to catch a falling leaf, so it's no surprise to see she has chosen a site with many escape routes, near the quarry I stumbled into. "It doesn't have as much shade as I would like ..." she says dubiously. That is one sizeable understatement. I crouch under the speckled shadow of a grass-tree. The real reason for her choice reveals itself in a loud cackle. "I really want to be close to my chooks, and thought the best place for them would be next to the garden," she explains. Chooks? A dog is bad enough, but chooks? I was picturing us going off on adventures, hunting and gathering food, not backyard farming. I assumed that everyone wanted the same thing from this year, but maybe not. The thought unnerves me.

Chloe takes us to several dead ends before finding her site nestled amongst the thick wet scrub near the creek.

"Well, you'll have a bit of clearing to do," Sam says, stating the obvious.

I pick a leech off my ankle. "You don't think it'll be a bit damp here in winter, Chlo?" I ask.

"Shade, I really wanted shade," Chloe says, her face flushed. "Maybe I'll incorporate the trees in my shelter, I don't know really." Her voice trails off.

"Hey, we're practically neighbours," drawls Ryan, as he leads us up the trail a little way and into his site. "It'll be one small sleeping room with a big verandah, kind of like a Queenslander," he says, already having picked up some of his host country's vernacular. Some of his considerations are not so sensible. "The fallen logs were the clincher – perfect for balance work." I look up to smile and catch his eye in recognition of the time we spent blindfold-walking across logs at the US wilderness school, but he makes a point of looking away. Okay, I'm not imagining it. He is avoiding me.

Maybe he's regretting his decision to come. I feel a bit guilty now, remembering how I described the land to him after the single orientation day I had spent here last winter. "It's got a great waterhole," I said (if you like brown billabongs); "The paths are sandy – great for tracking" (the topsoil has long blown away); "It's kind of open forest, so you don't feel so claustrophobic" (it's been hammered by logging and it's hard to find good shade). Spoken like a true shonky real-estate agent.

We walk back up to camp, the others joking together. I am quiet, aware that I'm the only homeless one. Sam clears the white-board and starts going through shelter design ideas as we munch on sandwiches.

I try to focus on the sketches, but can't. The muscles in my legs tense involuntarily. I knew this bit would be hard. Any time someone tries to show me something practical I seize up, too busy stressing out about not getting it to have any chance of actually getting it. Lashing knot – what's that? *Concentrate.* My eyes blur and the bread lodges in my throat. *Come on, get a grip; it's only the first day.* It feels like a week has passed already.

I tell the water welling in my eyes to dry up with some fierce blinks. Everyone else is intent on the lecture, taking notes and sketching. My chest tightens. Maybe I was kidding myself. Maybe I really can't do this.

I sink back onto the sawdust and close my eyes. The faintest of cool breezes caresses my cheek, releasing a strand of sweat-glued hair. I breathe in and let it out with a loud sigh. "Simplicity," I vaguely hear Sam say. "With primitive shelters, it's all about sim-plicity." There's that word again. The very sound of it echoes a sweet calm, like a pebble dropping into still water. I bob along in its ripple, remembering why I am here.

2.

'm lying on the floor of my office, staring blankly at the rainforest images flashing up on my screensaver, photos of the forest I am campaigning to protect. They zoom in and out just long enough for me to register a snatch of dripping green foliage, cold mist hovering above a clear, flowing creek, the slippery skin of a fist-sized snail. In one, a group of people join hands around an enormous trunk, their bellies pressed against its mossy bulk. They wear beanies and gloves, heavy hiking boots and daypacks. The image dissolves into a single figure standing atop a stump in the middle of a still-smoking clearfell.

I blink.

The blue carpet I lie on is thin and stained with splashes of coffee, the underlying concrete slab cold at my back. My body is at a slight angle, wedged between stacks of unopened boxes. Inside are thousands of fliers and postcards. "Stand Up for the Forests," they urge. *Stand up.* My limbs are pinned to the ground, as if held down by the weight of the boxes, the gravitas of their message. The hum of the computer grows loud in my ears and my eyelids droop.

I jump at the ring of my phone and fumble to take it from my pocket. Local ABC radio. Wanting a comment on the protest today, no doubt.

It's an election year. Following a tip-off that the prime minister, John Howard, was opening a building nearby, I had rallied the troops before dawn for a snap action. To the delight of the TV cameras, as his dark car pulled up, a *Lord of the Rings* "Ent" tree person extended a green gloved hand to greet him. I delivered the key campaign messages to the cameras as I had been trained to do – with a measured pace, pausing in between suitable sound bites, my tone rational and considered, never raised or shrill. Too much feeling is to be avoided; it makes you sound desperate.

My thumb hovers over the answer key. I really should take this. I try to clear my throat in preparation but it's clenched tight, as if blockading the sentences.

I can't do it.

I push the phone away. It vibrates and squirms on the carpet like a two-year-old in tantrum. *Stop*, I plead silently. *Stop asking me.*

My head releases back to the floor and I sigh deeply.

Words. I'm sick of them. Oh, I can play the role alright, deliver the radio grabs, create spectacles for the evening news. I can talk the talk, but that's all it feels like now. I'm a cardboard cut-out reading from the cue cards. It's a predictable script and an even more predictable ending. Politicians throw us a few tidbits to make it look like they're doing something, while business as usual continues and I'm left wrung out at the end of the greenwashing cycle.

Things aren't really going to change. I used to think that if people only knew, if they were shown what was going on with the forests, they would be as indignant as me. They wouldn't let it happen. It was just a question of ignorance and I could correct that. I could be the forests' messenger.

But I don't believe that now. I see how the words are deflected, shrugged off. There's just no space for them, no attention to spare. I spew the words out, hoping they will find a welcome place to land, to take root. But few do. How can I expect people to believe me when I don't believe myself anymore? I've become one of those pale-faced greenocrats – the ones who say the right words but have hollow voices, cut off at the stump from the very places that once inspired them. One of those people I vowed I would never become.

Right now, I'm too tired to care.

A few weeks ago I went to see a naturopath, worried about my flagging energy. "You could well be on the brink of chronic fatigue," she said sternly, writing me a list of supplements. I pictured myself tucked up in bed, a cup of tea and a pile of books on my bedside table. A broken leg might be even better – I'd be laid up for a couple of months. I couldn't believe I was thinking this.

My gaze falls on a column of photos pinned to the window frame, a messy album of the last decade. It rests on a close-up portrait of me, one corner ripped and curling. A necklace of threaded gumnuts hangs loosely around the neck of my rust-coloured woollen skivvy. Morning sun reflects the lighter streaks in my mousy brown hair, tousled from a night of sleeping rough. Gloved fingers wrap around a steaming mug, a wisp of campfire smoke curling from behind one shoulder. I look at the camera with my head slightly tipped, as if questioning, my eyes sleepy and soft. A smile plays at my lips.

I remember that photo being taken, almost eight years ago. Daniel was sitting behind me, our backs touching. Moments before, I had pulled the brown hoodie over his eyes as he quartered an apple in his hand, and laughed.

It was Daniel I fell in love with first, then the forest.

A friend introduced us. I had never encountered anyone like him, certainly not in my small-town upbringing, nor within the black-clad North Sydney crowd who were my journalism classmates. Instead of the cool apathy I was used to, he spoke quietly, passionately. He sang and danced without apology, showed me edible berries and named the wildflowers as we walked. He took me to my first logging operation. I stood next to him atop the remains of a brush box tree ringed with hundreds of years of growth, the sawdust still pungent and damp between my fingers. As I looked out over the field of stumps, a sharp pain shot up my legs and into my chest, where it became an ache of sorrow. I burst into tears and cried with the sudden realisation that we are destroying the very life-support systems we rely on. Daniel said nothing, but drew me to him.

I followed him to forests all over southern Australia, to where owls flew across starry skies as we lay huddled together in the leaf litter; to blockade camps, where we hung suspended like spiders from ropes high in the canopy as loggers swarmed below. He took my soft private-school hands and ground into them with dirt that couldn't be washed away.

When I finished university, the career goals of journalist and writer now seemed so flimsy. My blinkers had been removed, and I couldn't pretend I hadn't seen the destruction.

Daniel and I hatched a bold vision across rolls of butcher's paper. Together we would save the forests. We magnetised an ever-larger crew of activists and trundled out to logging coupes in beaten-up vans, documenting breaches in harvesting laws and finding the right noses to put them under. We ferreted in the dirt for koala scats and identified the V-notches left on trunks by yellow-bellied gliders. We talked with fiery eyes at rotary clubs and rallies, and staffed market stalls on our weekends. We shined our shoes and trawled the corridors of parliament and the press gallery. We were voices for the voiceless, for the creatures that howled and cackled around our campfires. It was the hardest I had ever worked, but I wasn't going to stop until we'd won. Which I had no doubt we would.

Daniel broke my heart not long before the government announced protection for the 65,000 hectares of forest between Sydney and the Queensland border that we had fought for. He told me his love was so large it could not be contained within one relationship, and that in fact it had spilled over already. I had won the forest but lost the boy. I went overseas, my backpack heavy with heartbreak and my parents' hope that I would return to the life they'd mapped out for me. I got as far and as foreign as I could. But still, sitting in the dry heat of the Syrian desert, I felt the wet tendrils of the forest tugging at me to return.

I was offered a paid position by the national environmental organisation that I had been volunteering for. It was perfect: I could assuage the guilt I carried about abandoning my career aspirations, as well as continue with my real vocation. I ignored the sticky feeling as I accepted the job, not wanting to acknowledge how tired I had been after the last campaign.

Everything changed once I was on the payroll. Gone were the spirited bush missions, the tribe, the magic. This was city campaigning by computer, sensible and sedate. The goals grew hairier as the ground crew grew thinner. Until it was just me. I tried to bring the magic back, upping the pace, working longer hours, telling myself what a privilege it was to have this job. I owed it to the members paying my meagre wage. I owed it to my parents, to the forests, to Daniel. To myself.

But the truth was I didn't feel passionate anymore. I just felt employed.

I shift and roll on to the other hip. The image from my dream a few nights ago flashes back. A white dove is soaring into a clear blue sky when a cage ensnares it, its journey thwarted. It's a gilded cage I'm living in, not just the job but my whole beautiful life: my fantastic friends, my boyfriend, the web of connections and commitments I am woven into.

It's just the *busyness* of it all. The relentless *onwardsness* of everything. Nothing's ever finished. Nothing ever stops. I fulfil one round of societal obligations and a new round begins. One guest leaves and another arrives. I tick something off my to-do list and another entry takes its place. The life that was once a consuming passion is now consuming me. I'm running around trying to keep all the plates spinning. If one topples, I know the rest will follow.

I could open the cage door at any time and fly out. But what else would I do? Who would I be?

I'm gripped by a sudden urge to kick off my shoes, walk out the front door and not stop until I feel the city streets turn to leaf litter under my feet.

*

"You need a break," my flatmate Jo said, noticing my staring out the window one morning a few months later, a bowl of porridge growing cold in front of me. She pushed a flier across the table. "Survival skills and nature awareness," I read.

I took Jo's advice and we signed up for the workshop together. When we arrived, Kate greeted us with a hug, wearing nondescript loose Levi jeans and a faded T-shirt. She glided rather than walked us over to where a small group crouched around a large wooden frame, rubbing away at what looked like an animal skin strung tautly across the rack with rope. Squatting down next to Jo, I stifled a giggle as she wrinkled her nose. The hide smelt like the day-old meat my brothers would use to bait yabbies. I scraped gingerly at one corner.

"Don't hold back," Kate said. "He's a tough old red, this one."

I leant into it, sprays of amber dandruff fluffing out into my hair and eyelashes.

Over the next few days, I learnt how to build a survival shelter from leaf litter, collected rainforest spinach down a wild creek, and had my first go at making fires from sticks. I pounded wattle seed for pancakes, sewed a corner of the hide into a pouch and slept by the fire. All thoughts of the election campaign and what I had to do that week vanished. When it came time for the much-whispered-about night stalking while blindfolded, I baulked. But an hour or so later when I emerged into the firelight, my whole body was electrically charged. I felt more alive than I could ever remember feeling.

On the final evening we gathered around the campfire, laughing and sharing stories. Kate shelled wattle seed while chatting with another woman. I watched her closely. She was attentive to the conversation but held herself back too, as if half of her was engaged somewhere else. Her presence intrigued me. She held a kind of unshakeable groundedness. A power. She seemed privy to secrets that I wanted to know. I casually took a seat nearby, eavesdropping as she told the woman about the year she spent in a primitive shelter in America, the thigh-high snow in winter, the rock-hewn hearth that she huddled next to during the long nights.

"I'm thinking of offering a year up the coast from here, if you're interested," I heard her say. I whipped my head around to find her dark eyes boring into mine.

Back at work the office felt stifling, my senses muffled and dull. I kept remembering the needle-sharp brush of fern against my thighs, every faculty pricked in anticipation as I searched blindly for the next step; and Kate staring at me with that presence of hers, inviting, challenging.

An entire year. What would it be like? I fantasised endlessly. No emails, no phone calls, no 5am media releases. No people to please or disappoint. No *Magic Pudding*-style refilling to-do list. No more feeling like the fate of a football field of forest rested in my hands that day. No more having to dress up in 10,000 different pretty ways the simple fact that we're fucking up the planet. No more having to remind myself to care that we're fucking up the planet.

Out there, just a summer breeze on my cheek, the palest of pink dawn skies, the raw truth of splinters in my hands, the scent of soot-soaked skin, the icy shock of the creek on a winter's morning. Out there, I wouldn't demand anything but would take only what was offered: the glimpse of a kingfisher feather in flight, a soft bed of grass on the forest's edge to lie on and watch the clouds tangle and release. Out there, things would be communicated not by words but by feel: string in my hands, bark against my skin.

What would life be like whittled down to the barest of essentials? If I was answerable only to earth, fire, water and air? If my responsibility to the forest was not as saviour or spokesperson, but merely to belong to it? One more creature resting under its broad wing?

I longed to know. I was terrified of knowing.

While the visible me smiled pretty for the cameras and electioneered with seeming gusto, beneath the surface a campaign of equal intensity was being mounted. The wild-haired revolutionaries came to me in dreams, three gypsy women swathed in layers of dark cloth, feeding me steaming bowls of broth from a bubbling cauldron, beckoning me towards them with long bony fingers. I would wake with their smell of ashes and earth in my nostrils, with the faint tracks of their muddy bare feet across my sheets.

What really needed saving here? Was I too busy "saving"

something else to see what was dying within? Something just as wild, just as threatened, something only I could save? I had been doing too much talking. It was time for me to listen to what the forest had to say. What *it* wanted me to do. To immerse myself in its culture, its language, its law.

But that was unrealistic, impossible. The time for wild adventures had passed. It was one thing when I was young, and another when all my friends were packing away their revolutionary caps and getting real jobs, marriage certificates, mortgages, babies. It was a time for consolidation, for settling. I'd be fine, after a break. If I could just get through this election and take a holiday, I'd be ready for the next fight.

*

The breeze has picked up since lunch and wafts over the scratches on my legs, making them sting afresh. It's less like pain now, just sensation. Tingling. I tune in again to the lilt of Sam's voice: "Pitch is of utmost importance." It takes me a few moments to realise he's talking about roof design. My head is spinning slightly, my breath deep and slow.

I sit up. Everyone is still taking notes. Excusing myself, I pull my hat down and walk out into the clearing. I head out towards an area of the property I haven't explored yet, the sweat trickling down my thighs. Wandering down a side trail, I stop and lean against a stringybark to scull some water. My gaze lands on a stand of old banksias. The pea green of their new growth sways gently, as if waving me over. Their trunks are pockmarked with age, one dripping with red sap, blood running down a single gnarled leg. Stooping to stand under their canopy, I suddenly feel as if I'm surrounded by a gaggle of bingo-playing women, picking up their skirts and fluffing them out above me at head height. The shade they offer is well endowed but not smothering. Two of the women have linked limbs, forming a natural archway that invites me into their feminine domain. I step through to find a perfect circular clearing bordered by three ancient scribbly gums, all politely pointing their bulbous branches away from me. It's like a secret cavern – spacious and yet protected, far enough away from camp to feel isolated. "Is this home?" I ask, with my eyes closed. *Wisha wisha wisha*, reply the leaves in the wind. I'll take that as a yes. Banksia Lane. My new home.

The sun drops quickly down the western slope of the horizon. With no-one to carry me over the threshold, I waltz my swag under the archway and roll it out under a banksia.

As I settle in for sleep, the forest starts waking. Feathered wings hum and whir in unison above me. There is a yelp, squeak and gurgle from a large hollow in one of the scribblies. I reach out and throw both sides of the canvas swag over me, burrowing in as far as I can, sweat gathering under my arms. Nice forest, good forest. Something scuttles next to my ear and something else crawls up my leg. "Ahh!" I yell, jumping up and swatting wildly in the direction of the crawly. "Get off!"

The bush suddenly darkens, as if frowning at my outburst, the bingo-playing arms morphing into long-nailed claws reaching for me. I don't want to get back in the swag but feel totally exposed out of it, a sitting duck who has just drawn unwanted attention to itself. The attention of what, though? Come on, there's nothing here. I shake out my sleeping bag, flash my torch around in false bravado and tentatively climb back inside, blinking up at the bush. *This is what you wanted.* A hundred invisible eyes bore into me. I squeeze mine shut. Damn, I thought I was getting better at this. It wasn't long ago that I would cross my legs rather than face the terror of stepping even ten feet away from human habitation into the bush at night to pee. I'd been working on it in the lead-up to this year, training as if for a marathon – making myself walk further, stay out longer, even going on a solo multi-day hike. And it had been getting easier. But this is no practice run, and I'm a twig snap away from dipping out.

A suspended light is coming towards me, getting larger. What the hell is that? My heart is sprinting.

"Helloooooo?" It's Nikki and Chloe, picking their way down my trail by torchlight. I drop to my swag in relief.

"We heard you yelling and thought you might like company," says Chloe, with bedding under her arm.

"Oh, it was just a spider," I say, hoping they don't catch the quaver in my voice. "But, sure, first-night slumber party, why not? What were you two doing skulking around together, anyway?" From their glance, I can tell Chloe doesn't want to admit she was fleeing the same night monsters.

Sleep still evades me as flying foxes arrive and throw a wild screeching party overhead. I may as well be in a noisy nightclub. And yet, beneath the bustle of the forest's peak hour, there is a deep calm, a thrumming silence I have been yearning for. I'm glad to be awake now. Just to soak it all in.

The half-moon bathes everything in a luminescent glow, our mozzie nets shining like bridal veils, the three brides lined up underneath, silently breathing, waiting, watching.

3.

"TIMBERRRR!"

The sapling creaks and sways but refuses to budge. I swing my foot up on its trunk and push as hard as I can. It gives an indignant creak but clings on. Stubborn thing. I force the saw back into the cut. The tree bites down on it so hard I can't get it out. In a contortionist act, I push one foot against the trunk again, while reaching between my legs to force a few more abrasions with the saw. I'm glad no-one is watching.

Despite the fact that my first word was "tractor", I have never been a particularly practical lass. Outdoorsy, yes; handy, not so much. With ballet, drama and tennis lessons, I couldn't really fit in DIY dolls-house building. Although Dad didn't bar me from the tool shed, it didn't cross his mind to teach me the workings of its greasy metal implements. The shed remained the shadowy domain of men's magic. Unlike my three older brothers, I was never privy to the nether regions of a lawnmower, never taught the Queenslander hitch to tie off a gate with a piece of eight-gauge wire, never shown how to deliver the punishing crunch to a steer's testicles (I was perched on a fence just out of view, covering my ears against the bellow that would ensue). While the boys were building billy carts, I was collecting flowers with my sister to make witches brews. When the boys were helping Dad build a retaining wall, I was helping Mum prepare lunch. Was I naturally not interested or was this falsely assumed? I don't have time to work it out now. I've got a shelter to build.

"TIMBERRRR!" I yell again, this time throwing my whole body against the thin trunk. It squeals loudly as it leans precariously to one side, releasing a sharp whip crack as the last of the fibres give way and it falls with a bounce onto the undergrowth. Sawing off the top branches, I hoist the log to rest on my hip and head for home like a proud hunter. The log marks a single drag line across the cleared circle I've made over the last couple of days. With the mattock as my bulldozer, I've peeled the bush back to a patch of earth that's the size I think my habitat needs to be. Just a few shrubs to go.

I've been surprised by how smooth the switch from tree hugger to tree feller has been. It's been made easier by the fact that I had to remove only two trees each the size of my thigh, and I plan to use them as building materials. But there has been an undeniable pleasure in the marking of my territory, the satisfaction of imposing some order on the chaos of the bush. Chipping up another shrub, I add it to the neat pile. I walk over with the mattock to the last remaining bush and squat next to it. It has nondescript small green leaves, spindly and spiky like most others. I went to remove it yesterday and felt uncomfortable, so thought I'd leave it for today. Crushing up the leaves, I breathe in their sharp tang. I don't know why, but I can't uproot it. Funny little thing. It makes my shelter site look like a bald head with a tuft of unruly hair sticking up – or two tufts, if you include the baby grasstree I've also left. I grab the folding shovel and begin digging another post hole.

I have a plan (of sorts) now. I tried doing some research before I left, finding one fantastic book on Aboriginal architecture, the only one in an otherwise non-existent genre. While it detailed shelters down to the placement of every stone, the relatively few east-coast examples were either temporary humpies or elaborate village-sized, palm-woven beauties from far-north Queensland. With still no concrete ideas for my real shelter, I've decided to cut my building teeth on the only model that I can actually visualise – a lean-to, with two tall front poles, two short back poles and a sloping roof. Simple. I'll sleep in it while my main shelter takes shape, then convert it to a kitchen. It'll be like living in the shed while the house goes up. The nearby paperbark swamps will provide the roofing. I reckon it'll take me a fortnight to knock up, giving me a good six weeks for my proper shelter (we're meant to finish our shelters within two months), which is plenty of time. Also, it gives me a chance to check out what the others are doing and borrow some ideas of what to do (or not to do).

As I'm methodically tamping down the soil around the last pole, I realise the Y-fork at the top is facing the wrong way. Two steps forward, one step back. I loosen the sand enough to twist the pole to face the correct way, the dark sweaty patch on my lower back broadening. I've been starting work not long after dawn, assuming I will want to knock off during the heat of the day, but I'm finding that most days I can push through. My movements become slow, as if underwater, swimming in the humidity rather than resisting it. It's almost pleasurable. It means I miss the midday group gossip down at the waterhole, but that's not such a bad thing.

Choosing the straightest pole from my clearing pile, I place it to fit between the back and front Y-forks, making a roof angle of about forty-five degrees. Forgetting the lashing knot Shaun showed me, I instead wind the rope around and around, securing it with a string of granny knots. If you can't tie knots, tie lots! Done. We're not allowed to use any metal in our shelters, but store-bought string is apparently admissible. I'll make primitive string for my real shelter.

I move straight on to digging the next hole. My arms are aching. Everything is aching, actually, but I'm loving the feeling of engaging my muscles, bending my limbs to a task. It feels so good, so natural, to be up and moving most of the day rather than sitting in front of a screen. My mind is just as busy as my body, entertaining me with a replay of events leading up to my departure. I'm catching up with myself, walking slowly back over the scenes that I didn't have space to really soak in, saying the proper goodbyes I didn't have time for.

Look at her go, she's checking the distance between the poles, good thinking. Now she's starting to dig the last hole. Let's hope there are no roots there. The commentator is another consistent companion, filling me in on exactly what I'm doing, in case I didn't know. Maybe it's a mental form of pinching myself that I'm actually here. I'm actually building my shelter – it's happening. I smile and pause mid-shovel to take it in. I can't imagine how different I'll be at the end of a year of this. Around the fire last night we took bets on who might leave early. I vacillated between Dan and Chloe. No-one guessed me.

*

"COOOOOOO-EEEEEEEEEEEE!" This is our version of a knock at the door. I give a slightly weaker cooee back. Shaun strides in, two climbing carabiners clinking on his belt. He cocks his head to one side, gauging how welcome he is.

"Just seeing how the backyard blitz is going," he says cheerfully. I think he's taken a bit of a shine to me, although he masks it with a brotherly concern for my shelter-building abilities. I stand back with him, surveying my baby proudly.

"Whoa, you've made those Y-sticks pretty small – you expect them to hold up a tonne of paperbark?"

My eyes narrow as I zoom in on the four poles responsible for holding up the entire structure. "What? They're wrist size, that should be okay, shouldn't it?"

The skeleton of my lean-to suddenly looks like Miss Piggy balancing on stilettos.

"Struts, she'll need struts on those beams." Struts? I trawl my mental dictionary for a word match. Shaun registers my confusion, picking up a stick and showing me the diagonal support idea.

"She'll be right," I reply brusquely, hurriedly applying them after he leaves.

Over the next few days I unleash my inner "Bob the Builder" – every knot an achievement, every problem solved a cause for celebration. I am the muttering master builder, brow furrowed, deliberating on architectural nuances. New neural pathways are being forged, bulldozing through the blocks that say, "You can't build," and replacing them with, "How about I use dried bangalow palm fronds to fill in the gap at the base?" *Brilliant*, replies the commentator. I start writing "Zen and the Art of Shelter Building" as I go.

Even though I'm not giving any thought to aesthetics, happy to have anything vaguely upright, primitive shelters are the original shabby chic. One morning Shaun and I return from a reconnaissance trip in his ute, down the road to an abandoned logging operation, with a treasure trove of wide and sturdy sheets of stringybark. I remember reading about the pioneers making roofing shingles out of them, but there aren't enough for that and the work's too fiddly. Three hours later, with a bit of digging and jigsaw puzzle play, I have walls (in the broadest definition of the word). On a whim, I leave one wall half open for the view. Grabbing a thick piece of flat wood that I found in the log dump, I trim it to fit on top of the half wall. Hello, breakfast bar. I picture myself sitting up to it in winter with a steaming teapot, spreading bush berry jam on homemade damper.

It's time for a roof. I'm grateful when Shaun offers to accompany me on my first mission into the swamps. I dip one new water shoe into the inky reed-choked waters. The cold swirls up to my shin, and I shiver despite the day's heat. One more timid step and I've entered another world, all sunlight rejected by the dense cover of the paperbarks. Rainbow lorikeets shriek and flap overhead. Sweet nectar fills my nostrils. The water deepens, swishing softly around the base of my knees. A giant spider hangs between two trees above my head. I duck unnecessarily and wade over to where Shaun waits, one hand on the machete strapped to his side. I'm conscious of mine bumping against my thigh. I smile involuntarily.

I've always loved paperbarks. I see them as a keeper of the waters, in a similarly revered role as the weeping willow occupies in Europe, but giving off a scent that is uniquely Australian – a summer storm after rain, the first breath of fresh air after a stuffy car ride. I love the grassy green of their slender leaves, which drip down in generous shady bunches along waterways and billabongs. I love the swirling mocha bark, peeling and frilled like a lacy skirt, full of cracks and crevices. As a kid I would write poems and letters on the bark. I love the way they unapologetically occupy an entire area, fully owning their niche, at home both with water up to their knees and with hard-baked sand around them. They are leaders, markers of weather and time – the oozing of rich nectar aboard their bottle-brush flowers signals the change in season from summer to autumn on the coast, drawing flocks of birds and bats at the first whiff of their annual beach holiday.

I've never before considered taking to paperbarks with a sharp implement, but here I go. Shaun and I silently signal to each other our first victims – the straightest, largest trees in the swamp. I place my hands on the bark, which feels tissue-soft on my fingertips. Sorry, I say silently, picturing my imagined roof by way of explanation. *Thwack*. I bring my machete down hard, making a horizontal incision across the top of my chosen piece. *Thwack*, a parallel cut down the bottom. I nervously stick my fingers in the crack, relieved when I feel the inner bark layer still intact. I don't want any ringbarking. *Thwack*. I wedge my fingers in the thin wound of the vertical incision and begin peeling back the skin. It lifts easily for the first few centimetres, then stops. The bark is stitched to the trunk by a mass of rootlets. I tug at a root. No give. I tug and pull and tug, my feet almost lifting off the ground. It snaps suddenly and I fall backwards with a splash, the bark ripped and hanging. Shaun hoots with laughter. The image I had of sheets of bark falling at my feet like wrapping paper sinks alongside me in the mud.

I move to a tree closer to Shaun. His dark curly hair is stuck to his forehead, his biceps pulled tight against his T-shirt. He's quite handsome, really.

I try a different tack with the roots this time, trying to pull each one through the bark without ripping it. A flock of lorikeets lifts up in a noisy cloud and departs. In their absence, I can hear the low creaks of frogs spread out over the reed beds.

"Hey Shaun," I say, easing the pressure off a rootlet just before it snaps, "why did you decide to do this year?"

Shaun leans forward on his embedded machete and looks up, as if struggling to remember. "Well, it all started with *60 Minutes* – you know, the TV show," he says, pausing to *thwack* the tree before continuing. "It was a story about a Danish prince who left his castle, carved himself a canoe in Polynesia, paddled to far-north Queensland and lived completely off the land for forty years. Well, I decided then and there that I wanted to build my own log cabin in the mountains and live in it."

"As you do," I say, my right arm disappearing under flapping bark.

"I calculated that I would need about $5000 for the gear and I didn't have a cent. So about a week later, I was walking near my dad's house and there was a blank envelope lying on the ground right in front of me, and, no joke, inside was $5065 – exactly the money I needed for gear and a bus ticket to the Snowy Mountains."

"Are you serious?" I stop, mid-rootlet removal. Shaun returns my stare with a quick smile and nod in my direction.

"I figured it must be for me," Shaun says, his voice thin as he strains up to the top of his bark slab. "So I bought all the gear I thought I'd need, managed to get my parents in the same room, played them the *60 Minutes* recording and told them I was leaving the next day.

"Mum put me on the bus and I got off in a little town, paid a taxi driver to take me as far into the mountains as he could and then started walking uphill. That night was absolutely freezing and I didn't have a sleeping bag. I realised I had bitten off way more than I could chew, so I rang Mum and got her to buy me a bus ticket home."

"What? You didn't buy a decent sleeping bag?" Having seen Shaun's collection of high-tech solar gadgets, I knew where the money went instead. Shaun doesn't answer.

"Well, after that, my parents nailed me into getting a job, and so for the last year I would leave the house in a suit, hide in the front yard, then change after they'd left and head out to a camp I had made in some bushland nearby."

"Ha – an urban bushranger!" I laugh, looking for signs that he is lying or joking but finding neither. "So when you heard about this, you just jumped aboard?"

"Pretty much," Shaun says, giving me his lopsided grin and sloshing off to find another tree.

I'm glad he didn't ask me the same question. All the reasons are still there, and I could probably articulate them, but now that I'm here, the story doesn't seem important anymore. Perhaps if he asks, I'll just tell him the dream I had the night I handed in my resignation: I'm walking through a forest, looking for "the power tree". I suddenly see it; it's the oldest and largest by far. I approach it slowly. Around the other side, a red-bellied black snake is curled at the base. It wakes up and begins to wind itself around my leg. I'm scared and push it back down. On a nearby rock ledge, I reach into a crack and pull out a stone tablet. There's an Egyptian symbol on it and a word carved across the top in large letters. The word is "FREEDOM".

In some ways it didn't feel like I'd really made a decision. It was more as if one day I turned over a rock to find a decision I'd made long ago, waiting for me.

*

After a couple of hours my arms are shaking with exhaustion, fine paperbark powder stuck like asbestos to my every moist and dripping crevice, my exposed skin shredded by mosquitoes.

"Come on, slow coach, the rains are coming," Shaun says, giving me an affectionate tap on the back. I run my fingers over the inner sheath of my last sheet. It reminds me of my grandmother's skin the last time I saw her.

She had fallen ill and I drove straight over, parking out the front under the pine trees I used to climb after school. The green hammock sat lifeless at the back door. It's where we would gather on winter afternoons, sun streaming down on us through the hydrangeas. I would lie, my head on her lap, and close my eyes, listening to the slow *click-clack* of her heels on the wooden verandah as she rocked, her fingernails on my back sending shivers up my spine. Gran was the only grandparent I'd ever known, but I hadn't needed any others.

At her bedside I watched her breath rise and fall in shallow spasms, her skin so translucent that the veins were blue rivers down her sunken cheeks. I smoothed back the fine wisps of white hair around her face and took her hand in mine. She opened her eyes, and said loudly, "Hello, darling." In that hour I was everyone to her but myself. Her mother, her daughter, someone she had never met before and shrank from, scared. Her breath grew more rapid.

"It's okay, Gran," I reassured her, patting the back of her hand as she gripped mine tightly. She travelled back through her ninety-nine years, plucking memories like fruit from a tree, the sweetest and best. Unearthing potatoes with her father from his prized veggie patch; clutching the mane of her pony as she rode to school each morning; the round, aproned form of her mother handing her the spoon from the Anzac biscuit batter to lick.

I prompted her to recall my favourite of her stories. How she had turned down the richest man in town to marry Papa, the young parish priest with the horse and sulky, who gave half of his modest stipend back to the church. The one about her Aboriginal nanny, Gracie, who liked to hide behind the curtain and listen to Gran play piano. Her voice squeaked with emotion telling me how she had waited for Gracie to arrive one morning, ready for her customary bear hug, but never saw her again. "The moon went and so did they," Gran said, explaining how Gracie had disappeared, along with the whole mob who camped on the river, on the night of an eclipse.

She was bright enough to nibble on a few of her favourite ginger chocolates and sip a sweet Milo. I promised to return in a few days, not knowing this was to be her last.

I was almost out the bedroom door when Gran shouted to me with lucid urgency, "Darling!" I spun around. Her thin frame was straining forward, struggling to prop herself up with one hand. All the fog in her eyes was gone. She looked at me with an expression of pure love and said quietly, "Thank you for being you."

I registered the words in slow motion, hearing each one as if spoken within a cave. I pulled myself together enough to give her a shaky smile, blow her a kiss and lurch out the front door, where I collapsed on the swinging hammock and wet the green canvas with my tears. I cried because I didn't know who I was anymore. And because one of the few people in the world who did wouldn't be here much longer to remind me.

A few days after Gran's funeral, I called Kate. "That year in the bush, I want to do it."

*

Back home, the day's largesse equates to barely a third of a roof, which would be fine if it was watertight. An afternoon storm quickly destroys this illusion. The rootlets are like little water slides, giving the rain a free ride straight in. I reluctantly unfurl a new blue tarp over the roof.

Night creeps in like a robber. I crash out before the mischievous night elves can start playing tricks on me.

4.

I t's either me or the grasstree. I hoped there might be room in this lean-to for both of us, but it'll only work if I'm willing to be poked in the eye with a sharp needle every time I reach for the salt while I'm cooking.

Grasstrees are incredibly slow-growing creatures – the turtles of the plant world, busting out not much more than an inch a year. If you're lucky enough to stumble upon a clump of blackened grasstrees that reach over your head (do the maths on a six-metre one), you may find yourself spontaneously dropping to your knees and bowing your head in respect for the gathering of elders who pre-date you by a few hundred years. This one is a mere babe, a head with no legs. I can't help but think of Grug – the big-nosed bush wanderer of Ted Prior's kids books. A favourite of mine as a child, Grug is a gadabout grasstree, the epitome of a laid-back bush hermit, waddling around in non-verbal equanimity. If he could say anything, I'm sure it would be "no worries", but Grug junior in front of me has a whole lot of worries as I reach for the mattock. He seems to have grown overnight, defiantly stretching his wiry needles as far as possible, as if in protest. You can't halt progress, I explain.

There is a silver, if somewhat starchy, lining to this massacre – a chance to finally try what is apparently a bush-food delicacy. My bush-food guide says that the grasstree was a rich source of carbohydrates for the Aboriginal people in this region, who would beat off the head with a stick and then roast or eat raw the starchy pith where the trunk joins the leaves. It was a heavy price – the death of the grasstree for a few inches of starch, but judging by the plethora of them still around, the stocks were well maintained. I'm not about to go beheading grasstrees to find out, but being an opportunivore by nature, I'll be dining on grasstree hors d'oeuvres tonight.

The communal fire's already going by the time I arrive on dusk. I wonder who lit it, and how. Waving to Shaun in the kitchen, I pull up a log and begin Grug's preparations. It's a rather gruesome operation, requiring me to scalp him and dig out the grey matter with my knife. A kookaburra looks at me curiously from a low tree nearby. Smiling, I offer out some Grug on the end of my knife. Amber spreads in an arc across the horizon as the first star appears. I pause and take a deep breath of the first wisps of cool night air. The land does the same, scribbly trunks blushing a pale pink, leaves perking up from their daytime wilt, swaying gently in the imperceptible breeze. It almost looks pretty.

I hear Dan and Chloe guffawing loudly from down the main trail, and I stiffen.

"Hey, where have you guys been?" I ask as they enter the firelight, arms full of shopping bags.

"Town mission," says Chloe, glancing at me nervously as if gauging my reaction.

"Oh ... already?"

"Yeah, needed some things."

"Like chocolate," Dan laughs. Chloe turns her head sheepishly. I try not to look disapproving. I'm carefully planning my supplies so I don't have to go into town more than once a month. I thought we all were. I wonder if that counts as one of their thirty days allowed out of camp.

Chloe glances briefly at what I'm doing, faltering for a second before heading off to the kitchen. I've been hoping we'll just slip into our old friendship, but we haven't reconnected much at all yet. Chloe used to be the only one who didn't think it strange if I screeched to a halt on the side of the road to gather the fluffy flower heads of bulrush for tinder. We sneaked into park gardens at night to harvest basket-making plants and almost burnt my house down practising primitive fire making in the backyard. Together we discovered books that mirrored our mutual call to the wild, exclaiming over passages that felt like someone had stolen the words from our hearts. Chloe and I were the original recruits for the bush year, signing up with the excited agreement of, "I'll do it if you do." With Chloe equally enamoured of bush skills, it didn't seem so crazy. In the year since we've seen each other, I've been overseas while she has been finishing a uni degree and delving into a personal development program. I have the distinct feeling that she is having serious doubts about wanting to be here but doesn't want to tell me. I haven't asked, either. I just want us to go back to how we were.

Baked-bean toasties and Shaun's just-left-home special of a bucket-load of pasta and mouldy cheese jostle for flame space. Ryan makes space on the log next to him when he sees Nikki coming.

"Way to go, Nik," he exclaims, giving her a high five when she produces two eggs.

"Grasstree brains, anyone?" I say, offering the head around the communal fire.

"It's good," says Dan. "If you like munching on Paddle Pop sticks."

Ryan takes a tentative bite. "Hmm, a bit like nutty peas."

That's the most I've been able to drag out of Ryan since he arrived. I've been hoping we'd also fall back into the easy mateship of our US adventure days, but that's clearly not happening. I was confident we were just friends when I joined him on a Rocky Mountains camping trip, underestimating the romance of skinny dipping in pristine alpine lakes and napping on sun-soaked meadows. I'd assumed that he also felt our brief roll in the wildflowers was situational. But I'm beginning to think that his decision to do this year might have had more to do with me than I wanted to admit.

I'm a bit resentful about having to consider relationships at all. I left my boyfriend of five years to come out here. It had become not just him and me but a third entity – The Relationship – which was sapping ridiculous amounts of my energy to maintain. In some ways I wish I was anonymous here, free of the weight of past expectations. Then I could focus on the relationships I really want to foster, those of the non-human variety. I was surprised when Nikki told me the clincher for her to sign up was being part of a group.

"Want some?" Chloe says, extending a bag of town-bought chips. I pretend to be deeply absorbed in Grug, noticing a slight tone of superiority in my voice as I decline. She inches away.

"Hey Shaun, did you make the fire tonight?" I ask, passing around Grug's young inner leaves.

"Yep," he says proudly, holding up chafed palms.

"Wanna see my firestick?" Dan says, producing a lighter. "The sacred Bic."

Chloe laughs.

"Still working on your kit?" I ask.

"Nope, already done. I just don't like rules. If I don't feel like busting up my hands, I'll use a lighter. Simple."

"But ... that's the whole point of the program ... that's why we're here," I say, looking around me for support.

Ryan sighs, and looks at me pointedly. "It takes more energy to piss out here than most people use in a day. We don't have to do it all right away."

"All?" I say, a fire igniting in my belly. Fire is not just any old skill. Fire is life. Fire *is* all.

The first time I saw Kate kneel down and effortlessly produce a glowing red coal using a hand-drill, the same technique that would have been used on this land for tens of thousands of years, it felt like I was witnessing a birth – it was that intimate, that profound. The sheer simplicity of picking up one stick and spinning it on another to produce fire was the most improbable and stunning act of human creation I could imagine. I wanted it, badly. That was three years ago. Now I want it with a bone-deep hunger. I'd made a few hand-drill fires in tandem with one of the others since I'd been here, but none on my own. Not yet.

Kate and Sam have strongly suggested that we use only traditional fire-making methods, such as the bow-drill and hand-drill, but are leaving the ultimate decision up to us. "The greater the need, the greater the result," Kate told us. I didn't need convincing. Fire defines for me whether we are serious about learning real skills or, well, just playing with fire. I wish Kate and Sam had set more ground rules, or were at least around more to establish some cultural boundaries. I understand the gentle approach but the slope could get pretty slippery. In the absence of rules I've made my own commitment to making fire only with sticks for the entire year. Matchsticks do *not* count.

"Well, we'll all have our own fires soon, once our shelters are built," says Nikki, trying to break the tension.

I take her cue and shut up. Like it or not, I am part of a tribe. A leaking shelter will be the least of my worries if I end up the misfit. Maybe Ryan's got a point. It is still early days.

"Look up!" Ryan yells. Six heads jerk upwards as a shooting star gobbles half the sky in a spectacular burnout. There is a moment of open-mouthed silence before Dan's phone rings. It's unbelievable, firstly, that there's reception, secondly, that he's happy to keep conducting his social life like this year is some kind of backyard barbecue.

I bury my head in the task of shaving off the resin from the outside of Grug's root-ball to use later as a glue. My knife work is fierce, shards of dark amber spraying violently into my upturned hat. I feel tarnished, as if the purity of my year is already stained. What we need is something to sew us together, something to help us let go of the past, let go of our fears and set our collective boat on course.

*

"So, should we welcome in the four directions, or give thanks to Mother Earth first?" Nikki says impatiently, poised with a pen over the blank piece of paper titled "Ceremony" in her hand.

We shift uncomfortably. While we all agreed with Kate's suggestion of a welcome ceremony to the property we've nicknamed

"The Block", we are resisting it with every ounce of our habitual individualism.

"Ceremony needs singing. Maybe we can use that river flowing song?" suggests Chloe. Shaun groans.

"How about 'Twinkle, Twinkle'?" says Ryan, catching Shaun's eye.

None of us are aligned with a particular religion, and none of us can claim to be indigenous to this land, (although Dan is part Aboriginal down the line). Do we look to our Celtic ancestry? Ryan's German and Viking heritage? What songs and dances are ours? What is our relationship with this land? We don't want to culturally appropriate what is not ours, but we do want to claim some kind of innate connection to the earth. We don't want to invoke gods we don't worship, but we also don't want to end up with a lowest common denominator scenario because we are so scared of acknowledging anything larger than our own egos.

In the end we cobble together the barest bones of a politically correct, culturally non-specific ritual. Luckily, none of us are die-hard scientific reductionists, and we loosely share a belief in some kind of overarching consciousness or life force, which can withstand use of the word "Creator".

There is a jitter amongst us as we gather at dusk around the newly raked ceremonial ground, a stone-ringed fireplace in the centre set with a perfect teepee of kindling. Kate and Sam turn up looking harried and under-slept. It's the first we've seen of them in more than a week. We spit on creek rocks, rub them together and stripe one another's faces with red, white and tan ochres. Together we lay our hands on the dried grasstree flower stalk that is our hand-drill and ask silently to be blessed with the gift of fire tonight. Chloe begins, spinning the firestick slowly between her palms, grinding it down on a timber board until dust starts spreading into the notch. "Last one," she whispers, as Ryan takes over. We continue around the circle, keeping the stalk spinning continuously, one person starting from the top as another finishes. Within minutes a large coal rolls out of the notch. Nikki transfers it to the tinder, a nest woven with dry grasses, leaves and lichen.

Her breath slowly tickles it into flame. The fire hungrily roars to life, maintaining shape long after ignition. We stand in silent contemplation of this bush magic, this lively extrovert that was a mere whiff of smoke minutes before.

Kate waits until the flames subside before raking out coals into an abalone shell, smothering them with green gum leaves so that plumes of scented smoke erupt. She signals us to approach. I close my eyes to the *swoosh* of the hawk wing Kate uses to guide the smoke over me.

"We acknowledge the traditional owners of the land, the Gumbaynggirr people," she says. "May we learn to tread lightly on their homeland and may the ancestors bless our way."

It's our cue to welcome the other VIPs, which is the part we had argued most about. Chloe begins, turning to each cardinal direction, struggling to find words of welcome appropriate for the southern hemisphere. We clunk through the steps like a car without oil.

"You've gotta thank Mother Earth now," Nikki elbows Ryan into the centre as we stifle a giggle. Shaun's greeting on behalf of us to the Creator sounds more like he is thanking the bloke down the street after borrowing his drill bit. I feel a pang of longing for elders, sensing the empty places that they should occupy around the fire. It's almost nostalgia, as if I'm missing people I once knew. Whoever they are, I wish they were here.

It's time to step up and state our intentions for the year, with the hope that the all-star cast we invited to our party will grant us the staying power we'll need to uphold them. We shift in closer until our shoulders are almost touching. The fire leaps and licks as if in anticipation. When my turn comes to enter the circle, I'm surprised to find my throat thick with emotion.

"I come here as nature's apprentice," I begin, with a gravelly voice. "To honour the old ways, and learn how to live in harmony with the land." I reach forward and place the black cockatoo feather I brought with me onto the flames. I pause and take a deep breath. "Ancestors and allies, please help me find what I came here for. Allow the earth to shape me into a tool for the healing of all beings." I sense there's more to say but my mind is blank. Inching back, I watch as the feather catches, crackles and shrinks, dissolving into smoke.

Rather than "I intend to be the best survivalist," or "Grant me a mean spear-throwing form," the intentions we share are remarkably similar.

"I come here seeking self-knowledge, seeking wisdom ..."

"Let me be open to receive whatever it is I need to learn ..."

"Help teach me the ways of the forest so I can come back into relationship with the Earth ..."

"May I let go of my ego and discover the truth within ..."

The last intention falls like a leaf from a branch. We rest in its descent, breathing together, eyes on the flames. It's the first silence we've shared. The land huddles in closer too, as if listening, the night sky a shawl slung loosely around our shoulders. I imagine our intentions spiralling up with the smoke, then falling like ash onto soft mossy beds or pockets of leaf litter, between buttresses of tree roots and in crevices of peeling bark. Finding fertile ground and taking root.

Perhaps what unites us here together this year is greater than what separates us. Time will tell. I send a wordless thank you to my tribe.

Formalities over, we relax around the fire, glowing in the aftermath of group bonding. After a few minutes, Dan jumps up and starts singing a medley of eighties songs. Initially annoyed at this seemingly ill-fitting end to our night, I give in to the irresistible charms of yodelling "Eternal Flame" around our ceremonial fire. Soon we are up doing our best Peter Garrett impersonations, belting out "Beds are Burning" (Ryan's a bit lost on that one). We dance ourselves into ecstasy, competing for the best daggy move as we churn through Eurythmics, Bananarama, David Bowie. So this is the song and dance we have inherited. Our passion for them is far more authentic than for any solemn earth hymn we could have forced out. We boogie into the night under the sickle of the new moon.

5.

My immunity to the heat is fast waning, along with my enthusiasm for roofing the lean-to. "Simple", "shelter" and "waterproof" just don't belong in the same sentence. There ain't no such combination, not in caveman land. If there was, we'd still be living under thatched roofs. I develop a new theory: it was actually the need for corrugated iron that fuelled the industrial age. It's good to have walls and a breakfast bar, but breakfast isn't much fun with rain pouring in. And pouring in it has been, despite the second layer of paperbark Shaun helped me collect.

The honeymoon really is over. My arms, legs and face are red from scratches, bites and sunburn. Last night I walked straight into a giant spiderweb, taking the bulbous leggy creature for a ride in my hair. Twice yesterday I thought I heard my name being called, and even answered, but there was no-one there. Despite our ceremony, the group is splintering into cliques. I saw Ryan and Nikki dancing under the full moon in the quarry the other night, while Dan and Chloe have started their own private coffee club in Dan's kitchen, which he has decked out like some kind of inner-city cafe. Is that all he wants out of this year – to swap the furniture? This whole coupling-off thing is really getting to me. I came here to be alone by choice, not as the social outcast. While I can't bear to think of the year being frittered away on mindless chitchat and lighter-fuelled fires, I don't want to be the uptight camp warden either.

Chloe and I had an awkward chat the other day about our vibe. I told her I was feeling a bit sidelined. She said she was feeling judged, which I suppose is true. We hugged and promised to check in more often, but the next day the caginess was back. We are both simultaneously pushing and pulling each other, too scared to say what's really going on.

There was a sign pinned up at the US tracker school that said, only partly tongue-in-cheek, "No Snivelling". Well, today I am nothing but a big sniveller.

The jumping ants are on the offensive. I fashion a makeshift canvas dike around me, hoping it's enough to keep them at bay while I finish lunch. One of the many splinters in my palm has become inflamed and I pick at it, sucking in quick breaths through my teeth. "Fuck!" I yell, clutching my foot as a new pain is delivered to my big toe, courtesy of an oversized red ant. I brush the ant aside but it marches back, swaying like a boxer in the ring, pincers raised. It really fucking hurts, just like everything else here. Even the din of the cicadas is like a thousand jackhammers on my brain from dawn 'til dusk. I let out a little whimper.

I thought I knew flies and mozzies until I met the fellas here. These aren't the polite biteys who are inclined to take a little high tea at dusk, who wait patiently until you bring your limbs to rest, their dining sensibilities easily interrupted by the slightest movement. No, these are bourbon and beefsteak country lads, clinging on like rodeo riders, up for it any time of the day or night. Their assault is compounded by the fact that I have nowhere to hide, especially now they seem to have found a way inside my mozzie net. It's actually the smallest raiders, the midges, that are the worst, proving that size doesn't matter. I amend the Dalai Lama's motto, "If you think you're too small to make a difference, try sleeping with a mosquito," to, "If you want to make a difference in the world, become a midge and swarm the AGMs of Earth-destroying companies." It would shut them down in an instant. Midge strategy is simple and effective – descend in a tight swarm and create panic in the victim, weakening their defences, before going in for the kill.

44

I lie back on my swag, toe throbbing. I dreamt last night that the beautiful beach sharehouse I left has been looted, all my precious possessions stripped, except for a green Buddha statue. I miss my mum, I miss my friends, I miss my mozzie-free bedroom. It's only six weeks in. I don't know if I can keep going for another month, let alone eleven. A single tear squeezes from the corner of one eye, drying before it has the chance to complete its run.

*

A shiny black BMW four-wheel drive pulls up outside the central kitchen. I bound towards it, waving wildly.

"So good to see you!" I squeal, greeting my sister, Liv, with a spinning hug. She's en route back to Sydney from her honeymoon in Byron Bay with her new hubby, Dwayne. While I had initially been unsure about their suggested visit, in the last few days I have been hanging out for it.

The strong scent of Liv's shampoo reminds me I probably don't smell too good, and I pull back. Her shiny hair is tied up in a high ponytail that swings between her shoulder blades, and she tugs on the hem of her denim miniskirt as she looks around. Squinting despite dark wrap-around sunglasses, Dwayne extracts himself slowly from the air-conditioned car and turns a slow, shocked 360 degrees. I follow his gaze. Half-burnt branches from last night's fire lie upturned on the gravel; flies swarm around something rotting near the water tank. I'm suddenly embarrassed, not sure I want them to see me here.

"What's that?" Dwayne yells back to my greeting, struggling to hear over the cicadas.

Liv tries to mask her dismay with an upbeat, "Well, show us around, then." It's slow going, Liv stopping every five seconds with a loud "ouch" – twigs stuck in her thongs, flies biting her bare legs, or some other mystery bug that we can never find. It's far too hot to light a fire for tea, and the tannin-coloured waterhole is not exactly enticing to a couple fresh from the blue waters of the Bay, so I'm not sure what to do with them but don't want them to leave. Liv produces cold ginger beers from an esky, and we roll a log into the shade to sit on while we sip them.

"So, you two, how does it feel to be heading back to normal life?" I ask.

"I'm kind of looking forward to it, actually. It's been such a big few months," Liv says, squeezing Dwayne's hand.

"I'll guess I'll have to carry you over the threshold," he laughs.

It's good to see Liv so happy. Growing up, she felt pressure to be like me, comparing her modest trophy collection to my over-flowing collection of academic and tennis awards. Four years younger than me to the day, Liv is often mistaken for the older sister. With the successful corporate career in fashion, the hubby, and the mortgage on their Sydney beachside home, my little sister has really grown up.

"So, are you having fun?" Liv asks, holding the beer to her forehead.

I hide the threatening tears behind a big cold slurp. "Sure, yep ... I mean, it's hard – the heat and the flies – but that's all part of it, I guess, isn't it?"

Liv eyes me carefully, as I snap twigs around my feet with my free hand. "Mum and Dad are asking how you're going with your shelter."

"Well, you've seen my lean-to. You can just say I'm going great," I say, remembering the last conversation I had with Dad before I left. He had taken it upon himself to pack my car, mumbling as he weighed up how best to persuade the mountain of stuff into my old station wagon. I tried handing him a bag, but he brushed me aside with a sweep of his hand, his brow furrowed in concentration.

"You see, if I roll these blankets lengthwise, they'll fill this dead space as well as stop the pans from rattling," he explained with satisfaction.

"Dad, I'm going to be building my own shelter in a few days. I think I can pack a car."

"Well, you never know, you might need my help on that one too."

"No, Dad, that's the point. I want to do this on my own," I said, a little too vehemently. "Besides, you always did tell me I could do anything I wanted in life," I stirred, knowing that building my own shack of sticks and leaves was not exactly what Dad had in mind.

I conceded to him this last opportunity to be indispensable. Although I hadn't properly lived at home since I left at the age of eighteen, somehow this time it felt like I was truly leaving.

"You know, Claire, I don't pretend to understand why you're leaving a perfectly good job to live in a humpy for a year," he said, shoving the last bag in with a bit more force than necessary, as if annoyed the task was done.

A wave of guilt washed over me. "It's just a year," I replied almost apologetically, the boot slamming shut.

*

"Well, we'd better get going, then," Liv says, looking at her watch. My heart sinks.

Dwayne gives me a hug, before pausing on the car step to take another sweeping glance around him. He looks at me with a mixture of confusion and empathy, turns to no-one in particular and says, "The Australian bush is a harsh environment." I nod and look down, messing with the gravel underfoot. The kisses that Liv blows me from behind tinted windows are lost in their departing cloud of red dust.

The tears that I'd been holding back stream down my face. That could have been me. On my way to a comfortable house with a comfortable job and a comfortable routine. Drinks with friends on Friday night, a Sunday night movie. I suddenly long to swap places with her, to cruise down the highway with my man, on a sealed road heading in a straight direction. Why have I chosen this track instead? It's lawless out here: no signposts to tell me where the track leads, or whether in fact I'm lost, having taken a wrong turn somewhere way back.

*

In the late afternoon, I listlessly wander the trail near my shelter. I had tried to distract myself from self-pity by digging another hole for my loo and fiddling with the lean-to walls, but the hours dragged. Now, as the shadows stitch together into a dark blanket spreading over the land, I wish for those hours back. My fear of the dark spontaneously returns, the adrenalin floodgates opening, pumping tension into my limbs and sending my heart into quick steps. My thoughts stray again to what Liv might be doing. Probably sharing a homecoming chardonnay with Dwayne, condensation dripping onto her fingers as they toast the good life.

I veer off the path and into the bush, with no care to direction. The bush begins to open out, the trees old and large. I slow a little, my hand resting on the trunks as I pass. And then I see it. The power tree. It has a girth twice as wide as any other nearby, the buttresses falling to the ground like draped white linen. My feet make small involuntary steps in its direction, magnetised not so much by its stature, but by the feeling that I know it already. As I approach, a dark stump at its base shifts and takes the shape of a curled black snake, its red belly just visible in the fading light. I gasp, and freeze. The snake stirs and slithers inside a hollow at the base of the tree, as if inviting me closer. I walk with silent footfalls until my forehead and palms press up against the cool trunk. I close my eyes and breathe. I can sense the snake inside, perhaps mere centimetres from my hands. My breath tightens, as if the snake is wrapping itself around my chest. I resist the urge to move, and concentrate instead on the pulsing in my palms, energy flowing down my arms and cascading through my body. I stay with the feeling, with the snake, breathing alongside it.

What is it that I'm frightened of? Is it really the dark? Or is the darkness a reflection of the shadows that flicker at the edge of my awareness; the places I'm afraid to see?

I open my eyes to blackness. A small breeze whiskers my cheek as I pull my face away from the tree. Gradually my eyes adjust enough to make out the boat shapes of gum leaves gently swaying, backlit by a stage of tiny flickering stars. All fear is gone.

I turn and walk slowly and steadily back to my swag, knowing that there is no going back.

6.

"I'm going to teach you a skill crucial for wilderness survival, and all you have to do is sit," Niko, our bird expert, told us on the first day in a series of five bird-language workshops. "Find one place that calls to you. Know it by day, know it by night, in the rain and wind. Know the stars and where the four directions are. Know the birds that live there and the trees they live in. Know these things as if they are your relatives, which in time, they will become."

This place, he explained, is a "sit spot", and in the cool of first light every morning I am busy holding auditions for mine. Rubbing my T-shirt over the lenses of the binoculars slung around my neck, I pad barefoot down my shelter trail as the sky reddens in anticipation of sunrise. I've already scoped out the area in which I want my sit spot – an easy walk from my shelter, at the junction of two trails, in the transition zone from dry, scrubby banksia forest to wetter eucalypt forest near the creek. Like the fertile breeding ground where freshwater and saltwater meet, any edge where one ecosystem type collides with another is a multicultural mixing pot, and should make for the liveliest show around, if I can find a good seat – somewhere comfortable (preferably with a backrest), with good cover for small birds and clear space for wallabies, a view of both ground feeders and canopy high fliers, ideally with a water feature. I'm talking dress circle only.

Perched on a mossy log, I can barely see past the tangle of vines in front of my face. No good, move on. I begin to feel like Goldilocks testing out different chairs: too low; too wet; ooh, too many leeches; too prickly; too visible. This is taking way too long. I begin to crash through the bush impatiently, exactly what Niko said not to do. When I have my sit spot, then I can stop.

"Ouch," I exclaim, as my big toe stubs on a tree root. A bird flaps up noisily from the ground nearby. I hobble down the trail, trying to regain composure. After a while I start to feel a familiar tugging, as if a string tied around my waist is pulling me forward. I pick up the pace, my heels landing with loud thuds on the ground.

Stop! I will myself to a standstill. I'm in the middle of a forest that is sweetly chorusing the dawn. The whole day, hell, the whole year, stretches out with nothing I *have* to do, and yet ... I'm rushing. I can feel it in my limbs, a kind of not-quite-bodily sensation, an urgency, like I'm always a step ahead of myself, never quite touching the sides of my experience. When I rode my bike back from Kate and Sam's yesterday, I was gunning it, pumping my legs to get back as fast as possible, in case I missed something. Missed what? A log burning? Hello, my name's Claire Dunn, and I'm addicted to busyness.

At least I'm not wearing a watch, having banished it to my car as soon as I arrived. Recently it has sneaked back into my lean-to (albeit "hidden" under a pile of blankets), and I find myself taking guilty peeks at it throughout the day, comforted by the guidance it gives me on when it's appropriate to eat or sleep. Its presence is beginning to feel superstitious, though, a talisman protecting me from something.

Stretching my arms wide, I consciously expand my vision, wiggling my fingers at the furthest edges of my frame of sight to remind me how much I can actually see. "Wide-angle vision," Niko calls it. As I soften my gaze, my mind also relaxes, that string around my waist going slack. Loosening my knees, I drop my centre of gravity and start taking slower steps. Each foot falls naturally on its outside edge, testing the ground first before rolling the ball inwards, the heel barely brushing the path before my weight shifts. I give up control to my feet, letting them weave a roundabout path through the forest. My body tingles in enjoyment at the meander, filling up at the sensations of the small dips and rises, as though I'm drinking in the land through my soles. The wide catchment of my gaze registers subtle movements of leaves, scuttling skinks in the undergrowth. The waking forest sings with snaps and crackles, as if I can hear the new growth bursting through buds, shoots and tips.

Circling to the east, I suddenly see it – my sit spot – a giant uprooted scribbly gum lying along the edge of a trail. Running over, I climb to the top via the ladder of exposed roots. A flat platform at the base of the trunk allows just enough space to sit cross-legged. My back is perfectly supported by the roots, which extend up behind my head like a webbed throne. I try out three different positions in which I can sit or lie comfortably. The sky and ground are equally visible. Small bushes are on one side, an open trail on the other. A bracken fern partly obscures my sitting figure. A crevice in the tree has collected water, and a family of blue fairy-wrens splash and preen not metres away. I have found my spot and it is *just right*. It's like a neighbour has just brought over a casserole and welcomed me to the community.

And make myself at home is what I do. For about an hour a day I sit like a forest princess and observe the doings of my new furred and feathered friends. I'm so excited by the anticipation of what might show up that I'm able to maintain a Zen-like stillness despite fierce attacks by biting insects. True, I do come dressed like a Bedouin, with layers of flowing clothes and a mozzie net draped over my face, but I'm finding that the more I focus on the action around me, rather than the frustration of being eaten alive, the less the insects seem to bother me.

This sit spot will be my classroom, the place where I can turn the pages of the book of nature, learning the language of my new forest home. Birds are my way in. They're the most visible, charismatic, demonstrative, diverse and responsive creatures around, and will be the key to unlocking the complexities of jungle law.

I'm not an entirely new recruit to the world of feathered friends. On request, for my thirtieth birthday I was given a pair of binoculars and a bird guidebook, my twin brothers inscribing it with, "Happy birthday, sis. Ornithology rocks, eh?" Okay, so it wasn't fashionable, but I found ornithology really did rock. When I held those magnifiers to my eyes, birds that had been background music began to take on shape, colour and personality. I realised that they were there sometimes and not others. Rather than one call, they had several. It was as if I had been surrounded by exquisite original paintings all my life and was only just noticing them.

The birds at my sit spot don't disappoint. This is no prim English suburb. No, this neck of the woods is the migrant part of town, noisy and raucous, with family dramas spilling into the central piazza. I am pinned to the soap opera playing out in front of me – the constant feeding frenzies, territorial skirmishes, petty fights, games and courtships. Most dominant are the families of neurotic white-cheeked honeyeaters, who keep a vigil against marauding wattlebirds wanting a piece of the banksia flower action. Eastern spinebills are unfailingly graceful as they hover like hummingbirds, their new-moon beaks curving into the tubular red bells of the mountain devils. Finches flock for seed in the grasses, throwing up their red underskirts like flamenco dancers. Thornbills are social butterflies, whirring and purring around me, and whipbirds cut the air like lightning. On the ground floor, matronly wonga pigeons waddle and peck; while above, golden whistlers are sun-drenched suitors showering the forest in a lyrical symphony. As well as the regulars, there is the buzz of drop-in predators such as the collared sparrowhawk, and rare and quiet visitors including the topknot pigeon and king parrot.

Summer is a heady season for a novice twitcher. I am on a birdy bender, drunk with the thrill of each new find. After each sit I race back to my lean-to, sketch the unknown specimen and cross-reference several books until I have a positive ID. I keep a daily log, full of observations and questions. Not just what is it, but where does it live? How far does it roam? What does it eat? Questions lead to more questions. I am a detective on the case, sketching my suspects, posing hypotheses, conjecturing, the journaling helping to keep my nose on the trail and sniffing.

One morning there is a new call, a loud and repetitive whining coming from the rainforest. I can't stay in my seat. Slinging my binos over my back, I crawl along wet leaf litter following the sound. I finally spy the source: a family of baby spangled drongos perching on a low branch. They would have disappeared to Papua New Guinea during the winter months, but now they're bringing up babies in my neighbourhood. Mouths wide open, the babes flick their fledgling fish-tail feathers, the whining turning into a squealing, "Pick me, pick me," as exhausted Mummy flies in with a bug in her beak. I'm oblivious to the multiple leeches taking hold of me as I lie amongst the thick carpet of leaves and watch the family. I sketch my drongos and wonder what other creatures lie hidden, what kindred spirits I have yet to meet.

Niko's expert eye helps to swing the doors of the forest wide open. Instead of the hostile island I've been living on, I start to see the hidden charms of my home, which transports me to a storybook land where giant owls kidnap parrots and possums by moonlight; where wrens and warblers weave silken sacs of huntsman spider babies into their nests. I can now nod to the ringtail possum as it sleeps in its dray, in a casuarina tree on the main trail, and know that the disappearance of a golden orb-weaver spider overnight signals that the golden-tipped bat, its only predator, has visited.

"If all you do this year is learn how to sit, how to watch and how to walk, you'll have achieved the greatest survival skills of all," said Niko cryptically. "Because what they are is a doorway to awareness. It's up to you how far down that rabbit hole you go."

*

In the dusk twilight, Shaun is pacing around an unlit fireplace when I arrive at the Gunyah.

"D'ya hear that?" he says excitedly. I thought I heard something at my sit spot this afternoon but presumed it was a cicada-induced hallucination. Cupping my ears in the direction he is pointing, I make out a dull throbbing beat.

"I reckon it's a bush doof. I saw some kind of alien sign on the gate to the property across the creek the other day," Shaun says, hopping from one foot to the other.

"Huh, bizarre," I reply, feigning uninterest, knowing exactly what he is about to propose.

"Come on – camo mission!"

"Shaun, I'm actually really tired. I've been paperbarking all day, and I've got to get up and do it all again tomorrow, so I think I'll give it a miss."

Shaun shoots me a "told you so" look. He accused me the other day of being too busy to play. While I suspect he is wanting to play in more ways than one, the accusation stings with its thorn-of truth.

I walk off to collect kindling, the bassline now a clear rhythmic thump from the east. Dammit, he's right. It would be fun. We could, of course, walk straight into the party, but it's a perfect opportunity to test out the scout awareness skills we've been learning. It's a pity Ryan's not here.

Rather than Baden Powell badges and knee-high khaki socks, the scout class that Ryan and I signed up for at the tracker school referred to the revered Native American Apache scouts, infamous amongst white settlers for their Houdini-like ability to escape any enclosure – to quite simply disappear. The scouts, specially chosen in childhood, were set apart from the tribe and trained intensely in the arts of survival and bird language, healing and endurance, intuition and body control. Legend has it that they could bilocate (appear in two places simultaneously) and read minds. Their role was to be the protector of the tribe, warning their people of danger from enemy tribes, and directing them safely to the next food source. I was intrigued to see how this ancient lineage would be passed down to a hundred fee-paying students in a week. I quickly found out it was through three tools – mud, sleep deprivation and blindfolds.

Mud was our camouflage uniform, coating us from day one. Our groups of ten were never (and I mean *never*) to leave one another's side, and we had to dig invisible "scout pits" (think: graves) in which to catch the two or three hours' sleep we were afforded. During the days we spent most of our time down at the swimming hole, blindfolded while walking across logs sprung with swinging buoys, learning martial arts or walking around the forest for hours. At night our missions required us to travel barefoot for miles out of camp, moving silently and invisibly along the sandy edges of the pine woods, being tested by various "awareness triggers" such as tripwires, ambushes and motion sensors, and also by the real need to avoid the often gun-toting locals. The mud-encrusted line at breakfast was alive with stories of the previous night's adventure, everyone's eyes bright and fiery. I pictured myself training as an Aussie ninja during my year in the bush, rising at dawn to don my blindfold, tuning my senses to finer frequencies. I feel instead that I've mostly been carving a deeper rut in the track from shelter to kitchen to sit spot and back again.

"Okay, Shaun, let's do it," I say.

*

We use a soft whistle to locate each other at our rendezvous spot by the creek. The forest is skittish, with harried flaps of wings and scuttles in the brush, as if the day creatures are rushing to get home. With the moon fat and almost full, perhaps hungry owls are out early. Crickets and cicadas meet at the day's edge in overlapping waves of sound, a harsh staccato punctuating the smoother track of the evening. A night bird suddenly peals with a hooting cackle from somewhere above us. I startle, the hairs on my neck prickling. As I look up, a winged creature momentarily blots out the evening star. The throb in the background ratchets up a notch in pace and volume. Is it the doof or the sound of my heart beating in my chest?

Already half covered in ash and silhouetted against the darkened greenery, Shaun looks like a ghost. He's a funny fella. I certainly wouldn't have predicted buddying up with the young army dude. I'm careful to keep my boundaries, but, really, I'd be pretty lost (and roofless) without him. I join him in applying the foundational layer of my camouflage, the ash serving to dull my fur-less human shine.

"Not so heavy, Shaun. It's moonlit, remember?" I whisper as he stripes the backs of my legs with powdered charcoal. I smear it over my front in zebra-like patterns, overlaying it with patches of cold, dark mud dug up from the creek.

"Don't forget your face," Shaun smiles mischievously, slapping a mud pie on top of my head and across one side of my cheek. I wet a bracken frond with white clay and flick it over us, mirroring the moon's splattered shadows through the underbrush. A final roll in leaf litter and our make-up is complete.

I gasp as Shaun crouches at the base of a tree, his camouflage almost completely disguising his outline. I strain to make him out, his only giveaway the two large, round whites of his eyes staring up at me.

I, too, feel myself growing diffuse, fading into the dusky light. The weight of the clay and mud hanging off my body wills me to stoop and crouch closer to the ground, and I have a sudden desire to drop to all fours and prowl through the wet rainforest brush, growling. I giggle at the thought of what my friends would say if they could see me.

"Time to party?" I ask the young animal in front of me.

With a thumbs up, Shaun falls in step behind me, as I cross the bridge and break in to a quiet jog along the edge of the track. When the music gets louder, I drop to a fast crouching walk and move until my shoulders barely touch the tree line, ducking under branches, step-hopping over twigs, bending and flowing with the vegetation. Any tiredness has vanished. I feel wide awake, shapes and colours more distinct, the smell of ripe nectar almost sickly sweet. All I can hear is the soft patter of our bare feet on the clay verge. My body feels lithe and flexible, my movements precise and concentrated, as if I'm running over slippery rocks. Shaun is a moving shadow, his bright eyes flashing back the excitement in my own.

At the first sight of car lights, we sink and fade into the brush, waiting as they sweep over us and turn uphill. With a nod Shaun takes the lead, commando-rolling across the road and cutting through the bush to join the car's tracks on the fire trail. My thighs burn as I follow him in at a low crouch. When we crest the hill, the full blast of the doof hits me. It sounds like an industrial machine stuck on a grinding loop. A few yards away, a hundred or so cars ring a cleared area where small figures move under flashing lights and video projection screens. Shaun turns to grin at me, his white teeth floating independently of the hazy outline of his face.

Using hand signals we plot our approach. I cling to cover and lead the way around the edge of the forest, heading for the back of the party. Scanning the field for movement, I almost stumble into a swamp before I see that the ground has turned to water. Frogs plop from waterlilies as I wade in, bubbles rising from the muddy bottom. I bend over until I'm almost parallel with the surface, the swish of water around my legs barely audible. On the other side I grab some mud from the bank to touch up my camo, giving Shaun a quick thumbs up before moving off again, deciding to take a risk and follow a back fire-trail rather than continue around the edge of the bush.

An owl-like whistle from Shaun alerts me to company. I freeze. Voices are approaching. I search for cover but there's none, only a grass patch on the side of the road. Damn my impatience.

I hear a slurring male voice turn in my direction. "This way, boys, there's a track."

I dive in beside a grass tussock and wrap my body around it, my heart pounding.

"Gonna find some hot chicks tonight, fellas," one laughs in a gravelly voice.

I feel totally exposed. *Trust your camo,* I tell myself.

The laughter gets louder, but I will myself to focus. Filtering out the sound of their voices, I visualise myself becoming smaller and smaller, a tiny speck of sand falling to the ground, burrowing deeper and deeper into the earth. The ground shakes with the hard stomp of boots next to my head, but instead of the howl of shock I'm expecting, the voices quickly fade into the music. Not realising I'd been holding my breath, I gasp for air and let myself feel again the full spread of my body on the earth. I can't believe I wasn't seen. Shaun creeps over and lies next to me, looking equally scared.

Chastened, I'm happy to follow Shaun as he guides us in on our bellies, under a shrub to a vantage point metres from the main stage, where hundreds of young bodies splattered with psyche-delic patterns convulse and writhe to the unrelenting beat. I feel like an owl, watching the human creatures, with bemused indifference, from an invisible perch. It's good to be one of the midnight observers, the watchful rather than the watched. There's no need to fear the dark when I'm one of its shadows.

I follow the movements of one young woman, her long dread-locks flying, eyes closed, body pulsing as if in a trance. Years ago it would have been a fire and drum that she danced around. Under our civilised skin, there is still a pull to the forest, a desire for wild abandon. I wonder whether she can find it within the generator's electrified beat. With my painted costume dried and cracking, I feel like I'm entering a trance myself as I lie here. The musk-scented earth is so warm, so soft, so inviting, not just below me but all over. I shift slightly just to reassure myself that I'm not actually sinking into it; to remind me there is a distinction between this body and the larger one under me. I feel so safe that I could curl up and sleep here, except I'm not at all tired. Even Shaun, usually so restless, lies next to me still and silent.

When we finally rise to leave, my limbs are coffin-stiff but quickly find fluidity again. A mist has descended on the creek trail. Entering it, I feel as if I'm half flying, my feet barely touching the earth. I look back to see Shaun stepping exactly into my prints, mimicking the direct registering gait of a fox, with me as the front paws and he the rear. I move fast, but, for once, I'm not rushing. The doof noise fades in and out, gradually overtaken by the swell of the crickets. We break our silence with a screeching splash into the waterhole.

*

As I fall into my swag, the sky is clearer than I ever remember seeing it, the stars bolt-holes of pure light. Strange sounds punctuate the quiet, creating glorious mysteries. I want to unwrap them, one by one, if only I could stay awake. I rub my eyes with oncoming sleep, while the furry and feathered creatures of the dark blink theirs awake, meeting me at the dream junction. As the soft underbelly of night takes wing, I let my heart yield to the whispers, the secrets that crawl into my bed and curl up next to me, warm and beating next to my still body. Sleep transports me gently, as if I'm being carried by the current of a wide river, snaking its way further into the forest, drifting deeper into the darkening night.

7.

The writhing snake nailed to the kitchen pole, blood dripping from its mouth, snaps me out of my dreaminess following a spell at my sit spot. What the ...? Ryan raises his eyebrows, mirroring my sentiment, and reports flatly, "Dan killed a snake at his sit spot this morning."

"Killed – are you sure? Looks more like a crucifixion to me!" The diamond python is at least three metres long, the golden geometric patterns on its back stretching and contracting as its body contorts wildly.

"Trust me, we bashed it so many times that it can't possibly be alive. It's just its muscles twitching."

I can't take my eyes from it, magnetised by the same macabre curiosity that has me staring at car accidents as I pass, shocked out of my everyday illusion of immortality by the reminder that death is everywhere and could come at any time.

Dan must be having a very different experience from mine at his sit spot to want to bring one of his neighbours home in a body bag. My morning sit-spot visitor was also reptilian – a gecko, fingers as fine as the spokes of a spiderweb.

Vegetarian Chloe is next to arrive. "What the *fuck*?"

Dan, having retrieved his hunting knife, marches in looking both defensive and incredibly nervous. We stare at him, waiting.

"Look, it was just there sitting next to me, and I warned it three times that if it didn't move I was going to eat it. I figured it must be meant for me, so I picked up a stick and killed it, or tried to kill it, but it just kept on wriggling."

Silence.

"Well, we're here to learn to survive off the land, aren't we?" he says, trying to convince himself as much as anyone. "Or are we just pretending?"

Dan lunges in to take hold of the snake's neck, as if also in doubt of its dead status. Unhooked, it drops to the ground, continuing to spin out in short spasms. Dan bursts into tears. Watching on from the shade, with a frozen grin of shock and bemusement, Shaun walks over and leans one foot on the snake's spine to help anchor it, as Dan plunges the knife into its neck. I turn away, hearing a groan as I imagine blood spurting onto his hands.

Hunting, survival, food: these issues had to come up at some point, but I wasn't expecting them to be shoved in my face quite so soon. And not at breakfast.

The bush telegraph is fast. Hundreds of flies descend on the exposed flesh, and then spread to me and the mung-bean sprouts I am rinsing. As I contemplate who I will enlist to help me light a fire to repel them, I see Dan rush over to the fireplace and strike a match. What? He's got to be joking. The hypocrisy almost makes me laugh.

I stomp out of the kitchen, grab a handful of kindling, prop it together a few metres away and begin furiously spinning a hand-drill stalk in protest.

"There's one going already," Ryan says wryly.

I channel my silent reply into fierce spins of the firestick, producing more smoke than I ever have before. For a moment I think I might actually get it, but, as usual, my forearms shudder and give out, tears springing to my eyes as I throw the kit on the ground.

Nikki, Chloe and I have been successfully spinning fire together over the last couple of weeks, but alone I don't yet have the oomph. I hate the position this puts me in – desperate to maintain my primitive-fire stance and yet still dependent on others. I find myself bustling to the communal area on dusk in a bid to manipulate proceedings towards real fire lighting, batting my eyelashes at Shaun to persuade him to help me. If the fire is already alight, I eye it menacingly, trying to deduce from the quality of flames the origins of its life, trying not to sound desperate as I say, "Hey, Chloe – success on the sticks tonight?" and wait with bated breath for the answer that has me either loving or hating everyone. I stalk the camp like a stern schoolmarm, trying to dissuade talk of town trips and matches, a little horrified at myself. Without some rules, though, this could easily slide into a lame hippie camp.

I tried to enlist Kate's help but she was unmoved.

"It's up to each individual," she said sagely. "Whatever they feel called to do. Just follow your own heart."

Just do your own thing, girl! I wrote in my journal last night. But here I am again. This is precisely why I need to get on with building my real shelter, I remind myself, trying not to look at the butchering behind me.

The naked snake looks like a giant earthworm, white and slippery. Dan slices it into chunks the size of bread rolls and drops them into a camp oven along with some garlic and spuds. Ryan and Shaun skewer some onto sticks and hold them over the fire. My mouth waters as they begin sizzling.

Dan holds up the skin. "It's a man-bag," he says, folding it over and parading around the fire.

All I can think of is a moose head mounted on a hunting lodge wall.

Ryan's gaze shifts and I follow it to where it rests with satisfaction on an approaching Nikki, with the injured lorikeet she found a few days earlier perched on one shoulder. She looks a bit like one of her chooks this morning, barefoot and skinny-legged, her hair ruffled. Finding a seat next to Ryan, she lets him lean in close to explain the snake situation. Looking at Dan in silent shock, Nikki continues feeding the hungry lorry, chewing birdseed into pulp and leaving it on her bottom lip for the bird to grab. "Ow," she says, as it nips her lip, Ryan laughing with her when she taps its beak in mock punishment.

"Want one?" Shaun smiles, extending a snake kebab in my direction.

"No, thanks," I say, despite the saliva gathering under my tongue. I've been craving meat. My vegetarian phase years ago was disastrous, my iron levels hovering around anemia no matter how many lentils I consumed. The few cans of tuna I've eaten here have only taken the edge off, but I'm *not* eating that snake.

Catching my look of disdain, Dan looks hurt.

"I can't do it, Dan ..." I trail off. "It just doesn't feel right to eat it. I don't know ... I guess I don't feel like I have permission yet."

"What, are you going to wait until some elder taps you on the shoulder and hands you the sacred spear, when they deem you ready? Maybe in a perfect world, darlin', but not this one. We've gotta make it on our own here."

Yeah, just like you did with fire ...

I know what he means. I don't want to feel like a tourist anymore either. I want to feel at home in this country rather than just a camper skimming the surface, to see even a little of it through native eyes.

That ultimately means killing. Only taking life would sustain me here in the long term. And only through entering into that predator–prey relationship am I ever really going to be woven into the familial web of this land. Once I step over that threshold with a clear intention, it will indebt me to the land for life, but I'm still just making the land's acquaintance. Maybe canned tuna is just as hypocritical as matches, but to kill something now would feel like I had marched into a stranger's house and helped myself to the contents of the fridge.

*

"Look here, this bloodwood sap is magic stuff. Heals any cut," explains Mark, a local Gumbaynggirr guide who's here for the afternoon. He gathers a sticky gloop of dark red sap seeping from a wound in the tree and smears it on Ryan's bleeding toe. "Like one scar healing another, eh?" he laughs, his dark eyes twinkling. "The cure is always right next to the cause. You just gotta know it. If the giant stinging tree down in the rainforest gets ya, chances are cunjevoi – elephant's ears – is right there too. Crush it up and it takes the sting right away. Don't eat him, though – poisonous stuff."

Mark grins like a cheeky schoolboy. We grin back, bunched up right behind him.

"Jeez, you lot are quiet," he says. I think we're all a bit starstruck. It's the power of his presence: as if all the gentleness and optimism of the bush on an early spring day, after a shower of rain, has been bundled up, boiled and distilled into an essence, which oozes from his every pore.

"Ow," Dan exclaims, as a jumping ant nips his heel. Pulling a bracken fern out from the roots, Mark mushes up the lower stem in his hands and rubs the juice onto the bite. "Wow, that really works," Dan says, watching the red swelling disappear.

As Mark points out the food surrounding us, the wall of green starts to break up into individual forms. "Up here, native grape," he says, pointing above my head. I look up, humbled to realise I hadn't before noticed the thick bunches of purple berries hanging from a vine on the path to the waterhole. "Makes an alright jam, this one."

"Yum," says Nik, passing around the bunch. I pop a few in my mouth and stash a bunch in my pocket.

Back at camp, Mark lights a small fire to cook some of our collected roots. Chatting as we prepare our supper, no-one notices Sam approach until he's standing next to us, a goanna slung over his shoulder, its eyes glassy. He lays it next to the fire gently, his hand lingering on its rough-skinned back. Only then does he stand up and greet Mark with a hug. "Great to see you, old friend."

"Ah, you got us a *gumgali*," Mark says, patting the goanna. He makes space in the coals with a stick before laying it on. "Best bush tucker around. My uncle showed me how to hide in the bushes with a stick, wait for him to come along. Sometimes waiting hours," he says, eyes wide in emphasis. "I was a young thing and I'd be itchin' and scratchin' but, no, I'd have to sit still. Bush meditation, eh?" He laughs. "Back then there was food all over. Four hours a day, you get a plenty big enough feed for the family. Eels, fish, crays, mussels. And plants – yams, hundreds of 'em. Not like now; there's hardly any left."

As the stories flow, the smell of slow-roasted meat wafts through camp. I'm starving, the berries being all that I've eaten today.

Mark turns his head to listen as he taps a stick on the back of the charred goanna skin. "Ready for him? Ya betta be, 'cause he's ready for you," he laughs, breaking the skin open with his knife and handing us each steaming limbs of pink flesh. There is no hesitation from me. It's different with Mark here, and Sam knows the land well too. I juggle the meat on my tongue until it cools enough for me to chew. The first mouthful is down before I register the taste. I savour the second, tasting of gamey roast beef, but way better.

"Marshmallows for dessert?" Mark says, separating the two fat sacs that I assumed were lungs from the back skin and carving them into chunks. I follow his lead, dangling a piece over the fire on a stick until it browns and sizzles.

"Oh my God, this is way too good," says Chloe with her mouth full. "Just how I remember crackling." Dan looks at me and laughs as fat drips down my chin. Mark's visit has burnt off all the earlier bullshit.

After a billy of tea, Mark rises to leave. "Well, folks, I gotta go. Got another group to smoke. It's bloody busy these days; not enough time for fishin'. I'll be back, though," he adds, seeing our crestfallen faces, before breaking into a belly laugh. "I gotta see how wet you get under them humpies!"

The fire gives off a large crack. Mark stops, a serious look coming over his round face. "What you're doing out here is important. We gotta keep the old ways alive, and it's not just up to black-fellas anymore. We gotta get back to Mother Earth, teach the children. Youse are all like six leaves just dropped from a branch, some spinnin' quick, some slow. But youse are all fallin'. You're all gonna hit the ground sooner or later." He looks in my direction with a wink. "I know it ain't easy, but hang in there."

"*Yarri yarang*," he says with a wave, and starts the engine.

Don't leave us, I plead silently as his tail-lights disappear. We can't do this alone.

I walk heavily back to my lean-to.

In an ideal world Mark would stay and hold our hands as we learn to walk the old ways. He would be our bridge, passing on the customs and gestures appropriate for this land, explaining away our awkward attempts at familiarity. His presence would melt my fear that maybe we can't do this, maybe we will always be strangers in a strange land. But he can't stay. In a way, Dan's right – we need to learn to do this on our own, as clumsy as it seems. We don't have the luxury of sitting under a mulga bush with a gnarled woman, waiting until she shows us the dance that will animate the land within us. And yet the world needs a new dance more than ever. It needs people who feel so inextricably linked to the Earth that to damage or destroy it is akin to ransacking the family home.

I want to be one of those people again.

*

Goanna grease still clings to my chin in the morning, as does the warm memory of the man in my dream. Tall, slim and with a mop of brown curly hair, he is attentive, romantic, his long limbs moving as fluidly as water towards me. I'm wary of him at first and keep my distance, watching him from afar. He comes closer, smiling warmly, smelling of freshly cut grass on a summer's afternoon. I allow him nearer, sensing the extraordinary in him. Although I have never seen him before I know this man is my soulmate. Stepping forward as though to embrace, we pause centimetres from each other. We are so close, and yet the distance between us is still so vast.

8.

change in season ripples through the forest like a
shiver, two weeks before the calendar deems it ready.
It's as if someone has ever so slightly turned down the
volume: a subtle but visceral recalibration, the high-
fluted melodies of summer somewhat muted, a slower, steadier
bassline emerging. I walk around for a couple of days feeling that
something is missing before realising it's the channel-billed
cuckoo. "Storm birds" Dad calls them. No more will I wake at first
light to their harsh screech, to the promise of rain they oftentimes
break. I wish I had caught the moment they lifted their heads to
an invisible beckoning, smelling something on the breeze perhaps, and rose en masse, tilting their long white wing-tips north-
wards, trusting their wings to deliver them back to the same
valley, maybe even the same tree, they left months earlier. Their
absence seems even more palpable to me than their presence did.
Perhaps we only come to know some things by the spaces they
leave behind.

Birds are one marker of the season change, but there are
others. The bloodwood flowers are drying up, the flying foxes
and lorikeets trickling back to the coast after a wild summer of
nectar-fuelled drunken parties. The wattle responds to the exodus by rebelliously letting loose masses of yellow pompoms. On
foggy mornings they are Christmas baubles set against the stark
white of the scribblies. The banksias are also blooming late (much

to the delight of the honeyeaters), while the geebungs are dropping their flowers. The abundant berries of the native grapevine, which we have been feasting on since Mark's visit, are withering. Their replacement is the aptly named sour currant bush, which I just discovered fruiting on the path to my shelter. They're apparently higher in vitamin C than any citrus, so I snack as I go – at least I won't die of scurvy.

One morning I wake shivering under my summer sleeping bag and scuttle around to find a blanket. If this is any indication of the winter to come – which I have been told is pretty fierce, temperatures getting down to seven below – I need to give some serious thought to my real shelter. The lean-to that was meant to take a fortnight to build is still leaking (and hence still tarped) after two full layers of bark and two months of work.

I've begun to scale back my grand design. I imagined a round shelter made with thigh-high wattle-and-daub walls in the old pioneering style – woven wattle branches coated in a "survival cement" mix of clay and grasses – with a paperbark roof supported by saplings lashed like a teepee at the apex. Ryan was quick to point out that clay and mud are not so thick on the ground near my shelter, and that I might be ambitious to assume I could personally wheelbarrow in enough from the quarry. What a killjoy. I had been picturing myself hitching my skirt and stomping up to my knees in mud and grasses like a jolly winemaker.

I switch on my head torch, wrap the blanket around my shoulders and reach for my sketch book, flicking through the pages of my design ideas. One thing I am not willing to concede is the shape – I absolutely have to live in a circular shelter. Who ever decided on the four-wall rule anyway? It's cheaper, I suppose. But the idea of building corners and straight lines here seems completely out of sync with the circular shapes all around me: trees and raindrops and planets and berries and fly bums. I haven't as yet seen a square leaf. I want to be hugged by my shelter, encircled by it, the centre of my own little universe.

Design ideas go round and round in my mind. How can I make it waterproof and warm *and* also let light in? What would a primitive window look like? I try sketching a thatched shutter, but it has "leak here" written all over it. "Simplicity, simplicity, simplicity," I murmur, looking beyond the overhanging roof to the larger roof of stars above me. That's it! A roof of stars. I've been trying to design a house, but the forest is my house. All I need is to create one room within it that provides protection from rain and cold. The other rooms – dining and lounge, bathroom, rumpus room, home theatre – have already been built for me.

I draw the simplest design I can picture – an igloo-like dome, made by bending a dozen or so saplings into the middle and lashing them to their opposites, a central fireplace with an underground air tunnel and a chimney. I pause on the roof plan. Despite my troubles with paperbark, it's hard to concede the dream – the no-fuss primitive equivalent to corrugated iron. It was too good to be true. I'm going to have to thatch with grass. Bundle by bundle. The thought is completely overwhelming, but we all seem to be coming to the same conclusion. Shaun has already almost finished thatching his treehouse with blady grass, and it looks like it might work. I guess millions of peasants throughout history can't be wrong.

That's the design taken care of, but what about labour? I know I can't do this alone. I think I've burnt out Shaun's help for the time being, and the others are fully consumed with their own shelters (and those of their besties), so there's no-one else. I stay awake watching the Milky Way, wrestling with my fierce desire to do it alone and the reality of what it will take to make a space to be alone in. I finally conclude that there's only one way I'm going to get this done.

*

"Hi, Dad, um, you know how you said to call if I needed you, well ... I think I do," I cough humbly into Dan's phone the next day.

My parents respond to my lifeline call with the same gusto as if I had asked them to help move me into a dorm room at Harvard Law School. "Of course, we're happy to help," Mum said, after Dad had passed the phone over. I'm relieved, but a bit surprised. There previously would have been a provisional "Yes, but (as long as it's something we approve of)." If I had pulled this stunt ten years ago, they would have had a whole lot more to say about it before picking up tools. Perhaps things really are changing. After watching five children, and their friends and classmates, grow up and try to find their places in the world, some keeling over from the pressure or falling by the wayside, my parents were softening into a wisdom befitting their sixty-four years, one that said the only thing that really matters is that their children are happy and healthy. Maybe this could be a bonding activity, fun even.

"So, where do we start? Which wall should we tackle first?" Dad says, within ten minutes of his arrival. I see he's unearthed his old moleskin trousers for the occasion. I think he's secretly excited. With a skilled eye for beauty, form and function, Dad loves a good building challenge.

"Well, it's all just one wall, actually, Dad. It's round, remember?"

"Round?" he says with a frown. "Are you sure? Four walls'd be easier. We'd have it knocked up in no time."

I sigh. This is going to be interesting, especially with me as the foreman and Dad as my lackey. We have a chequered history of working together. In fact, unless I relinquish all control (which I never do), relations often strain to breaking point. The front car-seats turned into a navigational battleground during a three-week driving trip through Europe with my parents some years ago. It didn't help that Dad assumed I could successfully direct us through Paris with a map of Europe. Mum was the backseat diplomat, trying desperately to keep the peace. Perhaps it is this memory that spurs her to gather us together on the first morning for a pep talk.

Mum perches in a ladylike manner on a log and smooths down her bobbed hair before putting on her folding travel hat. I eye the goodies packed neatly in the picnic basket next to her.

"Now, Bob, this is Claire's shelter so we need to remember that – we're just here to help. Agreed?" Agreed. Next thing he's off with saw in hand, headed for the nearest patch of leggy saplings, while Mum and I trail behind.

The first tree is down before I have even sized it up.

"Dad … I just need to lay my hands on the trees first before we cut them, okay?"

"What for?"

"Oh, well, I kind of check in with it. It's just something I do." Well, something I've just decided to do. I want the shelter building this time to be a bit more ceremonial. And, besides, if I would do it with an animal I was about to kill, then why not a tree? I kneel and lay my hands on the next intended victim.

"Any screaming?" Dad asks, but I'm too distracted by him watching me to feel anything.

Dad sets a cracking pace, cutting and hauling as if a snowstorm were on the horizon. It feels at odds with the slow, quiet movements of the bush I've been getting used to. By the end of the day we've knocked up half of the poles. I should be overjoyed and grateful, but instead I'm resentful. My shelter feels foreign, forced and tainted. This is not how I want my shelter to be built. I pictured myself kneeling beneath each sapling, gently asking if it would sacrifice its life to become part of my home, sinking them into holes sprinkled with herbs and aligned with the four cardinal directions. The reality is me struggling to hold Dad back for a few seconds while I perform a perfunctory, 'Um, so I really need another pole, do you mind, yeah great, thanks.' *Chop*.

The next morning, summer has returned, the ground hot before the sun has even peaked over the tops of the stringies. We eat breakfast in silence, despite Mum's attempts to lighten the mood with updates from home. I sulk into my oats, gulp down my tea and stomp over to where Dad has already started.

"Dad, can you just wait a second before putting that pole in? I'm not sure it's directly facing east."

He sighs. "I just measured it. Come on, we haven't got all day."

Well, we *do* actually, I think, swallowing my retort.

"Dad, let me tie the knot. I know how to do a clove hitch."

"Dad, can you wait until I bless the hole before you put it in?"

He leans heavily on the crowbar as I sprinkle in some native mint.

By morning tea the tension is rising with the thermometer. I take the tea Mum pours me from the thermos and sit by myself watching Dad work on, claiming, "No time for tea." His hands move deftly, throwing up the crowbar and catching it on its way down, a move he tried to show me yesterday. "Energy efficiency," he explained, but I turned the other way.

He suddenly looks old, tired and sad. What am I doing? I'm acting like a spoilt teenager. Something has to give here. Dad already has given something just by being here. It's my stubbornness grating between us, my clinging onto ideals that is the real source of any impure energy hanging around.

Picking up the crowbar Dad fashioned for me from a sapling yesterday, I join him on the other side of the hole, pounding the earth in syncopated rhythm. I catch his glance as our bars float up, and we grin at each other.

"Hey, you're getting the hang of this," he says. "Don't forget to put mint in the last hole."

Mum gives me a thumbs up behind his back. Soon we're joking around, bouncing ideas off each other. Having decided to use only natural cordage, I show Mum how to make string from the bark of wattle, separating the inner from the outer bark, softening it on the back of a knife. She quickly picks up how to reverse wrap the two strands, making a crude but incredibly strong cord. We slip into comfortable roles.

With the frame in, it's time for the nerve-racking process of bending them together in the centre. Pressing my whole body against a pole, I reach my hands up to grab its top, lowering it gently over my head, the curve of my body supporting the curve of the tree. I can feel it stretching, like ligaments pulled tight, the water in the veins of the tree bubbling as it bends. Dad stands at the ready in the centre to catch it, crooning to it in the same hypnotic language he reserves for rounding up the cows.

"*Easy* does it ... *there* she goes ... just a *little* bit further ... yep, yep, yep, *that's* right, you can do it."

I breathe in and release the tree a little, breathe out and pull down a little more. It feels like we're breathing together, Dad, tree, me – breathing the shelter into being. Eventually it yields enough to rest in an almost horizontal position.

Mum's not so sure. "Ooh, Bob, I think that's enough. It'll snap." Dad and I smile at each other as we reply simultaneously, "She'll be right." And it is, mostly: the trees are incredibly forgiving, except for the one that really does snap. Even then Dad and I look at each other with a "She'll be right" smile, applying a wet wattle-cord bandage around the strained fibres.

To the frame we attach four rows of horizontal runners from smaller saplings, Mum working double time to produce enough string. The chimney slows us down. I quickly cut off any talk of an inside fire being too dangerous. If it's good enough for millions of Africans, it's good enough for me. There is no way I am going to freeze my butt off outside all winter. As I've recently finished carving my kit, I show Dad how to make a bow-drill fire. Using a stringed bow and spindle is a hell of a lot easier than the hand-drill; however, with no evidence of it being used in Australia, and with a shoelace as a cord, it's nowhere near as sexy. Still, Dad's impressed. We sit around the fire long into the night, deliberating on chimney designs. How can we allow air to escape, but not let rain in? Several times I catch Dad muttering, "If we had nails ..."

When the billy is empty and there is still no resolution, Dad turns to me and says, "You know, Claire, when I can't work out a problem, I sleep on it, and somehow during the night the knot unties itself and the solution is right there, clear as day, in the morning."

Lo and behold, the old fella is right. Although I stay awake for a good long while trying to grind out an answer, in the morning an exact replica pops into my head in 3D form. Dad has also been struck with inspiration over night, of an entirely different kind. Amazingly, he concedes to my simpler design – three concentric

74

rings made from wattle, spaced at intervals and gradually narrow-ing, a wide bangalow palm-leaf sheath secured to the top. In theory, smoke will escape between the rings and rain will drip from the bangalow capping onto the thatch, and then, hopefully, slippery-slide to the ground below. It is fiddly work, carving the inside of the wattle to make it more pliable, lots of "She'll be rights" ending in a sharp snap and curse, but by the end of the third day an elegant spherical skeleton of my shelter stands adorned with a seriously cute top hat. With a feather stuck in it, I wouldn't be surprised if it started whistling.

After we pack Mum and Dad's boot with most of the guff I arrived with, we spend the last morning in the shade of the gum trees in the nearby paddock, laughing and chatting as we uproot the first of what I shudder to guess will be many loads of blady grass. As my pile grows, I look over to where Dad is barely visible, bent over in the grass, humming a Chuck Berry tune. It's the same one he'd play whenever it was haircut time, lining the five of us up for matching bowl cuts. I join in with my own harmony hum. He looks over and gives me a wink. As I feared, our seemingly enor-mous pile of grass bundles up to cover one single small panel of roof. It's daunting, but I'm just relieved to have a frame to hang it off. Now it's just sweat and hours ahead.

It was initially hard to see my decision to enlist the help of my parents as anything other than a serious compromise of my integ-rity – selling out my desire to craft by my own hands and in my own way a place of retreat, in exchange for a instant shelter forged from the values of "just get it done". But it doesn't feel like that now. It actually feels important that they were part of it.

As we've been weaving together the foundations of my first ever home, it is like we've been weaving to completion the role that my parents have played in my life until now. Starting in the east, the place of dawn and birth, I travelled to the farthest side of the circle, rejecting outright many of the values of my upbringing. Now I find myself walking back around to meet them, able to accept the gifts and shed the burdens that my parents, as every parent, passes on. I'm able to have gratitude for both.

Our easy enjoyment in each other, as we tie on the first bundles of grass with the string Mum has made, is laced with nostalgia, as if we all know something is ending. It is. It's more than a shelter. We're weaving me a cocoon. A second womb. A place in which I can cast off the remaining skins of childhood. Without it being said, our teary goodbyes recognise that nothing will be the same again.

AUTUMN

*

*Believe one who knows: you will find
something greater in woods than in books.
Trees and stones will teach you that which
you can never learn from masters.*

SAINT BERNARD DE CLAIRVAUX

*

THE SACRED ORDER OF SURVIVAL:

1. Shelter
2. Water
3. Fire
4. Food

1.

efore enlightenment, cut wood, carry water. The water barrel I'm attempting to lift into the wheelbarrow catches on the rim, threatening to tip the whole thing over. I strain on tiptoe to steady it, employing one knee to push it over the edge. Tin roof, tank, wheelbarrow, plastic jug – it's not exactly the picture I had of kneeling to drink from a free-flowing river. I did recently experiment with a survival filter on our creek. Cutting the flat end off a two-litre water bottle, I stretched a T-shirt around the drinking end, packed in layers of fine sand, ground charcoal and grasses, and filled it from the creek. The water that dripped through was definitely clearer and smelled good, but after I learnt of the chemicals dumped by the blueberry farms upstream, I'm not about to drink it. It's fine for an emergency, perhaps, although again that hinges on my having a plastic water bottle handy. The old "plastic fantastic" is still a crucial part of my umbilical cord to society. It's difficult to imagine that before white settlement you could drink from just about every water source. The land would have felt so much friendlier, so amenable to carefree wandering.

I pull up at a wattle and draw the knife from my belt. It's definitely losing its ninja novelty now. For a while I was conscious of it against my hip as I moved, but it's just become part of the bush uniform. I make a two-inch incision and tug at the bark. It falls from the trunk like orange peel in a long, loose spiral. For ages I couldn't work out why sometimes the bark would crack and split, while other times it practically fell into my hands. I finally saw the pattern: in the mornings or on really humid days, sap swelled and rose in the cambium cellular layer, making it moist enough to harvest. On hot, dry days, the tree conserved water, the bark clinging hard onto the trunk. It's high-school science knowledge, really, but my wattle cordage experiment is making the results very tangible. Of course trees are going to be different at different times of the day – just like me. When I rise every morning and take a big swig from my water bottle, I imagine the trees around me doing the same. I suddenly feel surrounded not so much by solid wood but by mini pump stations, drawing water up out of the soil, into their veins, and out into the leaves that stretch turgidly to salute the sun. Hidden waterfalls are all around me.

Surely this is the place for a survival slurp. Ryan and I experimented with cutting a sapling and sitting the base in a bucket. Four hours later, a cup of sweet eucalyptus-flavoured water had dripped out. It was good in theory, but in survival terms it's a "hole in the bucket" scenario – first I would need a saw, then a means of lifting it back into a standing position, and then a vessel to catch the water. Even the simplest tasks are deceptively complicated in the wild, and time-consuming – thatching with wattle string, for instance. After I tied on the first rung of grass with natural cordage, I realised that to do so for the entire shelter would mean stripping all the wattle within a radius of many kilometres, and six months of twiddling my thumbs to make the string. This morning's harvest is for frame reinforcement (which must remain pure), but from now on I'm using made-in-China sisal string for thatching – plastic fantastic to the rescue again.

There's one plastic item that's now redundant (hopefully). I've optimistically de-tarped my lean-to after completing the third layer of paperbark. Manoeuvring the wheelbarrow down my trail, I smile at the new vista, my site feeling more habitat than hobo camp without the lairy blue roof. The recent layer of paperbark, while yet untested, is my last. I'm not prepared to strip one more tree, and I don't think the shelter could support it, anyway. It was a bittersweet finish, though. I was rushing on the last paperbark and carelessly cut too deep, the tree spurting fluid like a burst water pipe. I pressed down on the wound, trying to stem the flow. Despite my learning that the tree is a great source of potable water, there is a chance that my haste has killed it. I bandaged it and mentally logged its position so I can return to find out in six months. Still, I celebrated the roof opening by donning my favourite moss-green woollen vest in camouflage camaraderie.

I unload my water outside the lean-to, sit cross-legged with my machete in front of a timber board and begin to *thwack* a clean edge on handfuls of grass, the roots a growing pile of witchetty grubs on the sand beside me.

God, it feels good to be alone. It's the first full day I've had to myself in what seems like ages. It's been really bloody busy: in the last few weeks there's been another two-day bird workshop, a land-scape awareness day with an ecologist and a four-day bush-food workshop. And, in between, grass, grass and more grass. Again, if Shaun hadn't offered to help me with that, I'd be stuffed. In the late afternoon we can often be found gloved in the paddock, the rhythm of our grass yanking sounding much like cows at mealtime.

Nikki has dubbed us the Blady Bunch, which sounds like a happier family than it is. There are fun times, but more often there is simmering tension, especially when we're all together. You can almost hear the clang of our unspoken hopes and fears bumping into each other. I thought it might have settled down after summer, but the only thing that has settled are the cliques and the chasms. Ryan is still stiff and surly with me and that hurts, but not as much as my strained relationship with Chloe. I miss her company but avoid her at the same time. The other day I found her in the Gunyah, painting a rooster on canvas, and made some subtly demeaning remark about her use of time. No wonder I'm dreaming of a neurotic, tight-lipped old woman.

The only real tribal camaraderie I feel is when Nikki, Ryan, Shaun and I are on mission together. Something about that com-bination works, maybe because there's a fair bit of bitching about "the twins", as Shaun calls Chloe and Dan. It's a fair call; they act like naughty kids up the back of the classroom. I'm not sure whose authority they are trying to rebel against, or why, but it's annoying. I spent the last two days with them and Shaun, building our floors. Flooring was not something I had considered until the last rain, when I realised that rising damp was going to be a severe understatement unless I got my bum six inches off the ground. So, contracted together by mutual necessity, we wheelbarrowed in hundreds of loads of gravel to one another's sites and tamped it down in a rough rammed-earth style.

At the end of the day Chloe pulled me aside and asked, "What does our relationship mean to you?" I didn't know how to answer her. The comforting memories of how things were between us bump against the painful reality of how they are now. I'm confused about why she's resisting being here, resisting what I thought we both wanted and needed. But just her asking that question seems to have lifted some of the tension.

Even though we're still bound together by the need for physical labour, for communal tools, utes, trailers, food and fire, I've made a small but significant shift away from the group by moving my breakfast supplies to my lean-to. It's amazing what a difference this has made, not to having to tiptoe around the couples or worry about how the morning fire was lit. Now I just have to hold out until I can *really* move in to my shelter and begin a proper solo life. I hear there are big rains coming, so I'm madly trying to make grass bundles while the sun shines.

*

As I cut off lengths of string, I arch my back and stretch out my legs. The pile of grass looks as if I've hardly made a dent in it. A couple of scarlet honeyeaters land directly above me, fire-engine red feathers stunning against the yellow banksias. Despite my pleasure in taking some time alone, I can't help but wonder what the others are up to today.

Here's the story, of a bunch of bladies ...

That damn song is stuck in my head again. That's another thing I thought would have settled down by now – my brain. It's actually sped up, or else I'm only just noticing how crazy it is. The commentary flits between planning (finishing shelter, skills to master, places to explore), grumbling about the group and random memories. Today I've been at a New York cafe with the cute waiter who asks, "Is that chai on soy?" to which I coyly reply, "How did you guess?" I sometimes feel as if I'm deliberately generating these space fillers, avoiding silence like a nervous host.

There are chinks in my thought armour appearing, though. In the campfire game last night, I could *not* think of a four-letter word beginning with "m" that means "a lot". And on the way to my sit spot this morning, my mind dropped into my body, sinking below the level of thought, as I fox-walked. When gaps in thought appear, I know them only in hindsight, my signal a warmth that suffuses my chest, a bodily pleasure in momentary stillness. I pause to take in a centipede riding the lean-to post, its legs rippling in seamless coordination. What will happen when these moments of stillness open windows that extend the view to vast horizons of open-sky mind?

Taking a bundle that is just wider than the circle made by my thumb and first finger, I roughly tap the roots into line before cinching them together with a surgeon's knot. The first few are a bit rough before I find my rhythm.

The Blady Buuunnnnch ... the Blady Buuuunnnnnch ...

It's been interesting to watch the other shelters rise up out of the dirt and assume the likeness of their makers, in either form or function, the way a pet might. Shaun has bravely pronounced his "finished" (a word that sits right alongside "waterproof" in its relative meaning). His shelter is a treehouse crossed with a rickety Thai beach hut, and he gallantly scales a knotted rope to his sleeping loft, only as wide as his shoulders, from where he can look out over the old quarry through his monocle – like a pirate. His roof looks like it's just stumbled out of bed, blady grass sticking out at awkward angles from the A-frame corners. I wouldn't have thought thatching was a method particularly conducive to patchwork, but Shaun keeps poking in a few more bundles to try and tame the roof's mane, earning him the nickname "Ten More Bundles". I think his "ten more bundles" refrain may be the excuse he uses in front of the boys for why he keeps accompanying me to the blady fields. Not that I'm complaining.

Dan's shelters are progressing in short bursts of frenetic activity. First came the kitchen, then nothing happened for weeks. After that, he worked a fortnight of twelve-hour days notching logs to form a waist-high rectangular wall, in the style of a log cabin, which he sealed with clay. With another burst, he erected a roof frame of curved saplings like mine. Dan's first foray into the blady fields quickly burnt up his remaining enthusiasm, and his shelter is now a blue-tarped mushroom that's empty inside. Besides, he's got other things on his mind – a love interest with a fella that was brewing before the bush year started has recommenced with ferocity via mobile phone and days away from camp. I just don't get it, but it seems I'm the only one here who could quite happily don monastic robes this year.

True to her noncommittal style, Nikki has only just sunk her first post holes. Her shelter plans are the inverse of mine – a large, open lean-to. I can't imagine how she will keep warm in winter, unless she plans to snuggle up with Ryan. If he finishes his shelter before winter, that is. Ryan's Queenslander took a sharp turn when a miniature model illustrated one key design fault: the gently sloping grass roof did almost nothing to prevent a bucketload of water from falling straight through it. Instead he has borrowed from the wisdom of his home country, by beginning construction on a teepee of a size and stature to rival those of the Mohawks – a five-metre-high handmade ladder his only access to the top. To service it Ryan has created an outdoor woodworking studio and laid a tessellated, seven-sided raised floor, making his shelter big enough to raise ten kids inside. I'm in awe of the sheer amount of grass (and time) it's going to take to thatch. He's quick to cut off any doubtful talk, though: "I've always wanted to build something, so this is my chance. If it takes me all year, then so be it." Spoken with Zen acceptance yet with not a small edge of defensive anxiety.

If Ryan is living in The Block Heights, his neighbour Chloe is in more of a working-class suburb. Like me, Chloe decided to live in the shed while the house went up. But as with many DIY-builder jobs, the shed has become the permanent dwelling, with various mismatched add-ons and extensions – a bit of a stringybark roof here, a bit of a thatched wall there. The one sloping wall that she covered in forest debris is proving to be a rodent haven. Still, it has a kind of impulsive, ramshackle charm, just like its owner.

And that's how they became the Blady Bunch ...

Now for the fun part. The hours of bundling translate quickly into rungs on the roof. I bunch the grass up tight and comb the edges together affectionately, as though running my fingers through someone's hair. Fixing the last bundle, I step back to survey progress. Wow, that's actually a quarter of my shelter thatched. If I really go hard, I could be done in a couple of weeks.

And then what? The question lands with an empty thud in the pit of my stomach, the wide-open space I've been hankering for suddenly becoming a cliff edge I'm walking towards.

*

As I drape my clothes over the fallen limb at the edge of the waterhole, I look down at my naked body. My arms are brown and buff, and I've definitely dropped some weight. My feet appear to have grown a size since being unshackled from shoes. They're tanned and leathery, the soles etched with mud-stained cracks. After numerous stubs to one of my big toes, the toenail is threatening to fall off, while the skin of the other is peeling underneath. There are two other tender places on my feet, as if splinters are buried there, but I can't find them. I'm still sporting the scars of the hundreds of tick bites I collected on one blady trip, the red dots that I've been scratching joining up to look like the rash of a venereal disease. I'm getting used to being dirty and bitten, and I'm not craving hot showers much at all while the waterhole is still warm. We humans are adaptable creatures, really. One welcome change is my hair. My no-shampoo experiment in the city was an oily disaster, but here the tannins in the water are licking it clean and shiny.

Easing myself into the shallow bend of the waterhole, I let out an audible sigh of relief. As I float on my back, gentle ripples massage the ache in my shoulders, my legs tingling from the day's accumulated grass cuts. I breathe deep and long.

Bathing in water is almost as crucial to my survival as drinking it. Day after day it embraces me, soaking my dried-up inspiration to make it plump and full again. It reminds me that there is nowhere else I want to be but held in the cricked elbow of this nameless waterhole, feeling myself – if only for a moment – forget the sound of my own name.

2.

"March-fly bum, anyone?" Ryan says, offering the winged morsel he has just slapped on his thigh. I screw up my face and take a Thumbelina-sized bite of the hindquarters, trying not to flinch as a wing brushes my gums. A shot of honey-ish liquid bursts out of the sac onto my tongue.

"Sweet revenge, eh?" chuckles Bill, the laid-back woodsman who's arrived to give a two-day advanced cordage and rope-making workshop. Laying out a cow skin rug, he tips a large knotted-string bag upside down, releasing dozens of balls of homemade cord in varying shades of brown, green and cream, some sturdy as sailor's rope, others thin as fishing line. The skill that has gone into these is clear – there's not a hint of a frayed edge or bumpy splice. That's a piece of art right there, I think, eyeballing them eagerly.

"All here?" Bill asks. Jessie the dog races into the Gunyah in front of Dan, who collapses against the back pole. Chloe's face is pinched and drawn as she writes in her journal; Shaun stands at the edge, tapping his foot. I nod politely from my cross-legged position down the front, Ryan and Nikki next to me.

"Welcome to the wonderful world of string and fibre," Bill announces gaily, his face becoming serious as he leans his elbow on one knee and says, "Now, I reckon string has been given pretty short shrift in the scheme of things.

"Think about it – you need string for shelters, fire making, fishing nets and lines, snares and deadfall traps, baskets, lashing spears and stone tools ..."

"Sewing," Nikki jumps in.

"Yep, sewing clothes ... I reckon it's in the running to be pretty damn essential, don't you?

"Now, we're not going over the stuff you know, because two-strand reverse wrap is baby's play. Nope, I'm talking three-strand, double reverse wrap, splicing, tanning ..." he says, getting visibly excited.

"Your mission by the end of two days is, in two teams, to make four metres of triple-strand tanned rope and then see if we can't have a good ol' tug of war!"

The group is silent, except for Dan, who lets out a heavy sigh from the back.

"Nah, it's not hard. Come on, let's get started," Bill says, mistaking our lack of enthusiasm for intimidation at the task, not realising that the real challenge is the idea of working together – all except for the one undaunted team player.

"Cool, okay, who's on my team?" asks Nik, jumping up.

My string envy overcomes my resistance to yet another group activity, and I wander over to where Bill is explaining the different materials.

"Lomandra and dianella – absolute gems." They're both abundant around here, but I tried using them fresh and wasn't too impressed with the results. "You gotta strip 'em green, hang 'em to dry, then re-soak 'em," Bill explains.

Holding out his wrist, he pulls hard at a fine thread bracelet to demonstrate the strength of the gymea lily, well known around the Sydney sandstone area for its enormous single red flower. Bill sets Shaun to work on its large flat leaf, showing him how to pound the thick central vein with just the right strength to loosen but not break the fibres, then clean off the snotty cellulose with his thumbnail. To Chloe and Dan, Bill offers the rainforest options – cordyline leaves, bangalow palm flowers and leaf sheaths, and the inner bark of fig and stinging trees. Ryan takes hold of the New Zealand flax that Bill pinched from a park garden on his way here.

"And now for my hands-down favourite," Bill says, unwrapping a long bundle of damp hessian to reveal two long skinny saplings. "Native hibiscus." Picking a leaf, he hands it to me, the rough edges giving way to a tart lemony flavour in my mouth.

Unzipping the bark from the trunk in one long cut, I lay it flat and use the back of my knife to scrape off the green outer layer, until the starchy white of the inner bark is all that remains. Bill coils it up and swaps it with some he has had soaking for two weeks. "Perfectly ripe," he says, with a glint in his eye, the dripping bundle he hands me sporting the distinctive smell of rotting vegetation.

I watch as Bill pushes the belt of bark together so that it buckles up in paper-thin layers, which he separates off with his thumb. Compared to the coarse wattle, it's like weaving with white chocolate, the string falling from my fingers in easy cream rolls. It's such a pleasure that I can almost block out the noise of Dan updating Chloe on his love life.

"So, how's the shelter building going, folks?" Bill asks.

"Finished," says Shaun.

"Taking way too long," I say.

"As long as a length of string?" Bill grins.

Ryan looks up at me sharply. "What is it with you and time? Ever since you've arrived everything has been, 'Can't do it, it'll take too long.'"

"Well, sorry, but I do actually have other plans this year, apart from playing with grass." My face flushes.

Bill looks perplexed. Poor fella, he doesn't realise he's just happily waltzed his string bag into a smouldering volcano, the pressure of several months of communal bush living cracking the thin crust of niceness and civility to form ever-wider fissures. My brothers' jokes about *Lord of the Flies* don't seem so far-fetched now. Our small community, which I hoped would provide mutual support for each other's exploration of the wilds, seems intent on focusing on human drama. Perhaps a Buddhist monastery, or an ashram in India would have been a better choice for me to find the space I crave? But I know I don't want to be shuttered within four walls; I want my meditation to be a sensory experience, with the forest – and not a dusty text – as my guide.

Jessie chases a butterfly, taking with him all of Ryan's carefully split fibres.

"Is it too much to ask you to control your dog?" Ryan says to Dan, with a death stare.

"He's not meant to be at the workshops anyway," I say, already pissed off that I was woken last night by the roar of Dan's van, Kylie Minogue's latest album blaring, when he drove right up to his shelter, despite the no-vehicles rule on the property.

"Okay, folks, now I'm gonna show you the best way to stop this rope from fraying," Bill says, demonstrating how to splice the end of the rope back in on itself.

Ryan sniggers. "Too late for that."

"I don't get it. Where does this bit go?" Dan says, looking as dark as charcoal as he wrestles with his rope.

"Look, you just pick up this piece and divide it in two," Nikki explains.

"If you just listened for once, you'd get it," Shaun mutters, frustrated at his own mess of knots.

"What was that?" Dan says sharply.

Ryan sighs and turns his back on everyone. I struggle to secure my own rope ends, as everything unravels around me.

"Hey, Ryza, do you remember when we made that deer-hide rope in class?" I say, Ryan shrugging in response. Why did I feel the need to say that? When I'm not being the camp warden, I'm mopping up after everyone, trying to keep the peace. I feel like screaming.

Bill hands me the mallet. Perfect. I whack at the fallen gee-bung, chipping the bark loose before dropping it into a pot of water boiling on the fire. The ropes wrap themselves around one another in the pot, turning a deep shade of blood red in the simmering water.

*

The night is hot and I drift in and out of sleep. I dream that I'm driving a huge bulldozer with L-plates on. It's awkward and unwieldy, and I'm stuck in gridlocked city traffic. When I arrive at the demolition site, everything is being sucked into a vacuum and vomited out as a thick metallic sludge spiked with nails. Even my bulldozer gets pulled in and pulverised. I climb a leaning pole and watch as the grey lava beneath me swallows everything in its path.

*

On the morning of the second day of the rope workshop, Dan is pacing the Gunyah perimeter like a caged animal. Ryan and Nikki have obviously had a falling-out, Nikki red-eyed and quiet.

Nikki, Shaun and I team up, silently weaving our strands together. I'm so exhausted and on edge that I struggle to remember how to spin the fibres correctly.

No-one has spoken for a good hour, with even Bill lost for words to slacken the tension that is cinching in tighter and tighter.

Jessie races in pursuit of a fly, this time straight into my neatly coiled string.

"Piss off, dog," I explode.

"That's it!" Dan shouts, red-faced and fuming. "Get me the hell outta here." And, with that, he disappears.

*

I shut my journal with a snap as Ryan approaches the waterhole. I don't bother looking over to gauge his reaction. I'm so raw right now that, for once, I just don't care. He walks by me with the barest of nods and squats at the water's edge, as if waiting.

"What's going on, Ryan?" I ask, the question verging on rhetorical.

He lifts his head to watch the clouds, one skidding on an air current to catch up to the mass.

"D'ya know that I walk around half the day having arguments with you in my head?" he finally offers.

I snort, surprised at his honesty. "Sounds fun. What about?"

"Oh, everything ... and nothing. Just fighting with you."

"Well, that makes two of us."

We lapse into silence, watching the clouds pull apart like fairy floss. A currawong swoops in low, landing in a nest above our heads.

Spinning around, Ryan looks me in the eye.

"You know what? Being around you is too much like looking in a mirror."

A moment of mutual recognition flashes between us. He turns back just as abruptly and dives steeply into the centre of the waterhole, surfacing almost out of sight.

We are all swimming in a sea of our own toxic shit. All the accumulated stink of our patterns and prejudices, usually contained within our comfortable routines and distractions, have nowhere else to go but out. We're sweating in a cold-turkey haze, in the throes of a giant collective detoxification; the old structures of our lives are disintegrating into black mud, which we fling at each other daily.

I dive in to the other end of the waterhole and search for a log to cling to. That's about as solid as it gets around here. The current is far stronger than I anticipated, and I hang on desperately, trying all the while to keep from drowning in a river of my own muck.

*

It's time for my evening torture session with the hand-drill. A foreboding air accompanies me behind the kitchen, pre-empting the lashing I will no doubt give myself in a matter of minutes, my firestick more a cane for self-flagellation these days than any survival implement.

Everyone has produced a hand-drill coal except for me and Nikki – and Nik hasn't even been trying since a few weeks ago, when her neck spasmed and froze as she was play-boxing. A trip to hospital allayed any serious fears, but she was told not to lift a finger until it healed.

The other day I watched Chloe sit down cross-legged and calmly produce her first coal. "Cool," she said, as if it were nothing more than finding ten dollars in the grass. I've upped my practice to twice a day, despite the pain from the large blood blisters on both of my palms, but sometimes I can't even coax smoke out of the bloody thing.

"It's all in the technique," Kate told me recently. "Strength is not the most important thing. You need to learn to draw energy up from your core – don't just rely on your upper body. Trying negates the effort. But, most importantly, you need to have faith in yourself."

That comment gets me smoking every time. To think that it's somehow my attitude holding me back ... it just makes me fume. No, if it's a hand-drill I need, then a drill sergeant is what's required. I've started doing push-ups every day to build up my biceps.

Tonight could be the night.

Grasping the stalk between my palms, I pause for a moment and pray with gritted-teeth fervour. For a moment my vision goes blurry from the intensity of the pain, as the blisters press together. I focus my attention instead on the movement of my arms, pumping them back and forth like pistons. Keep going, just keep going. The pain numbs into a general burning sensation.

"Frickin' smoke, hurry the frick up," I urge.

Like a spinning top losing momentum, the stalk starts rocking violently from side to side, and my forearms are losing their grip. With a single bum-puff the firestick jumps out of the notch, and with it, any hope of fire.

"Fuck you," I yell, hurling the kit into the scrub. Burying my forehead into the sand, I sob hot tears of rage and injustice, just like the previous night, the one before that and the many others since I arrived.

You're a failure. It's almost April, and you still haven't got a hand-drill coal. Look at you on the ground, crying. It's pathetic. You're just not trying hard enough; you're not committed enough.

Just admit it, this whole year is a failure. You *are a complete failure.*

The accusations rain down like stones, and I curl into a ball for protection.

Scrreeeechhh!

My herd jerks upward at the piercing cry of black cockatoos. Three silhouettes wheel and turn, sprays of yellow tail feathers glinting in the sun. They circle and land in a nearby wattle, tearing branches apart with their beaks in search of grubs.

Whhheeee-ahhhhh!

My skin prickles. I know the call well, even though they rarely flew over the family farm. "The goosepimple bird" I called it as a child, before I knew its name, referring to the effect on my body of its call, as it echoed through the valleys and hills like thunder. "Rain's coming," Dad would say, if three blackies flew over. He also reckoned that they flew over more often when I was home. They would frequently appear when I was in logged forests, circling over me as I stood atop the charred stumps, looking down across blackened gullies. It would sometimes feel as if the Earth itself were looking down at me through those black eyes, crying a melancholy lament.

The cockatoos take off with a shriek, looking back as if beckoning to me. Peeling myself off the sand, I'm almost under their new perch when they rise up, landing just within sight. As I break into a jog, they leapfrog ahead again, and I quicken my steps to catch them, crashing through spiderwebs and ducking under branches, eyes focused on the flashes of black and yellow ahead. I burst into a large clearing. The birds have landed in the top branches of a single stunted fig. When I reach the tree they take off, circling above me once, before banking sharply to the west and disappearing.

I run my hand over the mosaic of lichens on the trunk, frilly pinks next to lime greens. Old man's beard lichen hangs like mint-dyed lace. The tree reminds me of the huge figs I half lived in as a kid. Hoisting myself up, I climb to a high limb and straddle it, nestling my cheek against the bark. It's still warm from the late afternoon sun, and I sink my weight further into its embrace. A kangaroo lopes in to feed beneath me, figbirds perch on a branch nearby. I close my eyes, a breeze tickling leaves on my neck. It's the touch of my grandmother's fingernails as I lay on her lap, my cheek resting on the rough wool of her skirt.

"Why have I come here?" I whisper to her. "What should I do?"

3.

alcolm ... can you hear me?" Skype crackles and fades. Kate warned me their internet connection was slow, but I was hoping for a miracle. I switch off the video setting.

"Claire – hi there, how are you?" a deep male voice booms.

I suck in a breath of relief.

Malcolm was an instructor at the tracker school who gave me the sense he could see me in ways that I couldn't. He lived alone for a year in a primitive shelter decades ago, and I have a feeling he is exactly the elder I need right now.

My story tumbles out in a waterfall, the words tripping over each other in my urgency to unload them.

"I'm kind of here but not here ... I want to be alone but can't seem to leave the group. I love the skills but can't make fire. I'm rushing around trying to do everything at once. I had such great expectations for this year and they're all slipping away. I'm just not sure what I'm doing here anymore ..." I'm trying not to break down.

"It's clear what's happening here, Claire," Malcolm cuts in. "Your whole life, you've been conditioned to *do*: to achieve, to be productive. It's what you equated with self-worth and approval. Now you've stepped one foot outside that world, your ego is desperate to maintain the status quo. It probably feels like you've got a civil war inside you."

"Well, I know who's winning," I grumble. "But I had a great childhood, really, with affection and encouragement. It wasn't like I was pushed ... well, only with good intentions. This level of agitation just doesn't add up."

"Claire, the messages we receive from our culture run deep. It trains us to be human doings, rather than human beings. Your upbringing was particularly strong in this.

"For a woman, in particular, this comes at a great cost – separation from her true self. The most important task for you this year is to return to the feminine."

My heart jolts, my hands rising to rest on my collarbones.

"What *exactly* do you mean by that?"

"The feminine is guided by feeling and intuition. She learns to listen to the impulses arising within her, and acts according to her own sense of rightness. Her heart, not what the outside world deems to be success, is her map and compass. This is the seat of her power."

My shoulders droop forward, as if the strings holding them up have been cut.

"What I want you to do is simple: I just want you to feel. Feel *everything*. Unmoor your emotions from the judgments that will arise and come back to your heart. Ask yourself, 'What do I *feel* like doing now?' And then do that."

My shoulders snap back to attention.

"That's it? You're saying that my whole project this year is just to feel? What about the skills – fire and tracking?"

"The Earth is a great healer. If you release into her, she will teach you what you need to know. Surrender."

Surrender. The word resounds like a bell inside me.

"Claire, understand this," Malcolm's voice drops a register, "your mind got you there on the premise of learning skills, but you are there for something much more important. You are there to heal, to shift from being a girl buffeted by her external environment into the full power of a woman. Start with an experiment. Give yourself two days off – a holiday – and just do whatever you feel like. Be flighty, be spontaneous, be wild ..."

"Just be myself ..." I say quietly.

Malcolm leaves me with a warning. "Change is not easy, transformation less so. As each brick crumbles, it will feel like you're falling apart. Life does shatter us, just as the seed shatters the pod. Take care out there."

With that, my cyber-elder disappears, leaving me alone with a heart beating in nervous anticipation.

Closing the door behind me, I tilt my head towards the sun and let its rays soak through me like a shower of molten rain.

*

I rifle through my barely touched crate of books. There it is, down the very bottom, its pages yellow and musty: *Women Who Run with the Wolves*. The torn front cover shows a painting of a naked woman chasing her shadow across a moonlit desert landscape. The image jumped out at me from a pile of books in the back of a second-hand shop, years ago. I found it again when I was packing and threw it in at the last minute.

I turn over to the back cover.

The wild woman carries with her the bundles for healing; she carries everything a woman needs to be and know. She carries the medicine for all things.

I sink onto a stump. Two yellow robins cling to a nearby tree, watching. I draw my knees up and open the first page.

The spiritual lands of the Wild Woman have throughout history, been plundered or burnt, dens bulldozed and natural cycles forced into unnatural rhythms to please others.

We may have forgotten her names, we may not answer when she calls ours, but in our bones we know her, we yearn toward her; we know she belongs to us and we to her.

... then we leap into the forest or into the desert or into the snow and run hard searching for a clue, a remnant, a sign that she still lives, that we have not lost our chance.

I close the book with a shiver. The robin flits in front of me.

What do I *feel* like doing right now?

I stand up, wriggling my toes into the dirt.

What does Wild Woman feel like doing?

She takes one step forward, then another, and disappears behind a wall of green.

*

Wild Woman pads with silent bare feet through the rainforest this morning, leeches snuggling between her toes, bracken fern shivering the insides of her thighs. She plays snakes and ladders as she moves, feeling lithe and light – tiptoeing over fallen branches, crawling through burnt-out trees and swinging on hanging vines. She rests for a moment, then lets the sound of an unknown bird, a forest of tiny fungi or some other new friend seduce her.

Wild Woman plucks basket reeds from the heart of the lomandra, binding the bundle with roughly made string. Chewing on the white fleshy bases of the reeds, she gasps as a brush turkey stalks out of the undergrowth in front of her.

Wild Woman drapes herself along a log, making shapes from scudding clouds. White-naped honeyeaters feed at the mountain devils near her face. Fairy-wrens dance within inches of her toes. She rests in the silence between visitors, between breaths, between sunbursts and clouded shade.

Picked up by an afternoon wind, she rises to run down sandy trails, hurdling logs and ducking low-hanging branches, her mind wholly absorbed in the task of finding the perfect placement of every footfall, until eventually she falls into the leaf litter and traces wings with her arms.

Wild Woman finds a nest of moss woven with tiny twigs. It's time for some nest work of her own. Diving under the steep far bank of the waterhole, she forages with fingers in reeds and rushes until locating the seam of silk. Sleek as a platypus she surfaces with a quiet splash, before diving blind again, all noise underwater as she kicks to hold herself at the bottom long enough to unearth chunks of clay.

Returning naked on the backtrail with a full bucket, Wild Woman scoops out gravel and earth in a circle within the centre of her shelter. Rocks are moved and shaped to fit, the jigsaw cemented with clay spread thick as cold sliced butter. Her hands continue to move between the rocks long after they are laid, making hypnotic circular motions in the hardening rivers of grey.

Wild Woman sits back to admire the beauty of her hearth; her hands are tired but she is deeply satisfied. The shelter feels warmer, no longer a collection of sticks and grass thrown together but made whole, awake, staring back at her through this single central eye. She wonders what changes it will witness over the coming months.

At dusk, Wild Woman reaches for the caches of dry sticks that collect in tree forks and snaps them over her bare legs. She has been alone all day, and considers for a second replying to the beckoning call from the trailhead, wondering what invitation it brings. She holds silent, though, and glows in relief when her small fire offers the best company.

When the dark can get no darker, Wild Woman walks under the cuticle moon, past the flickering glow cast on the leaves and limbs around the home fires of her tribe, to where the forest shadows deepen. Her heart thrums to the rhythmic *whirr* of flying fox wings, thin and papery against the moist night air; she watches as an orb spider weaves threads as thick and golden as raw silk. As she enters a new trail, a scribbly gum beckons to her, one limb twisted in a perfect circle, standing with hand on hip. The closer she walks, the more strongly she is drawn to it. She nestles herself amidst its sprawling toes, and rests.

*

I unwrap the bow-drill spindle slowly and turn it in my hand. This is not just any spindle, it's the magic spindle. I haven't once failed to get a fire with it, usually within minutes. Once I realised its special qualities, I decided to keep it for emergencies and special occasions only. It hangs from a beam in my shelter, wrapped in a special cloth. I'm comforted by the knowledge that it's there.

I nestle my foot close up to the notch, the side arch stained cigarette-yellow from its close proximity to the friction. Jamming the bow between my right hip and the ground, I free up my hands to loop the spindle around the bow. Grabbing the wattle handhold, I fit it down over the upright pointy end of the spindle. I check my pose: left knee at a right angle, elbow wrapped firmly around my shin for stability. Good to go. I pause for a few moments longer than usual before lightly moving the bow back and forth, settling the spindle down into the notch before applying pressure. Smoke starts to waft almost immediately from the friction point. I speed up, the smoke billowing so vigorously I can't see the board. I don't want to wear the spindle down anymore than absolutely necessary and ease off as soon as I sense a coal.

With the fire crackling away, I settle back on my swag and open *Women Who Run with the Wolves* to a random chapter. It is a fairytale titled "Red Shoes".

"Once upon a time in a village there lived a poor motherless child who had no shoes ..." I read.

Over time the child saved scraps of cloth and sewed herself a pair of red shoes. Even though she was poor, and spent her days foraging for food in the woods until past dark, the shoes made her feel rich. They were rough but she loved them.

One day as she walked down the road in her red shoes, a gilded carriage pulled up next to her. Inside was a wealthy woman who promised her a world of riches, and so the girl went with her. Despite her new and fine garments, the girl grew sad, for she was made to sit still and not speak. When she asked after her red shoes, the woman told her they were burnt along with the rest of her clothes.

I'm unable to stay awake and drift into a dream. I, too, am wearing a pair of bright red shoes. However, instead of being homemade, these are mail-order, cheap Chinese copies of the original. The left strap is broken, and I stick both legs up in the air in a compromising position while a man tries unsuccessfully to fix it.

I wake heavy and read to the fairytale's end. The girl forgets her homemade shoes when she's given a brand-new, fire-engine-red pair. So enchanted is she by their beauty, she is deaf to any warnings. Dancing and dancing in her precious red shoes, her ecstasy turns to horror when she discovers that she cannot stop. Instead of dancing the shoes, the shoes dance her, onwards and onwards, threatening to dance her to death. In desperation, she eventually begs an executioner to cut off her feet.

Tears of recognition spill down my cheeks. I know that girl, I know that dance – that relentless, spinning, crazed dance. All this time I've been wearing someone else's shoes, dancing someone else's dance. A wave of exhaustion sweeps over me, and I collapse back onto the swag.

How long ago did I trade in my own shoes? When did I exchange them for inferior reproductions? The feeling of a memory whose image won't surface causes me to shed fresh tears.

It has been Wild Woman calling me all these years, rapping at my door, howling in my ears, winding roots around my ankles. She watched as I allowed myself to be seduced by counterfeits, to follow dead-end roads paved with inherited expectations, but still she came looking for me, leaving a trail of breadcrumbs dropped from a hole in her skirt pocket, in the hope that I would someday come to find her. I'm here now, with a homemade patchwork shelter and the wild woods all around me, but there's no telling yet if it's all smoke and mirrors.

Malcolm's words take on a new gravitas. I need to find my original shoes and stitch back together what I lost years ago, what was taken from me. And, at the same time, I must find a way to shed the shiny imitations before it's too late.

4.

"Darlings, by the end of this workshop, you will hand me every single metal item from your kitchen," Claudia, our primitive pottery teacher, informs us with a deadpan German twang.

Seated on the ground, she spreads her legs, as thick as fence posts, around a tub. Her hands form a dragnet in the murky water, fishing out a grapefruit-sized chunk of red clay, which she begins to knead ferociously. Blood-red water runs up her forearms, staining the edges of the khaki shirt rolled to her elbows. At intervals, she brushes back the loose brown curls that have fallen over her eyes with her left wrist, leaving a smudge of rust across her forehead.

"Sweeties, this is how it goes. You will rise at dawn. You will join me for two hours of yoga. You may swim. You may eat. If you're lucky you may even sleep. Otherwise you will be with the clay. If you sit on the toilet you work the clay. If you walk to the kitchen you work the clay. We have such short three days, and much to do. Do I have your 100 percent?"

The six of us are straight-backed and silent, spellbound by the sight of this Amazonian woman punishing an innocent ball of clay.

She raises one eyebrow. We're obviously meant to answer.

Shaun clears his throat. "Well, if it's okay with you, I'd like to keep it pretty flexible. I'm not sure that I'm really into ... you know

... pottery." His voice trails off when his suggestion is met with a steely glare.

"Really? Girls' stuff? Too easy for you?" Claudia says, arching one eyebrow higher than I thought possible.

"Sweetie, that not okay with me and not okay with the clay. The flesh of Earth Mother deserves more respect than that. You either stay now or go."

Shaun looks down.

Wow, I like this woman. Kate said she was known as the primitive Martha Stewart when she lived for a time in the US wilderness, her thatched shelter emanating the smells of slow-roasted roadkill and blueberry acorn pancakes, all cooked – of course – in her own pottery. To enter her domicile with a skerrick of plastic or metal on your body was to do so at your peril.

I've been looking forward to meeting her. I've also been looking forward to the workshop. Not just because pottery sounds plain fun, but mostly because I share her vision of a metal-free kitchen. In just three days' time I could be stirring a bubbling ceramic pot, hung with homemade string over a homemade fire, spooning out my meal with a short-handled clay ladle into a bowl made so my fingertips just touch as they wrap around the warm earthenware. That's when things will really start feeling primitive. That's when Wild Woman can really feel at home.

Claudia throws us each a smooth ball. The clay is cold and harder than I imagined. I struggle to make a dent in it with the base of my palm.

"We not try to make anything. We say hello to the clay," Claudia says. "Tune into what it wants to give, how it wants to be moved."

My clay seems to be telling me it wants to be a rock. After a few minutes my fingers are tired. I look over at Claudia, her sausage-thick fingers massaging deep into her clay.

"You are not controller of the clay but servant to it. Ask not what you want, but what it wants of you."

I'm impatient to start a bowl. There's no need to rush, I remind myself, we've got three days. The clay gradually begins to yield, the warmth from my fingers softening the ball.

Claudia eventually moves us onto pinch pots. The good ol' pinch pot. It's a term I have not heard since I was making play dough in preschool. It puts me right back there, the smell of salty red dough and squashed bananas in lunch boxes. This is a bit like adult preschool, I think with a smile. Shelters and mud pies and fires and berry picking and bare feet.

"Finished," says Shaun, holding up a lopsided pot.

Claudia looks over in disdain. "Would you build a house on top of that? The pinch pot is the foundation. We don't go anywhere until is perfect."

I concentrate hard to make the walls even, the base not too thin or thick. None of us dare to suggest ours is perfect, and my belly is growling by the time Claudia directs us to the next step, demonstrating wordlessly how to build the pot up by rolling long, even clay snakes and laying them around the top rim, integrating them with a sweep of her thumb inside and out. Her hands work deftly, snakes coiling up quick and strong. In a matter of minutes she is cradling a bowl in her hands that I would be happy to take home. If it's that easy, by the end of this workshop I'm going to have a complete dinner set.

It's not. My snakes are lumpy sausages, breaking at the skinny points when I pick them up. The sides keep thinning out under the enthusiasm of my thumb, leaving a rim thin and brittle. I try to patch it up, but Claudia reaches over and squeezes it back into a ball with one hand and a firm, "Begin again."

We fall into silent clay-absorption. Dan's tongue hangs out as he works. He looks almost calm, which is quite a difference from our last intensive session. He actually did try his hardest to leave after his dramatic dummy spit at the cordage workshop. After his van wouldn't start, he walked all night with Jessie to get to the highway and stuck his thumb out. A day later and he still had no ride, which he took as a sign and limped back into camp, collapsing into his "rocking chair" (a sheet suspended from the rafters) where he stayed for the next two weeks, staring blankly out into the bush, even turning his phone off. When he appeared at the evening fire one night he was subdued, cutting off any questions with a cheerful, "Well, folks, seems like this place won't let me go." Something had popped, not just in him, but in all of us. We weren't schoolkids here by law anymore. We *could* check out if we wanted to. It was our entirely our choice to stay, and our choice what we did with our days.

For me that choice had suddenly become a lot more complicated. I wasn't here to just learn skills and unwind anymore. Apparently I was here to learn how to be a woman. A Wild Woman. The whole question of doing what I felt like was proving to be deceptively hard (like pottery). The two-day holiday was easy, because it was a finite amount of time during which I was permitted to do whatever I desired. It was fun, and outrageously self-indulgent, but I couldn't keep that up day to day. Who would thatch my shelter? The question of what I feel like doing has lately been countered by a terse voice telling me, "We can't always do what we feel like." And then I get confused about whether I'm doing something I *want* to do or feel like I *should* do. Other times I feel like doing two different things, and when my body droops and looks longingly at the hammock, I pretend I don't hear it.

*

An hour later my bowl is still struggling to progress past halfway, the middle-aged spread blowing out the top. My fingers are beginning to cramp, and I'm starving but don't dare mention it. Neither do the others, despite Ryan already having produced a damn good-looking bowl and started on his second.

"Chloe, sweetie, fetch me the tin," Claudia says, pointing in the direction of a round metal container on the trestle table.

Chloe opens it gingerly, as if expecting something to leap out and bite. She gasps. We crowd around the overflowing assortment of homemade chocolates. There are dainty milk-chocolate stars and moons, white shells, toffee-caramel crunches, and strawberries and citrus peels dipped in dark chocolate.

"Whoa," exclaims Dan, his eyes opening wide.

"Chocolate is antioxidant," Claudia explains, a smile playing at the edges of her mouth. "Two each."

I pick out a dark-chocolate almond cluster and a raw cacao bliss ball, and close my eyes to savour the taste. Good God, chocolate. I'd almost forgotten. The tin's presence proves an equally effective way to tame the herd. After lunch, even Shaun settles in without his usual ants-in-pants restlessness.

The sun arcs up and over our circle as we learn how to pummel, preen and paddle clay. On my eleventh attempt I manage to forge a reasonable bowl, albeit one with a definite tilt. Claudia gives it a wary glance but lets me sit it on the drying mat. I know it's far from pottery perfection, but I've got a whole kitchen to kit out. I reach for another clay chunk.

Nikki stops with a heavy sigh and stretches her head slowly from side to side.

"How's your neck, Nik?" Chloe asks, smiling at her unintended poetry.

"Not so great," Nik says, turning stiffly in Chloe's direction.

"Could you ... help ... move my chair?" she soon asks Ryan timidly. Annoyance flickers over his face momentarily before he jumps up to shift the folding camp chair out of the sun. Nik whispers a thank you and lowers herself slowly back into a seated position.

Poor Nik. She and Ryan have an arrangement whereby he pulls grass for her and she helps bundle his. But in reality she needs more help than that. Even craning her head to tie a knot is painful. It's a strain a new relationship doesn't need. I was surprised the other day when Ryan cooeed down my trail for no particular reason. I had the feeling he wanted to talk, but he stayed as clammed up as ever.

Claudia stands behind Nik, wrapping her large hands around Nik's neck. Tears well in Nikki's eyes at the unexpected touch. "At least I've got lots of time to spend at my sit spot," she says, with forced cheer. Claudia takes a long, noisy breath in through her nose, her half-closed eyes wavering almost imperceptibly. Nikki closes hers, two tears washing clear paths down her clay-stained cheeks.

"It was same with me in woods," Claudia says quietly, looking out into the fading light as if reliving a memory. "You get what you need ... not what you want."

Towards dusk Claudia appears from behind her campervan with a steaming pot of pumpkin soup, home-baked rye bread and another round of chocolate.

We are now as pliable as the clay in her hands, happy to be patted and prodded with matriarchal tough love. At first light the next day we all obediently appear for the "hour of power" yoga and pilates regimen, before settling cross-legged at the pottery circle.

My hands seem to have been practising overnight, guiding a new bowl upwards with some measure of skill I didn't have yesterday. Still, it doesn't come easy, and I struggle to contain the rim. Claudia has been eyeballing me all morning but not saying much. I get the sense she wants to, then pulls back.

Instead of our needing a chocolate incentive, today Claudia needs to remind us to eat and drink. Our entire focus is channelled into the bowls, pots, mugs and cutlery manifesting in our hands. She shows us how to attach handles using a slurry and cross-hatch surface glue, giving rise to an entirely new range of decorative dinnerware. On occasion she steps in, and with a few sure strokes massages the contrary piece back into line. Like ours, her fingers are never idle. If we flatter ourselves that we are getting good, Claudia sets a new benchmark with another gorgeous bowl, an exquisite ladle or new decorative print.

The completion of each piece is like a birth, and I'm flooded with oxytocin each time I deliver the final polish with the burnishing stone. It's only when I finally release it onto the drying mat that I remember I'm busting for the loo and starving. None of us have washed since we started, and we are all coated with a similar shade of ochre. Hour after hour we sit, as if under a spell, our usual fractious energy focused on the clay. There is a synergy to our learning too. Somebody will master a new skill (usually Ryan), and soon the whole group catches on.

My back and neck are aching, but I am almost oblivious to the pain, too intent on the clay creation. After a quick pee, a quick stretch in the sun and a handful of nuts, I'm back on the floor reaching into the clay bucket. This is what I *love* about this year. I'm crafting the tools for living from my own hands, from the earth; beauty and functionality are one and the same, transforming the mundane into the sacred. My shelter, my fire-kit, and now my pottery are my babies. Each piece is infused with the effort, struggle and inspiration that went into making them. I'm reminded of how I felt during that first skills course – giddy, like I was falling in love.

It's unusually cool tonight, and I've dug out the first of my woollen jumpers. The evening fire is like late summer sun on my skin, and we huddle around it as steam rises from our soup mugs. Chloe is giving Nikki a neck rub, while Jessie has collapsed on top of my feet. Claudia stands behind us just short of the firelight. I glimpse her face when the twigs Shaun is throwing on the fire flare momentarily. Her forehead is furrowed. Is she worried or just thoughtful?

"Sweeties, you have until first light to finish your pottery. Tomorrow we get ready for firing," she says.

Tiredness is heavy behind my eyes, my neck contracted in knots from hunching. I have a couple of decent bowls, and a cooking pot I'm fairly proud of. I could stop here. But I won't, not without at least trying for more. I've dreamt of having a water urn since I arrived. It's ambitious, at least twice the size of my cooking pot, but I've got all night.

"Should I stoke the fire?" Claudia asks, eyeing us curiously.

I look around the circle at the others, waiting for their responses. "Count me in," Ryan says. The others nod. "Definitely," I add, smiling.

"Alright, bring on the pottery party!" Dan says, jumping up to fetch more wood.

I arrange my nest for the night, sitting cross-legged on a grass mat with my back to the fire. Drawing out a large chunk of pure white clay, I close my eyes as the water drips down my fingers, imagining from what seam or riverbed it was drawn, how long it lay in the earth before excavation. Breaking off a small piece, I begin to work it between my palms. The others amble in, forming a loose circle around me. Nikki hums a familiar tune to which I add a quiet harmony. A plump moon rises above the tree line.

There is little talk as bowls and mugs, cooking pots, forks, spoons, plates and beads take their place around the fire. Every so often someone rises to turn the pottery a few degrees, baking the pieces on a slow all-night rotation, mirroring the moon's track above us.

The moon is tracking too fast for my task, though, the urn struggling to maintain integrity past its widest point. "Damn it," I say under my breath, as yet again it collapses inwards. Hot anger bubbles in my chest, and I slap more water on the rim. It's a quick fix, and one Claudia warned us against. She is watching me but still offers nothing when I smash it back into a ball and begin again.

"Fuck it," I say, as my third attempt ends in a flop. My neck is killing me and I bend over, groaning. Shaun has gone to bed, and I wonder whether I should too.

Claudia walks over and squats next to me.

"You're trying too hard," she says. I flinch. "Just *feel* what your fingers want to do."

There's that word again. It's what Kate told me about fire: "Trying negates the effort." I try to mirror Claudia's fingers but the rim blows out again. I cross my arms with a sigh.

"I don't get it – how do I not *try* to do it?" I ask.

Claudia takes the pottery from me and holds it silently for a few seconds.

"Look carefully at this bowl," she says, "and tell me what you see."

"A big mess?" I say, shrugging my shoulders.

Keeping her gaze on the bowl, Claudia continues as if she didn't hear me.

"A bowl is a circle, no beginning or end," she says. "It both receives and offers nourishment. It is empty but pregnant with possibility, like womb of woman. It is the embodiment of the sacred feminine."

I look up sharply.

"If you are to make this urn, you need to feel that bowl within yourself. The clay will let you shape it, if you let it shape you," Claudia says, placing the bowl at my feet.

I get up and walk to where the firelight is a pale glow on the white of the scribblies. I look up, the night sky curving over me, smooth and solid, a vast velvety bowl freckled with stars, the moon a stamp of its creator etched on the side. I breathe in and feel myself contained within the sky.

Returning to my mat, I roll my sagging bowl into a sphere, and with a deep breath, dig my fingers deep into its solid centre.

Quiet conversations rise and fall, as does the gentle crackle of the fire. The powerful owl hoots from afar. Dan heads to his shelter, Nik pulling a blanket over her by the fire. Claudia brings over the chocolate tin for the remaining three of us, then bids us goodnight, giving me an encouraging wink as she goes.

"And then there were three," Chloe smiles, halfway through her best bowl yet.

The clay is so white it's almost blue in the moonlight. The urn walls have risen strong and supple to their widest point, and I've started shortening the coils to rein it in. I'm not doing anything particularly different, but somehow it's less personal, as if I'm just assisting it to take its natural shape.

The faintest hue of indigo is smudging the eastern sky when Ryan puts the finishing touches on his masterpiece – a hanging lantern, with the face of a man who is a cross between Pan and Mr Potato Head. They grin at each other.

"Looks good," he says, glancing over to where I sit cradling an urn in my arms. I smooth the surface with a river stone. The clay is cold but I am warm. The yellow robin chirrups its first of the day. Chloe has crashed out. I stretch out next to her, two more clay sculptures nestled by the fire.

*

I wake to the hurried stamp of large feet next to my head.

"Not yoga," I groan.

"Yoga? No time for that," Claudia says, bustling about. Stopping abruptly in front of my urn, she turns, flashing me a look of lioness pride.

We light a fire at the base of a large pit, and the pots take their place along an inner ledge to dry. Between kips in the shade we turn them, the sun a welcome helper.

Before the dusk dew descends, we rake the fire out and move the pots onto the warm sand. My heart leaps as Claudia tips my urn on its rim and sits it in the centre. I watch as it disappears under a pile of sawdust, which will allow the heat to diffuse evenly.

"Feels like we're building a funeral pyre," Chloe says, as we start building the fire, small sticks first to take the weight of the larger logs on top.

"Hopefully it's more like a fire birth," I say anxiously.

"Yeah, and not the big bang," laughs Dan.

Shaun leans in with a lit twig and hovers low until a glow appears. We can hardly keep our eyelids propped open long enough for the fire to stabilise, before covering it with a couple of sheets of corrugated iron and crawling off to bed.

I jump out of my swag at dawn, yanking on pants and a jumper as I walk. Nikki, Ryan and Claudia are there already, poking sticks into the still-smoking pit.

"What's your vibe?" Nikki asks, as I approach.

"Quietly confident," I reply with a smile, before registering the look on her face.

I peek over the edge but know already. Shards. All of it. Smoking, charred shards. I gasp in disbelief and fall to my knees.

"Oh my godfather!" says Dan on arrival, covering his mouth with his hand and sucking in a loud breath through his fingers.

"I don't understand," Claudia says, shaking her head. "This has never happened before."

"Ha!" is all Shaun offers, with a lopsided smirk. I scan the pit for remnants of my urn, my cooking pot, my beautiful bowl. Bleary-eyed Chloe almost stumbles into the pit before realising.

She bursts into tears and collapses next to Dan.

With a jumper pulled over his hands, Ryan sifts through the remains.

"Look, a survivor," he says, pulling out half of his lantern, Mr Potato Head's smile now a broken grimace.

"What did we do wrong? Was the fire too hot? Were there air bubbles?" Nikki asks, pressing Claudia for answers. Claudia, saying nothing, gets up and walks away, her back to us as she stops in front of a tree and places two hands on the trunk, leaning in until her forehead rests between them.

Eventually she returns, lowering herself onto a stump seat with a sigh.

"When we leave the city and enter the woods, we must give up control or have it wrenched from us. This I know."

Nikki and Ryan exchange a worried glance.

"Nature, she will take you, work you like clay in the riverbed, wear you down and sift out impurities, until only essence remains."

She suddenly looks old, her grey hairs catching the early morning sun.

"Yah ... the pots maybe were not enough warm ... But in my book there are no chances, and no failures. There are only lessons for the learning. Maybe this fire asks – how deeply have you learnt to let go?"

I think back to my intentions for the year. How much control do I really have and how much am I a servant to some greater hand, something that cannot be forced into shape anymore than my urn?

Just as the fire worked the clay, so is the land working us, exposing our sharp edges, shattering the fixed ideas we held about ourselves: Nikki's neck forcing her to stop; the messiness of intimacy threatening to undo Ryan's cool detachment. For Shaun, being with a group that accepts him for who he is, and opening his closed heart to us, is cracking all the hard surfaces. Chloe is painfully aware that her resistance to being here mirrors her history of not finishing things, and for Dan, just being part of a group is enough of an edge to rub him raw.

"Garlic bowl going to the highest bidder," Ryan says, holding up some of the larger shards.

"I'll take it!" I say, suddenly hit by the ridiculous poetry of it. I begin to laugh. Chloe joins in, and before long we envelop Claudia in a guffawing bear hug.

I walk down my trail without an urn on my head, but with a bowl inside, a vessel brimming with a sweet yearning to dwell within this space and cradle all that arises.

5.

pad naked across the sand to squat at the water's edge. Light filters like pencil shavings through the leaves of the giant swamp turpentine, fine and curled, falling in shimmering arcs across the still surface, across my skin. I turn my head to look back at the tree, or "the keeper", as I've come to call it. It feels as if this tree maintains some kind of order down here: the benevolent boss of the billabong. Usually I run my fingers across its flaky trunk in greeting when I arrive, but after my recent discovery, I'm a bit reluctant to touch it.

Niko had instructed us to find anything a bird could snack on within a small area. While the others got down on hands and knees, I peeled back the bark of a tree, screaming when a writhing reptile sprang out at me.

"Small-eyed snake," Niko laughed. "A feast for a kookaburra. But poisonous, so be careful, especially at night when they're hunting."

"Do they hunt on the ground?" I asked warily, thinking of my preference for walking barefoot without a torch.

"Check it out for yourself," Niko threw back at me. He noted my frustration.

"Don't wish for answers, wish for more questions. The more you ask, the more you see. The number-one enemy of awareness is boredom. And boredom is just a failure to ask questions. When you find yourself without a question, look down to find the rut you're standing in."

That night with the help of a torch, I asked the question and found not one but *two* small-eyed snakes on the trail near the creek. Since then I've been reluctantly flashing a light in front of me every ten steps or so. What a killjoy. Maybe some questions are better left hanging.

A rufous fantail flutters in to perch on a melaleuca, its tail feathers a deep warm rust, darkening at the tips like a bushfire sunset. He spreads his feathers wide and prances from side to side piping a high, fluting melody. Flirt, I think, grinning. I've fallen hard for rufous. It is not so common as to be ubiquitous but appears regularly enough to form an acquaintance, and each of my sightings is sweetened with the knowledge that any day now rufous might leave for the tropics. Lately I've been thinking I see it, doing a double take and realising that it's actually just a leaf fluttering. This experience is not just restricted to rufous. I'll catch a flash of bird in my peripheral vision and swing my binos up to find that, more often than not, what I've spied is a bird shape in a bunch of leaves, a feather in the texture of bark or the hook of a spinebill's beak in a curved stick.

It's similar to when I was shelter building and the perfect straight sapling or the smoothest paperbark would jump out at me. They still do. It's like those books where the 3D images emerge from the flat picture, except in this case, what appears from the myriad of possibilities is what I've been paying most attention to – birds and building materials. There must be some tipping point, where after a certain amount of focus on something, the mind switches to autopilot and unconsciously tracks for it. Questions must work in the same way, as spotlights sweeping the land for possible patterns. Maybe it's like Niko said: a question will open the neural gate to allow one to see what couldn't be seen before. In this way everything could be a pattern – an emotion, an intention, a thought – and the more energy I invest in looking for it, the more likely it will manifest.

Looking down I realise I'm squatting next to a bunch of dog

prints. My fingers move to trace their outline in the air. Jeez, they're big. Two, maybe three dogs, at least. I wonder how big these fellas' home range is? And if my shelter is within it? Maybe that's another question I'd rather not know the answer to.

I think back to my dreams last night – children kidnapped or abandoned, my holding five deadly tiger snakes in the palm of my hand.

What questions am I really asking? What am I seeing and what remains invisible? What am I tracking, and what is tracking me?

*

I tie a sarong loosely around my neck and head back up the main trail, still dripping, stopping often to add to my armful of kindling. With the chill of winter palpable in the evenings, I've started seriously thinking about firewood. I have no idea how much I'll need, but if I'm having two fires a day, that's a lot of fuel. I should also stockpile it in case of weeks of rain. It's not good survival practice to collect directly from around your shelter; leave the easy stuff for if you're sick or injured. "Stocking the larder," Kate calls it. Without a chainsaw I can only burn what I can collect and split with my hand axe.

Fire making has also ramped up in urgency since Kate initiated a ban on matches and lighters for the next month. I pushed for the rest of the year but the boys whinged and asserted their personal rights to the Bic. Why are the the ones who can most easily pump out a coal using lighters? But we all agreed that for the next four weeks at least, it's sticks or nothing. If I was having dinners at my shelter I would be doubly nervous about it, but I'm still stuck at the kitchen in Camp Crusty. Well, "stuck" by my own inertia.

Turning into my trail, I pause to admire my shelter, to which I attached the last grass bundle a fortnight ago. It sits perfectly poised and empty, like a medieval museum piece. I sat inside it the other day. It was unearthly quiet and kind of sad. I'm annoyed with myself for not moving in but keep making excuses for why I can't yet. As much as I want to be alone, I don't seem to be willing to make the break away from the tribe. What am I avoiding?

Today, though, I'm getting the hell out of Dodge. It's autumn equinox and the gals are celebrating.

"Have you been waiting long?" I ask the other two, who are skimming stones at Snake Creek.

Group gatherings without clocks have been a little frustrating. We probably all have a watch (or a phone) stashed somewhere, but we've been experimenting with "pre-programming" our body clocks to go off at meeting times, much like waking right before the alarm. A more esoteric exercise has been listening for when Kate silently calls us in. "Couldn't you hear me yelling?" she asks good-naturedly when we wander in an hour late. A chain of cooees is the fallback when telepathy fails.

"Nah, not long," Nikki says, chewing the base of a blade of grass.

"Got water?"

"Check," I reply.

"Got tarot?" I direct to Chloe.

"Check," she says, pushing back the rim of her hat.

A few years ago I gave Chloe a set of tarot for her birthday. We really got into it for a while, dressing in sparkly scarves and sitting cross-legged on the floor with the spread between us. "The cards are talking today," we'd say. It'll be good to shuffle the pack again with her, if only for old times' sake.

"Alright, let's get out of here," Nik says.

I rock-hop across the creek to join them on the trail heading south-west, the new firesticks I found on the heath clicking together out the top of my daypack. The sun, between shadows, makes my skin tingle. The track grows grassier as it meanders through private land, before ending at a rundown fence, the border to the trackless expanse of national park. I've made it here before but baulked at entering the boulder-strewn hills beyond, for fear of getting lost.

Nikki consults the compass around her neck.

"This is where we're shooting for," she says. Chloe and I crane over her shoulder to watch her position the edge of the compass on the topographical map towards our destination, a patch of tight concentric rings levelling out in a flattened hillock.

"Uh huh," I nod. I pretty much understand what she's doing but wouldn't trust myself to do it yet. To get lost amongst the endless sandstone cliffs and ridges is a survival test I'm not ready for.

Nikki takes the lead, weaving us around families of tall grasstrees and hedgerows of thick wattle. The huge sandstone boulders we rub shoulders with could be marbles nudged over the ridge by giants playing games. Chloe poses two hands against one as if holding it up. I laugh and pretend to take a photo.

"Ohh," Chloe says, with a loud sigh. "It's so good to be off The Block!"

"Tell me about it," I say. I've just been thinking how much lighter I feel, as if I'm rising above the knot of camp politics with every upwards step.

"Still The Block, hey?" Nik says, shaking her head with a grin. As much as we'd tried to christen it with a more sophisticated name, none of them stuck. The Block it remains.

"What day is it?" I ask, realising I have no idea.

"Wednesday ... or Thursday?" Nik offers tentatively. "Does it matter?"

"No," I say, smiling. "It doesn't." I picture what my friends would be doing right now, mid-week and mid-afternoon, what I might still be doing if I wasn't up here on the side of a mountain.

Turning our noses to the sun, we begin a steep ascent, the forest thinning out to open grasslands dotted with grey gums and casuarinas. Blackbutt buttresses spill over rock ledges like candle wax.

"This is it," Nikki says cheerfully as we finally crest the ridge. A rocky outcrop offers a spectacular view of a woodland valley stretching to a horizon of sheer cliffs, a mirror image of its eastern counterpart, which we stand on.

With only a handspan of daylight left, we start setting up camp, Chloe collecting kindling, Nikki foraging for a tinder bundle, while I carve a new notch.

As the sun flushes its last rays onto our cheeks, we gather around the fire-board, holding it silently in thanks before beginning to spin. My arms move easily and rhythmically back and forth without strain, as I'm comforted in the knowledge that there's back-up.

"Last one," I say, Chloe taking over. The board issues a thick plume of smoke from the new energy. I breathe in the pungent scent of fire beckoning. I've forgotten how magical the hand-drill is. It's become a chore trying and failing on my own day after day. I gladly accept the invitation from the others to bed the coal in the nest woven with stringybark, banksia stamens and lichen, wrap my hands around it and breathe it slowly into flames.

We sit silently watching as the fire finds life within the monkey bars of kindling. It sways and dances to a breeze undetectable on my skin, the flames flickering like fairy lights from yellow to orange, to blue, green and white. A hand seeks mine and I turn my palm upwards to link in. Chloe does the same, our circle a tight ring around the circle of fire. I think back to summer, the days I could barely stand for the heaviness of the heat.

"We give thanks for the long days and light of summer, the strength of the sun from the north," I say, looking out to the smudge of red on the western cliffs. "May we now welcome in the coming winter, the cold and dark from the south."

"On this night of balance," says Chloe, "may we receive the guidance we need to come back into equilibrium with life, so that we may follow clearly our hearts' desires."

With a squeeze we drop our hands, Chloe reaching behind her to fish out a brown leather pouch. I feed the fire as she unties the beaded string that holds the pack and begins shuffling. Choosing one from the pack, she lays it on the dirt in front of her.

"The lover," she exclaims, blushing.

"Ooh, do tell," Nikki prompts, knowing full well the answer.

"Well, I'm not sure if you've noticed, but Niko and I are, well, seeing each other, you know, without seeing much of each other," Chloe laughs.

"Well, I'm not exactly shocked, Chlo," I say dryly, having long noticed Niko's binoculars pointing towards one particular featherless bird. Another couple. The tenacity of the human species in finding a mate, despite obstacles such as almost complete isolation, is quite astounding. That now accounts for everyone on the block except for me and Shaun, and I'm fairly sure he is angling to amend that.

Nik and Chloe giggle over the card, while I shift uneasily with the now-familiar feeling of being on a very different path this year.

I drop my head back to look at the sky as I shuffle, the broad sweep of the Milky Way overhead, and the smooth slip of the cards in my hands. I fumble the deck, and a card jumps out of the pack and lands face up in my lap. I tip it towards the fire. A woman dressed in furs sits alone in a cave by a fire, a single cooking pot by her side. My heart thumps at the image, as if wanting to leap into it. "That's me," I say quietly, with an ache in my chest.

"The Hermit," says Chloe, looking at me curiously. Switching on her head torch, she reads from the tarot book.

"With the light of summer fading it's time to turn inwards." She raises one eyebrow. "The duality of light and dark exists within humanity and in the work of spiritual transformation. The mystic must descend into the abyss alone to face her own inner darkness – the shadows of the ego – in order to emerge into the light. It is time to turn your face from the external world and go within. Do not ignore the call."

Above us, a tawny frogmouth strikes up a sonorous beat.

Niko's parting words flash back to me. "Sooner or later," he said with a strange smile, as I scribbled notes in my journal, "sooner or later you'll find that as you track the questions, the questions start tracking you."

6.

When we walk back into camp the next morning, Ryan and Shaun are bustling about in the communal kitchen amidst piles of boxes.

"What's going on?" Nikki asks.

"Kate's asked us all to be out of the kitchen by tomorrow – they're running a day course and need the space," Shaun says.

"Good excuse to get us out of here and into our shelters," adds Ryan wryly.

"What – *today*? But I'm not ready," I say, panicky, thinking of my empty shelter and all the fire preparations not done.

I hurriedly join in dividing up the bulk dry supplies into separate bags. Well, since I wasn't going to make the move myself, it seems I am going to be pushed. This makes the tarot card from last night look more like a premonition than guidance.

As I wheelbarrow my rations down the shelter trail, a wind picks up ahead of a rumble of thunder. I grab some firewood and stash it inside my shelter. Not that it's any guarantee of dryness. It hasn't rained for weeks, so my thatched roof and untarped lean-to are entirely untested, and now my back-up communal shelter is gone.

I recently tried starting my faithful old car, for the first time in over a month, to find the forest had lulled it to sleep. Although it was a buzz to throw away the last key in my possession, as I watched it being towed to the wreckers I realised how comforting

CLAIRE DUNN

it had been to know that a couple of kilometres away was a little metal nest, which I could crawl into at any time – and use to escape if I got desperate. Now, unless I beg or hitch a ride, I am a prisoner of The Block.

Heavy-set clouds overtake me on my way back to the kitchen. The first raindrop spanks the tin roof, the second follows a few moments later, a third and fourth coming rapidly. Shaun, Ryan and I look up from our packing sharply. D-day. My feet don't want to move, as I remember my dream from a few weeks ago, in which my lean-to was a giant sponge saturated with water. Oh God, if it isn't watertight, I don't know what I'm going to do.

Ryan bolts first, followed shortly after by Shaun. Curiosity finally sends me hurtling towards my shelter too, my heart pulsing in my throat. The rain picks up behind a gust of wind, battering my shoulders as I bound over fallen logs on a shortcut. Diving under the lean-to, I crouch and crane my neck into every corner, expecting a torrent of water to flood in any minute, as if through flywire. The rain throws down fierce bundles that splatter with muffled thuds on the paperbark. Okay, so far so good. But, more importantly …

My stomach lurches as I run to my shelter. Water droplets are sliding down the outside of the grass and disappearing into the sand. Please, grass, please work. It takes a few seconds for my eyes to adjust to the dim light. The wind whistles in behind me. What was that on my hand? Oh, it's just my hair dripping. Rain raps loudly on the chimney cap, as if demanding entry, misty sprays wafting in through the smoke gap. I search for signs of drips, but the rain *actually* seems to be staying on the outside. I can't believe it. Any drips on me? I'm so wet I can't tell. But I don't think so. *No drips.* Oh my God, my shelter is waterproof!

Hang on. What was that? *Splat.* And that? *Splat.* And that? *Splat.* Three raindrops collect in the sand near my feet in an almost perfect triangle. "Stop, stop, stop," I whisper, squatting next to them. Another drop lands in the middle of the trio. They join together in a huddled pool, waiting for back-up.

"Ouch!" My head bangs on a rafter as I stand. I run my hands along the runners, panning for signs of the intruders' entry points, but they've hidden their tracks well. I crouch again, frowning as the pool makes room for subsequent drips. I count the seconds between drops, as one does between lightning and thunder. I will them to stop. Fat droplets continue to splash in at five-second intervals.

Ryan bursts in, drenched. "Howzit going?" he yells.

I point down at the drops.

"Is that it?" he asks.

"I think so," I yell back. "You?"

Ryan gives me a thumbs up and an enormous grin.

"Dunny, we've done it – it's working!" Ryan says, grabbing me by the shoulders, before catching a drip in his eye. We burst out laughing. The drops slow to ten-second intervals. I guess if this is as bad as it gets, it's pretty good really, the drips close enough to the centre and slow enough not to pose much of an issue.

Back at the lean-to, a steady trickle is running in at the back but flowing straight out again. I reckon I can live with that too.

"Woohoo!" I yell, pulling Ryan out into the rain, water sliding down my upheld arms and my back as we twirl.

Shaun marches in, his face as dark as the storm.

"If it wasn't raining I'd burn it down," he thunders.

I flick my palms up in a question.

"Ten more bundles," he says definitively. "Ten more bundles and it'll be sweet."

Ryan and I laugh and grab his hands, the wind and rain spinning with us.

*

"This feels really strange," Ryan says, as we walk down the main trail together later that afternoon en route to our shelters. Around us the bush sparkles and gleams in post-storm bliss. I'm relieved that his coldness towards me is thawing, partly in response to my own warmth, but also, I suspect, because the honeymoon period with Nikki is waning.

I, too, feel jittery, both scared and a little excited about the first night alone with my own fire. *If* I get fire that is. It's a big if.

"Yep, I hear you. All you couples will be having fun without me ..." I say.

"Thought you wanted to be the hermit?" Ryan says, elbowing me. "But, anyway, I reckon I'll be the one who goes days without seeing anyone ... well except Nik, maybe," he says dubiously. We arrive at my junction.

"Well ... good luck. Hope the fire gods are good to you," Ryan says.

I laugh nervously, really wanting to follow him and his easy fire-making muscles.

"Yeah, night then ... see you ... whenever."

I walk, heart in mouth, to the start of my shelter trail. It is strange knowing there's no group fire to fall back on. This is finally it. I stoop under the banksia branch archway and look ahead to my destination. The wet paperbark roof is mottled with rusty reds and charcoal greys. Nestled between ancient white buttresses, the grass hut could be a hobbit home. It's so adorable I just want to squeeze its cheeks. All I need now is a flame to warm my hearth, and I'm home.

I stand between the two structures, deliberating. My swag is still in the lean-to. It's pretty crowded in there with all my kitchen stuff, but for some reason I haven't moved into my shelter. I haven't even had a fire in there yet. I'm not sure why, but I feel a bit guilty as I walk away from it.

*

Outside the lean-to, I lay my hand-drill kit down in front of me, piece by piece, like a surgeon positioning instruments. A tinder bundle sits expectantly on my breakfast bar, a teepee laid in the kitchen fireplace with precision.

I look down at the sticks. I'm feeling hopeful, although there's no reason why I should. What's to say today will be any different to every other that I have tried and failed? The other night Nikki mistook the squeal of my firesticks for the high-pitched whine of the resident plover. It's the noise of a novice – indicating that the wood fibres are glazing and becoming glossy rather than grinding, due to lack of pressure.

Kate has been giving me private lessons, but they usually end with me sulking as she effortlessly glides it home.

"How bad do you want it?" she asked recently. She was shocked as I held out my hands in reply, blood weeping from two stigmata-like blisters. Her next words were slow, carefully chosen.

"Remember: you have to want it more than anything, but give up the trying."

I wince at the first spin, the blisters sending piercing shots up my arms. The pain numbs to a throb but the blisters are still problematic – speed humps in the mid-point of every spin. Every millisecond of lost heat matters. I grit my teeth and press my palms more firmly into the stalk.

Just warm up the board. No need to rush. Wait until dust collects.

I maintain a steady rhythm, floating up the top of the stalk, trying to ignore the acidic pressure in my biceps. My breath is laboured and sweat beads collect on my upper lip.

Keep spinning. Keep going. You can do it.

The board starts squealing as it loses pressure. I switch to speed. Up-down, up-down. Sweat drips onto the sand. My forearms are shuddering, every muscle screaming at me to stop. I peek at the notch – the wood dust's not even half full.

It's no good. You can't do it. You're never going to be able to do it.

Anger stampedes through my body. I can't keep going. I drop my sticks to the ground in defeat.

*

Slumped on my swag considering whether to try again, I sit up when a stream of chattering shadows passes over me. The birds

gurgle as they land with a pancake thud against one of the scribblies. I run out with my torch. Yellow-bellied gliders! They let
loose another waterfall of chortles, taking off like a school of fish,
splashing from tree to tree. I'm watching them disappear when
something else swoops in low, alighting on one of the lean-to
poles. I turn towards it slowly, creeping in for a better look. A
bird, white as a whisper, balances on the edge of my roof with the
poise of a china doll, its only movement the blinking of its enormous childlike eyes. Strange and ghostly creature, blown in on
some passing mist, where do you come from? What is your errand?
It answers with the call I've heard most nights. This is no lost
traveller, but my invisible neighbour, the owlet nightjar.

"Good night to you too, sweet one," I offer, as it flies away, its
exit as silent as its arrival.

I am alone, blissfully alone, in the wild forest. At last. I begin
to dance a little jig between the two shelters. I don't give a hoot
what the others are doing.

The owl in the distance does, though – unleashing a *woohoo*
that booms across the forest like a foghorn. I freeze in recognition: the powerful owl, the largest of the forest owls and one of the
rarest.

It has shown itself to me only once in my life, at a forest blockade. It had been a dramatic week, with thirty loggers from the
local town turning up and threatening to physically evict us,
despite our attempts to befriend them with an impromptu sausage
sizzle and a slab of VB. Finally, we secured an agreement from the
government that the old growth would be left alone. While our
tents were being dismantled, I walked up a dry creek bed near
camp, full of gratitude for the opportunity to play a part in the
protection of hundreds of old trees and their inhabitants. As I lay
face-up on a mossy log dotted with milky fungus, my gaze was
drawn to a large tree hollow. Suddenly the space was filled with an
enormous bulk of brown speckled feathers. Two dark eyes stared
down at me momentarily before their owner flew directly overhead. I gasped, knowing it was the owl I had marvelled at in
books and heard spoken of in reverent tones. In my mind it existed

more in spirit than physical form, a mythical creature, and yet there it was, the powerful owl, right in front of me. I accepted its visit as an acknowledgment of our efforts.

Woohoo!

After sweeping the coals together, I launch down the main trail and across the bridge in the direction of the call, following the trail south to where the road dips level with a paperbark swamp. I stop. The forest has fallen silent, even the frogs pausing their symphony, as if also in wait.

Woohoo!

I spin around, the call so close it reverberates in my chest. I drop to a crouch, brushing spiderwebs from my face as I stalk into the brush. A cricket chirrups and I jump. The air is thick with expectation. I stop short of a swamp turpentine tree to wait for the next call. The hairs on my neck prickle. I feel as if something is watching me, the gaze weighty with presence. I look up, scanning the branches, at first seeing nothing but pale leaves and stars. Then my eyes lock with two huge yellow irises. The creature grips a branch with finger long talons, its mottled brown feathers embroidered with moth-wing intricacy. Its wings lift and shake, as if slightly irritated, before settling. My body has turned to stone. Breaking our stare, the owl lifts its beak skyward and puffs out its chest to deliver a ground-shaking holler. Unfolding broad wings, it looks down to demand my gaze for another split second before launching like a hang-glider into the night. I melt to my knees, swaying in the wake of its flight.

*

What a day, I think, as I walk back down my shelter trail. No fire, but a royal welcome nonetheless. I cast a guilty look towards my shelter as I crawl, exhausted, into my swag and crash out.

I wake in the middle of the night, my heart beating. It must have been a dream, I tell myself, and snuggle back down in my sleeping bag. Starting to drift back off, I vaguely register a slight rustle coming from the paperbark above. Pricking my ears, I realise the rustling is not the subtle stop-start of a skink, but one uninterrupted movement. A slithering. My eyes snap awake. I grab my head torch and shine it above me.

"Holy shit!" I exclaim, my torch illuminating the triangular head of a snake poking and prodding at my mozzie net, its scaly body suspended like a hammock between the net and a roof beam.

I hurl myself out of the swag and net. I spin around quickly, not wanting to lose sight of it. Exposing a red belly, it slides down the side of the net, searching doggedly for a way into my bed. I cringe as I imagine myself still asleep. With a figure eight, the snake turns abruptly to follow its tail back through a hole in the paperbark. Great, I've got a poisonous snake living in my roof. I weigh up my options: try to get the snake out (unlikely and dangerous), try to go back to sleep (unthinkable) or move camp. In one swift motion I undo my mozzie net and fling my swag outside, checking each layer to see there aren't snake babies writhing beneath.

Without even the wan light of stars inside my shelter, I can barely make out my hand in front of me. I wave my torch around to ensure the snake hasn't followed me in. There's nothing bar a few spiderwebs. Tossing my swag down, I tie the mozzie net to a beam and warily climb in. I cross my arms over my chest and wait for my heart to slow. The shelter smells of damp hay bales and clay. A few stray blades of grass sway in the chimney gap, stars twinkling behind them. My breath deepens. When my eyes adjust, I can make out the individual bundles. Divided up by the crisscross of the runners, my roof looks like a giant patchwork quilt arching over me, every square inch alive with the memory of the sweat and struggle of its creation.

I can't believe it's taken me so long to move in. *I'm here now*, I silently assure it.

I lie wide awake, staring up into the dark dome, thinking of all the coming nights we will spend together. The shiver of anticipation that runs through me runs through my shelter too, its grass feathers rustling. I look down into the hearth, the stones cold and stiff.

Flinging off my sleeping bag, I run out to scoop up the untouched kindling from the lean-to fireplace and prop it up in the shelter hearth, sitting the tinder bundle on a flat stone next to me.

I begin spinning the stalk: slow, slow, slow.

"Breathe through it," Kate's words come back to me. "You've got all the strength you need. Channel it up from your core."

Closing my eyes, I take a few deep breaths and pull back, my shoulders loosening.

Keep floating, keep breathing.

Barely able to keep the stalk moving in the notch from exhaustion, I visualise oxygen pouring into my limbs like liquid gold from the core of my belly, streaming down my arms and into my hands and fingers. I breathe long and deep. Suddenly I feel a shift, my arms gaining strength, instinctively pressing together and down, as if tapping into some kind of muscle memory. The sound changes, deepens. It is wood grinding to a dark powder and coalescing. Smoke fills my lungs and still my arms continue, up-down, up-down, in fast, fluid strokes, as if cutting through water. A warmth in my belly surges up and out through my fingers.

I know I have it before it arrives; I can feel it coming. I keep going even after I see a tiny red glow from within the black dust. Not until it rolls out of the notch and sits smoking independently on the bark cradle do I double over in front of it and cry.

I gather myself together and transfer it to the lichen-lined heart of the tinder bundle, breathing on it as one would a baby, long and slow, lavishing it with affection until it flares into flame.

As the fire crackles, I send out thanks to the creatures – even the scaly ones – who dared show me their dark underbellies and sacred feathers, who threw down a vine for me to climb into their night world, carrying me over the threshold and tucking me in. I snuggle into the swag under my grass doona, warm in the knowledge that this hermit is not alone at all.

7.

A pair of azure kingfishers swoops in to dive-bomb the creek in a lightning flash of luminescent blue, before coming to rest on a half-submerged branch metres from where I sit on the bank. In a woollen camouflage jumper, khaki cargo pants and bare feet, I am invisible to them. Even the mist from the teacup in my hand blends with the mist rising from the still surface. They're far too occupied with bobbing up and down, gazing at their reflections, to notice, anyway. I'd be a narcissist too, if I had their good looks. One of the birds arches back its neck and sopranos a long upward call. So it *is* you. Mystery number seventy-six solved. I switch back into wide vision. The two birds are stencilled animations against a painted backdrop of tiny white flowering tea-trees. A bark boat floats by, a shipwrecked spider tiptoed in the centre. Without warning the kingfishers alight, their beaks barely skimming the surface before they career upstream like jet-fighters, banking sharply between vines and fallen logs.

A sharp snap of sticks being broken over knees signals that Shaun's up. We've been at it again – shelter building, that is: a holiday house for me. My shelter site had started to feel a bit suburban, the once-wild frontier of The Block now gentrified with our well-defined paths and thatched roofs. I moved my cooee point further out but also started dreaming of a little shack on a quiet bend of the river. Shaun's assistance is his present to me before he leaves for the army in a couple of weeks.

It took us only an afternoon yesterday to knock up the holiday house, bar the last layers of paperbark we plan to complete this morning. The design is based on the standard survival shelter – a ridge pole held up at thigh height on one end by two interlocking Y-branches. Sticks resting between the pole and the ground are the frame for the paperbark roof. The steep pitch has given the paperbark a chance to redeem itself as a viable means of wicking water, passing Shaun's test yesterday of a bucketload from the creek. If this were a true survival shelter, we would include two or three feet of leaves for insulation. There's a reason those are called survival shelters, though – you don't want to spend any longer than absolutely necessary in them. I know, I've tried.

At tracker school, on day two they confiscated our sleeping bags and tents and told us to build a shelter. In that moment the oak leaves on the ground turned to gold. We ran to fill jumpers and sarongs, knowing every leaf would count in the bid to stay warm. Debris piracy was rife. After forty-eight hours of leaf hauling, I had created something resembling the bower of a burrowing Jurassic bird. Dressed in every piece of clothing I had brought overseas with me (including two pairs of undies), I painstakingly inched my way sideways into the narrow tunnel entrance. Once finally installed inside, I pulled a string to draw closed a door made of a leaf-filled sarong, sealing the airlock. I lay panting in the pitch black, my ribs rubbing up against the stick ribs of the roof. Bugs scuttled and scratched all around me. I was stinkingly, stiflingly hot but there was no room to strip layers. The mild claustrophobia that I had hitherto experienced was nothing in comparison to the sweltering panic inside that thing. Sweat poured from my underarms as I contemplated the roof caving in, imagining my screams as my mouth filled with suffocating leaves. There was nowhere else to go but into the cold night. I closed my eyes and focused on my breath, willing myself with every inhale to cool down. It was hard to tell if I had actually woken when my eyes opened to the cave's blackness. I felt weightless, floating in space or an inky womb, a cicada curled deep underground during hibernation. After a time, as if coming from the other end of a tunnel,

I heard the first muffled bird of dawn and emerged blinking into the light.

That was a survival shelter, not a holiday house.

I look across the creek to the paperbarks we stripped yesterday. The exposed bark is dark pink, like the new skin under a scab.

Rising stiffly, I follow the curl of campfire smoke to where Shaun squats, toasting bread. Bread is no longer an occasional luxury, as our neighbour Terri, who homeschools her two kids up the road, delivers six fresh loaves to our gate every week.

"Sleep well?" Shaun asks, with a grin, his dark hair flopping over his forehead.

"I did," I smile back. "Yep, it's a fine hobo shack."

"How does it compare to the pandanus?"

I've recently returned from a three-day solo trip to a remote beach, where I camped under the low spreading branches of a pandanus tree in the dunes.

"It was pretty awesome too," I reply, thinking back to the last night, when I sat under the broad arms of the pandanus, turning a bird on a makeshift spit over the fire, the ocean crashing gently onto the shore.

My belly growls loudly as I take over one of the toast forks. Shaun pokes me with a stick and I giggle.

"How're you feeling about leaving?" I ask.

"Well ... you know, sad, but kinda ready for it," says Shaun, spooning some of Dan's native grape jam onto a crust.

Shaun has been a bit of a wandering ghost since the communal campfire was extinguished. Several times he cooeed at my shelter and I didn't reply. It must look as if I've dumped him, but I'm really loving being alone at my shelter. I've been having fun cooking in the same cast-iron cauldron pot that as a girl I would fill with water and flowers and call my "witches brew". It's like I'm getting a second go at childhood.

"What do you think you'll miss the most?" I smile. "Apart from thatching, of course."

Shaun looks back at me intensely. I immediately regret asking.

I look into the fire. I'll miss him too. Who'd have thought my closest friend out here would be a young army wannabe? It's just easy; I don't have to try around Shaun. With him, what you see is what you get. While I'm a little worried about how I'll go without him, I'm more concerned about how he'll fare in the army. I don't think he realises how much he's changed in the last five months. Last night he said he felt native. I'm not sure if native is the word I'd use, but I wonder whether it's similar to the humming I sometimes feel when I'm out on the land alone, an energy pulsing through me.

"So, you up for the survival mission?" Shaun says, breaking the awkwardness. His one request before he leaves is for a group survival trip, where we take nothing but knives and the clothes on our backs.

"Sure. Wouldn't miss it," I say. I don't tell him that I'm still tired from my solo mission. It was pretty hard, despite the fact that I took some food with me.

"Are you going to check my pockets for nuts?" I laugh and spear another slice of bread.

*

"Watch your footing, it's slippery," JJ yells at us over the roar of the river, straddling two mossy boulders with his bare feet. With JJ's long blond hair shaved close on one side, his brown pecs flexed against his half-buttoned safari shirt and a leather pouch his only luggage, I don't think our survival guide realises he is the more likely cause of slippage than rocks.

"You doin' okay?" Shaun bounds up beside me, all smiles. So much for his knives-only rule – his head-to-toe Gore-Tex is a wearable tent. He did relax the rules somewhat, in the end, letting us each bring a raincoat and water bottle. But no nuts.

I give him a thumbs up. He leaps behind me to check on Chloe and Dan. Ahead, Ryan is backdropped by a distant waterfall spilling from a high rocky mountain. He walks apart from Nikki.

CLAIRE DUNN

I wonder whether they've had another falling-out.

Despite his warning, JJ practically runs over the rocks, and I concentrate hard to keep up. I shiver a little despite my woollen jumper and beanie. Camping in May without a sleeping bag, or even a tea bag, is a first. I certainly wouldn't do it by myself, and even with the group I'm nervous, especially considering the heavy clouds gluing together at the end of the valley we're heading towards.

JJ circles one finger in the air, signalling for us to group up.

"Smoko," he yells, reaching into his pocket and offering around a handful of bright red berries. Nikki does the same, having already identified the edible fruit of walking-stick palm.

"Everyone doin' alright?" he shouts.

"Whoa!" Dan yells, teetering on a slippery rock. He grabs Chloe, who slips and falls forward onto her hands with a yelp.

"Anyone bring a fire-kit?" JJ says, looking west to where thunder is growling.

"Not allowed," Shaun grins.

JJ looks slightly bemused, although there is a clipped edge to his "Onwards."

At a fork in the river, we fill our water bottles then follow JJ uphill until we reach a huge sandstone cave – just as the rain starts.

"Not bad, huh?" JJ says, extending his arms like a proud host.

The cave floor has room enough for a tribe ten times our size, the overhang an arched window, framing a view of thick bangalow palm forest. I look around at the walls, almost expecting to see painted handprints.

"It's amazing," I say, seriously impressed.

JJ nods, buttoning up his shirt and pulling on a brimless brown felt hat. "Okay, folks, treasure hunt time," he says, counting on his fingers: "tinder, bedding, food, firewood *and* ..."

"Firestick," Shaun finishes.

"We've got an hour before dark; let's get a move on," JJ says.

I'm glad I brought a raincoat as I step out into the steady drizzle. I can't imagine where to look for a stalk in the rainforest, let alone a dry one. I mentally prepare myself for a cold and hungry night. Seeing the boys heading downhill with machetes, Nikki and I stay up high.

"Hey, look!" Nik says, pointing to a log teeming with small white termites. Licking her thumb, she presses it down on the pack and pops it in her mouth.

"Really?" I ask. Nikki nods encouragingly. I chew quickly, mouth open and nose screwed up. To my surprise, the ants turn into a rather pleasant peppery paste in my mouth. It reminds me that I haven't eaten since our early breakfast. Gosh, I'd love a cuppa.

The rain is running in small waterfalls down the outer rock walls and the back of my neck as we pick our way back, arms loaded with firewood and pockets of tinder ferreted out from rock crevices.

Inside, the boys are huddled shoulder to shoulder, on their knees next to the fireplace. Nik and I dump our firewood and rush over.

"C'mon, you can do it fella. Bring it home," Dan says to Shaun, who is attempting to spin a stalk the width of a chair leg between his palms. With a cheek on the cave floor and bum in the air, JJ is whispering unintelligible words to the board with a fixed gaze.

"Walking-stick palm?" I whisper to Chloe. She nods.

"Bugger," Shaun says, as his hands fumble on the bottom-to-top changeover, the stalk jumping out of the hole. "Last one," he says, collapsing back on his haunches as Ryan takes over.

"Atta boy," Dan yells, as thick smoke appears. Ryan's lips curl back in a grimace, sweat beads condensing on his forehead. Nik stands behind him, palms hovering reiki-style over his back.

"We got it," JJ says quietly, before shouting, "We got it!" Scooping up the coal with his knife, he drops it into a rainforest fungus, which he doubles over. Holding it in one hand, he weaves figure eights around his body. We watch with held breath while the smoke thickens, trailing behind the moving bundle like a meteor. The fungus bursts into flame and he stuffs it into the kindling teepee, blowing it to life with a few long blows. The other six of us whoop in relief.

That night our dinner is termites and banglalow palm hearts, which taste like bok choy, roasted on the coals. They're by far the most satisfying bush-food carbohydrates I have tried, but still are more about boosting morale than filling the hungry hole. We crash out on the bed Chloe made from layers of dried bangalow fronds, spooning tighter in the night as clouds of misty rain float in.

*

"Come on, dinner's not going to come and bite you on the bum," JJ says, stirring us out of what looks like a fire-staring competition the next morning, as rain falls in a curtain over the cave entrance. Nik and Ryan opt to fish and set traps nearby, while the rest of us head upstream.

The dense rainforest is a maze of dripping wait-a-while and lawyer-cane vines, which scratch their appropriate names below my shorts a million times as I stumble blindly behind JJ. I poke listlessly under rocks in search of crayfish, shivering under my raincoat. The others mooch around, waiting, while Chloe and I spend half an hour digging a hole with our sticks to unearth a single finger-sized yam, our energy expenditure far more than its intake could offer.

My head is aching and I'm starting to feel shaky. Why did we choose to come to the rainforest in the cold and wet? This is the season in which the tribes of this land's traditional inhabitants would be heading for the coast, not the freezing mountains. What do we know about surviving in this environment? It's pure foolishness. I just want to be back in my shelter, cooking up some baked beans.

When JJ eventually stops, even Shaun is grim-faced. We must have walked twenty kilometres, at least. I pull off some more walking-stick palm berries and squat to nibble at them. They're starting to make me feel nauseated.

This hunt seems like it's going to be the opposite of mine last week. Although I didn't really intend to kill anything, I carved a throwing stick and carried it with me, and practised setting a few traps. I was trying on hunting to see what it felt like, giving it a test drive, and I was content enough with the few whelks, pippies and seaweed stews that I cooked up. In the end, though, the prey came looking for me. Walking along the beach at dusk on the last evening, I noticed a dark shape in front of me. It heaved itself up as I approached, before slumping back on the sand. A sea bird with a badly injured leg. My hand moved instinctively to stroke its back. The bird shuffled, looking up at me pleadingly as a sea eagle circled. I knew at once that it was for me. Crying, I cradled the bird and thanked it for its sacrifice, for the teaching it was offering. Placing a piece of driftwood under its head, I steeled myself for the kill, letting out a primal yell as I brought my stick down. In the last light I managed to gut and pluck it. It was the first animal I had killed and eaten, but it wasn't a hunt.

"I'm pooped," Dan says, hanging his head.

"Maybe we should head back," Chloe offers weakly.

"Okay, gang, I'm handing over to you," JJ says, his throwing stick turning a perfect two rotations in the air before landing back in his hand. "It's your call if you want to eat tonight or not. There's food enough here, you just have to get out of your heads to find it."

I scratch a notch in the leaf litter with my throwing stick.

"Put yourself in the shoes of the prey. Think like them. Where would you go on a day like today?"

"Home," Dan sniggers quietly.

"Use the rain to your advantage," says JJ, ignoring the comment. "It's masking your sound, right?"

It's enough to motivate Shaun. "I'm ready," he says, smearing mud over his face. My belly is twisting in knots of hunger, my eyes blurry. I really need to eat something soon.

"Yep, me too," I say.

Abandoning the hunt for the elusive crays, we fan out across the flat creek bed, JJ trailing behind. As rain bounces off leaves in loud thuds, my bare feet are silent on the spongy soil. Without anyone to follow, I begin to take more notice of where I'm walking, looking side to side and above, as far in front as the thick foliage allows. I squat to search inside fallen logs, part fern fronds and poke in tree crevices for signs of life.

I know you're here somewhere. Come out, come out, wherever you are.

Spying a bird's nest, I climb a vine to check for eggs. Between two tree buttresses is a burrow, and I carve off a leggy stick to probe it. A brush turkey mound is piled high with leaf debris, and I scour the ground for tracks.

Warmer, warmer, getting warmer.

The hunger pangs are fading, my mind growing sharp and alert. No longer shaky, my legs have a new energy, a bounding aliveness. I move upstream through the forest, feeling like a river myself, weightless and fluid. I pick up sounds beyond the thump of rain – distant birds, frogs, smaller rustlings. Catching movement in the tree above, I spy two doves, feathers flecked with the brightest pink, nestled together in the fork of a branch. As my awareness extends further into the nooks and crannies of the forest, I feel as if I am becoming diffuse, all thoughts of past and future gone, sucked into a single focus: food. All is sound, sensation, movement. I glance back behind me to see the others similarly bright-eyed.

We are all, literally, coming back to our senses.

The rain slows. A cloud parts, a single streak of sunlight landing on my face like a warm flannel. JJ jumps ahead and signals a gathering.

"Conditions have changed," he says. "What d'ya reckon is gonna want to be out in the sun?" We think for a moment.

"Snake?" Chloe asks.

"Correcto," says JJ, hinting at his game plan with a jab of one finger upwards.

Single file, we head west to where the rainforest ascends into giant blue gums, thinning to a steep grassy woodland. We scramble with our fingers up rocky scree. Far below, the creek ripples through the valley like a snake in motion, half-shrouded in mist.

I'm following Shaun along the ridge, and when he halts abruptly, we bump up against each other. Curled on a flat rock in front of him is a huge diamond python. Creeping forward, we form a circle around it, watching as breaths ripple down its spine in a slow swell. I don't feel like a predator. I have no thoughts of malice or violence, just sorrow and gratitude. The snake opens its eyes. They remind me of the bird's; small, black and beady, staring trustingly into mine. I turn my back as JJ brings his throwing stick down with a hard thump on the back of the snake's neck, before diving in to slit the throat. Chloe sobs as we lay our hands on the writhing scales. Just like with the bird, I think I can sense the moment when the twitching body beneath my hands changes, when consciousness leaves and the flesh is animated merely by the workings of nerves and muscles, the fire in its eyes dimming to lifeless cold.

Survival is violent. It demands blood and bark, burning the flesh of trees and animals alike. In the city, it is hidden under packaging and buffered by distance. We don't see the earth excavated to power our homes, the delayed effects of pollution blanketing the globe. Here it is in my face: ugly, raw and real. A letter arrived from a friend the other day. He asked me what I was giving back to the land. Perhaps it is this, the willingness to confront the violence that supports my life, to cradle the dying head of a snake with my heart swelling in gratitude. If violence could ever be beautiful, it is now.

My hunger resumes with a hallucinatory intensity on the way back to camp, as I follow the trail of blood dripping from the forked tongue of the snake slung over Ryan's back. While it cooks on the coals, JJ launches into a full rendition of *The Man from Snowy River* to entertain us. Firelight flickers on the cave walls like dancing figurines. I wonder how many camps just like ours this cave has witnessed, how many celebratory hunting parties.

It's finally ready. Oily juices run down my fingers from the roughly hewn chunk JJ hands me, and I join the others in loud slurps before ripping through the crispy-fried skin to sink my teeth into the white flesh.

When I wake the next morning the snake has come alive in my belly, writhing and squirming. Rain clouds are amassing again, and I'm glad we agree to leave. At the edge of the wilderness, we gather to give thanks for the protection that the valley has offered us: the shelter, water, fire and food. As we turn to leave, a diamond python lies directly in our path, this one farewelling us.

8.

'm curled like larva in a faded sleeping bag, under a tarpaulin sagging with pools of rain, enclosed by a circle of about ten feet in diameter, etched by the tired scuff of my footprints. My hips, bruised and sore from lying down without padding, shift at regular intervals to spread the pressure, a throbbing pink rash spreading down my neck from a tick bite. My tongue is white and pasty, and I can smell my breath against the freshness of the steady rain. I stretch my arm out to reach for the water bottle. If it wasn't attached to my shoulder, I would worry about it floating away. I concentrate to pilot my arm in on the object and back to my lips. The water tastes sour but I force myself to take a few gulps. Nausea washes over me as the water sloshes around in my empty belly, and I close my eyes to wait for it to pass.

Another fifteen minutes gone, maybe twenty. I peek my eyes open to check the day's progress. The vague glow of the sun behind the clouds has made no signs of movement up the trunk I've been measuring its progression against since daybreak. How is that possible? Never again will I complain about there being never enough hours in a day. There are enough hours to do most anything: write a book, compose a symphony, raise a family. An entire life could be lived in a day. I'm surprised Rome wasn't built in a day with that many people working on it. As long as there is a sentinel whose only job is to watch every excruciating detail of the Earth's turning, time will jam up, will slow to an interminable crawl. I now have direct evidence of this, almost three days' worth.

It feels more like thirty days since I arrived here, at first light, for the first of a four-day "vision quest". For Native Americans, the vision quest is a sacred ceremony in which initiates sit within a small circle on a mountaintop, fasting and praying for a vision. Many indigenous cultures have some version of it – the Aboriginal walkabout, for instance – a rite of passage involving renunciation and solitude in the wilds, a fast from all things familiar that is designed to break the habitual patterns of the mind and allow a deeper knowledge to arise. "The sledgehammer" is what Kate called it, a less romantic but perhaps more apt name for the fierce beating the ego receives every minute that passes with almost zero stimulation.

This isn't my first vision quest. When I began studying with Kate and Sam, I signed up for one. Wanting to confront my fear of the dark, I spent most of the four nights burrito-rolled in a tarp, quivering. But what I wasn't prepared for was how incredibly vast ninety-six hours could feel. The experiences of blissful reunion with nature and the cosmos that I expected were brief blips in an otherwise monotonous sea of tedium and physical pain. Perhaps like the selective memory of a woman after childbirth, the peak moments are the ones I remember most clearly: fearlessly dancing around my circle under the moonlight on the final evening, walking wobbly-legged back to the communal fire the next morning with the sense that I carried a precious jewel inside. For months afterwards, my life made perfect sense, the steps in front of me as clear as if I had already made them.

As soon as I'd heard Kate speak of that quest I'd known I had to do it, but for this one my decision was far less certain. It was the last scheduled group activity, marking the end of the workshops and the start of a calendar-free six months, an opportunity to align ourselves with our intentions for the final two seasons on the land. In the preceding days, I procrastinated about finding my site and organising the twelve litres of water and basics I'd need. It didn't help when Dan pulled out a few days ago.

On the eve of the quest, I was still packing the last of my things inside my shelter. I held out my hands to the dying embers in my fireplace. They roused and flared up momentarily, as if they didn't want me to leave. What am I doing? I thought. I don't want to go out into the cold and starve; I just want to stay here. My heart was a constricted knot of confusion. I turned to gaze into two unblinking eyes. What would Wild Woman do?

I found her face recently, while on an excursion to the local Aboriginal Cultural Centre, where we learnt how to make primitive eel and crab traps. During a break, I wandered inside the art gallery. Our eyes met: hers were yellow and scorching and held mine unwaveringly. She was on all fours within tall golden grass, her shoulders naked, her face streaked with white ochre. I walked slowly over to her, as if hypnotised. *Running with Wolves* read the picture's title. I took her home for twenty-five dollars and pegged her to a wall runner. I know I can never lie in front of this woman. She won't put up with half truths or pretty imitations of wildness. She demands nothing less than unbending integrity, uncensored passion, and the scratchy raw truth of things I don't always want to hear. She's a perfect reminder of my real task this year. I want to look into her eyes every morning and see in them a mirror of my own.

Go. Her eyes blazed. *Go to your quest.* My shoulders sagged. Of course, it was just resistance to the ordeal that I knew lay ahead. Last-minute jitters. No-one said it was easy to squeeze through the eye of the needle. No pain, no gain, right? I hadn't come all this way for a stroll in the park.

We gathered for a communal meal that night. I scraped at the remaining specks of soup with my spoon, tipping up the bowl to my mouth to gather the last few drops. The sight of the empty bowl immediately made me hungry again. Four days. I wished I could walk in right then, get it over and done with. It was like waiting for the signal to go over the trenches. The others joked quietly, biding time before the evening's ceremony that would commit us to silence. Sensing my turmoil, Chloe slipped me the pack of tarot. I slid a card out of the centre. A woman stood naked in a small circle by a fire in the desert, a rattle and drum in her hand. The vision quest card. I shook my head in disbelief. How much more confirmation did I need? The following day, as soon as it was light enough to see the trail in front of me, I walked to my site and stepped over the threshold into my quest circle.

*

The rock. *You need to put the rock out.* I groan as I unpeel myself from the sleeping bag, staying horizontal as I pull on wet-weather gear. Every muscle protests as I wobble to my feet. Rain thuds against the hood of my raincoat. My head clouds with dizziness and I lurch towards a tree, pressing my forehead against it until the spell passes. I stumble out to where a rectangular box bordered with bark lies on the edge of the main trail. Two rocks sit side by side within it, like bulging eyeballs. Another is heavy in my hand. Kate and Sam will check soon that it's in the box. If it's not they'll come looking for me and pronounce my quest over. I contemplate throwing it at a tree. Instead, I place it neatly next to the other two. Three rocks make it look like I'm three-quarters there, but it's a cruel trick. I'm only halfway. *Halfway.* Oh God, no, I can't do this.

The first day was almost enjoyable. I'd been craving time alone since Shaun's farewell. I had chosen a site with good sun and spent most of the day dozing and cloud watching. I sporadically got up and did the toe-heel stamp of the "quest dance" around my circle. I thought of Shaun. On his final evening, after we'd played a group game of sardines and cooked him tacos, he'd come looking for me. Cupping my face in his hands, he'd said he loved me and asked to stay the night. I'd sent him away with the first tears I had seen in his eyes. The next morning I'd found a note of apology written on paperbark under a rock near my trail. There was no need for him to be sorry. By dusk on my first day, the rain had closed in and I crouched under my flimsy tarp structure, shivering.

The second day blurred into endless, soggy misery. The steady rain was accompanied by a cutting wind, and despite the layers of clothes I was bundled into, I was cold, my body temperature dropping due to the fast. The blanket of clouds covered any indication of what time of day it was. Numerous times I was certain that the sky was darkening, and I stared at the horizon, praying for nightfall, but instead it brightened, as if laughing at me. The kookaburras colluded, several times prematurely announcing dusk. Most other birds avoided me altogether, my only visitors a family of wrens. I passed the time by building ant obstructions, weaving reams of string from the wet grass and imagining all the things I would like to eat. I contemplated stripping off and dancing in the rain, but I was starting to feel weak. Thoughts of leaving popped up, but I pushed them away. When I became bored, I got frustrated. I took issue with a large stringybark on the edge of my circle, barraging him with a litany of complaints. I slept fitfully, however, and woke this morning nauseated and so weak I could barely get up.

I look longingly down the path. My shelter is probably not even a kilometre away as the crow flies. I could be back by my fire within an hour. Just the thought makes my throat clog. I loiter at the box. Snapping twigs, I spell out *Help!* then scatter them.

I walk back to my circle, slow as a monk in meditation. The rain gets heavier, slanting in at the wrong angle. I wish I'd spent more time setting up my tarp. I'm shipwrecked on an island that is now smaller than my body and quickly shrinking. I scratch some shallow trenches around me and crawl back inside my increasingly damp sleeping bag. I read the washing instructions on the sleeping bag tag for the hundredth time. Halfway. What a detestable thought.

What am I doing here? What good is sitting in the rain being miserable? It certainly doesn't feel like a road to spiritual enlightenment. Oh, I know, I know, every experience in the quest is a teacher: the sore bum, the tick bites, the cold. I got that sense in the first quest – even the boredom had some substance to it, some grist to grind through. Even when I wanted to leave, I knew I wasn't going to. This is different. This just feels like wretched and unnecessary suffering.

Stringy is drenched, his bark creased and sagging like an old man's neck. I thought we were friends on the first day, but now he seems to be glaring at me with disapproval from his one-eye burl, as if reading my thoughts.

"What are you looking at?" I snap.

He lets loose a loud creak as two branches rub up against each other in the wind.

You humans. Your minds are so restless. I stand here every day, rain, hail or shine, and you don't see me complaining.

Cranky old thing. If you had legs, I bet you'd be outta here too. But then that's the practice. Denial. Restraint. This is the sledgehammer, after all. How else does the peppercorn get crushed into spice?

But what if I just want to be a peppercorn? Isn't it this year about learning to follow my heart? Doing what I want instead of what I should? The thought energises me. I sit up defiantly.

"Stringy, I think my heart is telling me to leave. What do you say about that?"

Stringy coughs and splutters in shock, as wind whips through his top branches.

Who dares leave the quest? Who thinks they know better than a tradition as old as dirt itself? Lazy is what you are! You just don't want it bad enough.

I fall back onto the wet ground. I just want out. But what's the difference between a passing desire and an impulse of the heart? And is the heart always right?

Stringy snorts a waterfall of sappy snot down his trunk.

Maybe he's right. Isn't sitting through interminable hours of physical discomfort and boredom the path of every mystic throughout history? I am lazy, a spiritual cop-out. Rain blows in and I huddle on my rapidly diminishing island, watching tree trunks turn into cascading rivers, until dark finally descends and I escape into sleep.

In my dream an anti-war protest is being waged outside a church. A V, for Virgin Mary, is carved large on the church door. The protestors grow increasingly angry, damaging a statue of the

Virgin Mary as well as another sacred object called the "sacristy".
I am upset about it.

*

I wake to a subdued dawn. The rain has stopped but a thick cloud
cover remains. I sit up and wrap myself in a blanket, closing my eyes
in meditation. My breath rises and falls, long and even. My thoughts
are as scattered and brief as the bird calls. I drop my blanket and
step barefoot onto the track of flattened grass at the edge of my circle. Raising my right foot, I bring the ball down hard, followed
shortly after by my heel. Toe-heel, toe-heel, stamp and stamp,
around and around, perambulating my circle, my limbs feather-
light. My arms rise above me and sway, the only visible movement
in a still forest. A hum vibrates my lips, pursing to a high note,
which rings out like a chime. I slow when I reach Stringy.

"I'm leaving," I say.

Stringy's burl watches me in disappointment. *So, you've made
your choice.*

I stand tall and strong-faced in front of him, with all the
appearance of assuredness.

I'm not sure at all, but I need to leave to find out. Something is
in danger of being broken, or perhaps it already has been. Something sacred – something pure, feminine and essential.

Dropping my last rock into the box, I skirt the edge of the
trail to hide my escape tracks. At the sight of my shelter through
the trees, tears spring to my eyes. I feel as if I am approaching a
church. Slipping my sandals off at the door, I tiptoe into the quiet
cavern. Everything is just as I left it. I'm surprised, as if three
years might have passed. I breathe in the musty air with relief.
Home. I begin at once to set a fireplace with the dry kindling
stacked inside the door, placing one stick at a time into the teepee
with care. Unhooking my bow from the rafters, I spread the kit
out on an altar of paperbark. Despite my muscle weakness, a coal

comes easily. Stripping off my damp clothes, I stand as close as I can get to the fire without getting burnt. The kindling sticks are bright candles of flame, to which I hold my outstretched palms. The warmth spreads over me in showers of shivering delight. Fetching some kitchen supplies, I chop a sweet potato, a carrot, seaweed and dried herbs into a billy of water, watching as they soften in the boil. Mixing in a spoonful of miso, I take a slow mouthful. Holy sacrament, sweet elixir of the gods. The warm liquid pools in my belly, hugging me from the inside, while the fire wraps its warm arms around my shoulders. I look over to Wild Woman from across the fire. She seems to be smiling, the hands I can't see perhaps holding up two fingers in a V for peace.

The sphere of my home is my circle for this, the last day of the quest, and I explore it like a new lover's body. Wrapping my mouth around mountain devil flower heads, I suck hungrily at the nectar, nuzzle my nose into fresh banksia flowers and pause to allow gum leaves to tickle the back of my neck. In the leaf litter, tiny ringlets of bark lie curled under gold-top mushrooms. I discover a red-legged spiky insect so unlikely that I wonder whether I am the first human to see it. A grasstree has pushed up an asparagus-like spear of new growth, the needles tenuously clinging together. I tease at them, plucking a few free before I break their hold with a single twist, and they spill out in a fountain of pale green. In my absence, the plant that I had spared in my shelter clearing has burst into sweet-smelling pink boronia flowers. I cradle them in my palm.

Towards dusk the sun pierces the cloud cover in a long furrowed opening of soft pink. I stand and watch, swaying in time to the slow beat of the frame drum I'm holding. I recognise this woman standing alone on the earth within her circle. This is what she was trying to tell me. My vision quest doesn't end at dawn tomorrow; the entire year is my vision quest. I don't have to take myself away and starve to be within its circle of transformation, just like I don't need to hammer down church doors and fight to find peace. Maybe all I need to do is knock.

Stoking the embers inside my shelter, I prepare for an all-night vigil but fall instead into a deep sleep. I dream of a baby boy lying beside me, sleeping. When I wake to first light, I reach for my journal, the lines I scribble more prayer than poem.

Perhaps grace too,
may one day tiptoe in under the cover of darkness,
wrapping a shawl of the softest fleece
around the sleeping one,
who, only yesterday,
gave up the storming.

Above: My favourite time of day was watching wildlife at my sit spot atop the root ball of a fallen tree. Over the year the birds came to know me and flew in closer. (*Australian Geographic*)

Below: Time is of the essence as I transfer a tiny coal from my fireboard into a pre-prepared tinder bundle of blady grass, banksia, stringybark and bracken fern. (*Australian Geographic*)

Above: Nikki, Lorry (the Lorikeet) and me after a day of gathering bush tucker for a community feast, including lilly pillies (in the bangalow palm basket), native scaevola, dianella, pandanus, pigface fruit, bungwall fern, bulrush and warrigal greens.

Below: The heath was a treasure trove of grass tree stalks for hand-drill and sandy trails full of animal tracks. This tree gives me a great view of the area. (*Australian Geographic*)

Above: Ryan, Nikki and I show off our tanned hides in this primitive fashion parade.

Below: The Blady Bunch (clockwise from top left) Ryan, Nikki, me, Shaun, Chloe, Dan.

Above: My quest for hand-drill fire caused painful blood blisters on both palms. Here I hold a fire-kit of grass-tree flower stalk and wild tobacco board. (*Australian Geographic*)

Below: My shelter was littered with handmade baskets, pottery and cordage in various stages of completion. Sporting my deer-hide top, I sit and weave string with the inner bark of native hibiscus. In the background hangs the wallaby-hide firestick bag. (*Australian Geographic*)

Above: A glimpse through the arched door of my shelter reveals me sitting on my swag and writing in my journal by the light of the central fire. An underground air channel from outside helps oxygenate the flames to keep the fire burning bright. (*Australian Geographic*)

Below: My smile lasts until the next rain when I discover my first hopeful layer of paperbark is not going to keep my lean-to kitchen dry.

Above: My parents responded to my shelter-building SOS call with gusto. By the end of three days we have created the frame of my shelter and are about to commence construction on the chimney with wreaths of wattle.

Below: Even the most carefully laid plans can go awry. Overnight our primitive pottery bowls, pots and mugs turn to shards in the fire.

Above: Without matches, fire by friction was the only way to light a fire. Here I attempt the indigenous method of hand-drill using a grass tree flower stalk. (*Australian Geographic*)

Below: It took three layers of paperbark to waterproof my lean-to kitchen. The fun of swamp missions was marred by vicious mosquitoes. (*Australian Geographic*)

Above: Immersed in the creek, I re-bait the lawyer-cane eel trap with meat. Unable to swim backwards, the eels find themselves trapped – in theory. (*Australian Geographic*)

Below: Making and maintaining fires in winter took up a good deal of the day. Here I relax by my alfresco dining area to work on a coil basket. (*Australian Geographic*)

WINTER

*

What is there, after all,
besides memories and dreams
and the way they mix
with land and air and water
to make us whole?
ROBERT MICHAEL PYLE

*

THE SACRED ORDER OF SURVIVAL:

1. *Shelter*
2. *Water*
3. *Fire*
4. *Food*

1.

wake to the cry of a solitary currawong, muffled through the grass walls. It sounds marbled, a lament tinged with yearning. I close my eyes to the tendril of light reaching in for me and instead let the dream images hovering on the edge of my awareness pull me back. A kitten, playful and curious, lost inside a noisy nightclub. I'm looking for it. Where has it gone? My grandmother, smiling at me encouragingly.

The vine of light has wrapped around my ankle, tugging gently. Groaning, I obey, pulling on thermals, parka, boots, beanie, scarf and gloves. Strands of blady grass brush my hair as I stoop under the archway door and step out into an ethereal white mist.

Steam rises from the snaking stream my pee makes in the sand. A piece of scribbly bark makes good enough toilet paper. Shrouded in white, my shelter looks like a giant forest snail. Winter becomes this forest, the mist softening the sharp edges, air-brushing the scars. Everything is slowing, contracting, having been pruned back to its pure form: the thump of a swamp wallaby moving north along its breakfast route, the drop of nectar hanging from the single remaining blood-red mountain devil flower, my exposed brown wrists collecting a bracelet of damp. Sporadic bird calls punctuate the quiet, like bells in a monastery. I focus on the spaces in between. There is no absence of sound in these gaps, though. A hum grows loud in my chest and legs. My shoulders drop, as does my centre of gravity. I thrum in synchronicity with the forest.

My heart swells with the fullness of this precious moment. I send out a silent greeting along the spine of the currawong's call to all who share in this dawn with me – the winged ones, the four-leggeds, the scaly creatures curled in hollow logs and burrows, the underwater dwellers in the cold creeks and billabongs, the invisible kingdom of insects, the soil munchers, the leafy green monks surrounding me, and the silent earth itself. The mist rises like a prayer, blessing everything it touches until it dissolves into the sea of blue above.

I didn't include two-leggeds in my blessing because there aren't any others. Just me. Kate, Sam, Nikki, Ryan and Dan left a week ago for the indigenous community of Mapuru in Arnhem land, the women to learn basket weaving and bush food, and the men hunting. I visited this community a couple of years back and had originally planned to join this expedition. But even the thought of reconnecting with my adopted family on their red-dirt homeland didn't tempt me away from my four-season vigil on this patch of turf. I don't want to miss a beat – not of bat or butterfly wings, nor of my own heart. It felt like a brave decision, going against my usual pattern of gobbling up every opportunity, but the chance to be here alone, finally – gloriously – alone, was far more appetising. Well, almost alone (why is there always a catch here?); Chloe stayed too, although she's currently away on a one-on-one bird intensive with the amorous ornithologist.

But right *now*, it's just me and wild nature for kilometres. Just me and this deep, deep quiet, this gossamer light inviting me to slow, to soften, to curl in on myself. Until now, my days and weeks have been hedged between shelter building, workshops, vision quests, group obligations. I've been holding back, hesitant, waiting. This is the season when time can roll and tumble unimpeded, can stretch until it's thin as a veil, so thin it may disappear altogether. When I can finally let impulse and whim direct my days, follow the shadow and scent of things rather than the things themselves.

I yawn, stretch my arms as far as they'll reach and let out a little squeal. The sound of my own voice surprises me. I shiver with excitement.

And cold.

To fire, or not to fire. That is the question. The promise of a hot cuppa overrides my reluctance to go through the rigmarole of rubbing sticks together, so I start gathering kindling, the sharp snap of twigs ringing through a forest still rubbing its eyes awake. A breaking stick glances off the blister on my palm and I yelp. Despite my breakthrough coal, most of the time the hand-drill still eludes me. If it wasn't for the bow-drill, my no-matches commitment would have been sent to the rapidly filling glass cabinet labelled "ideals".

The need to make fire is more palpable since the cold appeared, and the others disappeared. It's my sticks or nothing. Although the worst that could really happen would be that I'm cold and miserable and eating raw rice for dinner, my limbic brain is acting as if I am stranded alone on the savannah with wild beasts waiting to devour me. Fire constantly flickers through my thoughts, generating a worry cycle of imminent failure and sending me scuttling back to my shelter long before dark to start preparations. I have been engaging in some serious fire insurance activities – carving bow-drill spindles and notching them onto boards; collecting grasstree stalks, dry bracken fern, whiskey-grass seed heads and stringybark shards. On my last town mission I stripped the fibrous mesh from a cabbage-tree palm in the street and plucked seed heads of bulrush from the highway verge for tinder.

Looking down at the tender bloody lumps on my palms, I reach instead for the bow-drill kit. I have made solid friends with this fire-making method, although I'm still using parachute cord for the bow string, so I'm no maestro yet. Another thing on the list.

Smoke starts to billow vigorously from the friction point almost immediately. I stop for a peek. The dust is coarse and brown, fraying out rather than knitting together. The notch has already chewed through half the board. Hmm, the casuarina spindle must be too hard for it. If it's not one thing it's another with fire; it's as tempestuous as a two-year-old. I really don't feel like carving a new notch and am not sure my half-frozen fingers could coordinate the action anyway. Damn, I just want a cup of tea. I launch back into the bow with a logger's intensity, seesawing back and forth until the spindle breaks through the board into the dirt. With desperate hope I fan the clump of motionless wood dust. I'm about to stomp off when a tiny spiral of smoke erupts. A submarine coal. Crouching back down, I purse my lips close and whisper a breath. The coal gradually grows into a fiery orange marble, robust enough to be transferred to the blady grass tinder bundle and blown into flames. Soon I am sitting, smug as a Cheshire cat, under my paperbark lean-to, cuppa in hand and porridge bubbling away. The world is a wonderful place again, now there is fire.

Fire gurgles in baby talk, making self-satisfied crackling and popping sounds.

Happy now? It asks with a loud fart, as I poke a stick into its belly.

I smile and offer it a sprinkling of dry gum leaves. Fire claims the snack hungrily, thanking me with an explosion of bright orange sparks. I drip-feed it to keep it small, after discovering recently how easily fire can become overexcited if fed too much, the charred stain on the paperbark ceiling a constant reminder of this. I curl my legs around the rock fireplace and expose my belly to the flames. We rise and fall with purring breaths.

A flutter of wings in the banksia alerts me to the arrival of my breakfast companions – a flock of small birds that have banded together in some kind of food cooperative, seemingly using the power of (wing) numbers to flush out more insects. I reach for the binos hanging behind me on a hook. The brown thornbills have a strong showing this morning, feasting away in the mid-storey. A family of wrens bounces along the ground, a grey fantail fussing over it all from above. Eastern spinebills and white-cheeked honeyeaters are the other regulars in this core collective. This morning is quite a party, the grey shrike-thrush and white-naped honeyeaters joining in, even the scarlet honeyeater making an appearance. They aren't at all dissuaded by my fire; in fact, they seem drawn to it. Perhaps passed down to them is the memory of insects swarming the fireplaces that once dotted this landscape on winter mornings. My kitchen fireplace is one of three dining areas I can now choose from, the latest an alfresco space out the front of my shelter, with a log backrest and a tripod to hang my billy on. It's all part of the primitive IKEA binge I'm on – gathering, carving, whittling and weaving gadgets to feather my nest. If I'm going to hibernate, I want to do it in style and comfort. Like a true first-home owner, I'm fizzing with ideas for interior design improvements: baskets to hang my veggies in, as well as more intricately woven baskets and dillybags; coal-burnt wooden utensils and bowls; string hooks to suspend my pots over the fire; gourd water bottles. I'm keen to give pottery another go and can picture some naturally woven matting for my kitchen floor (which I've discovered floods in heavy rain). Then there's tanning hides to make clothes, rawhide lamps and water containers. I also want to experiment with bulrush flower heads and hardened banksia cones dipped in animal fat to replace candles.

Shuffling through my mental list of "things to make and do" excites me enough to fetch the bangalow-palm-leaf sheath that has been soaking overnight. It's great material, so far doing a stellar job of keeping rain out of my chimney. I've also had success with stripping it into ribbons and making a coarse cord. This piece is hopefully going to replace my plastic bucket. I fold one end in on itself like I'm wrapping a present, and pierce it with a wide-eyed needle threaded with gymea lily cord. Knotting the end, I tug the cord through in gentle pulses. Bone needle, I add to my mental list, as I cross-stitch down the fold. A warm contentment spreads through me, as my fingers find rhythm with the work. Like the palm made soft overnight, I become absorbed too, swelling and softening with the task in my hand.

The last week of crafty days has felt like one big pyjama party, indulging my desire to be a homebody and simply *potter*. The word itself is almost as pleasurable as the activity: pottering. The art of doing lots of little things with the feeling of doing nothing much at all. Or perhaps it is the art of doing nothing much at all with the feeling of doing lots. It doesn't matter. The pleasure comes not from ticking things off a list, but from flowing between things on a whim, physically moving through a space, absorbed by the act of pottering itself. I know I've had a successful potter not by the number of things I've achieved, but by the sense that I too have been fluffed up, rearranged and adorned with fresh flowers.

When I was growing up, pottering was a luxury squeezed between more important activities such as competitive sport, study and part-time work. My occasional mornings of aimlessness felt stolen and decadent. Those weekend afternoons when tennis was washed out, and I could stay home and read or cook, were some of my happiest. But when the sun shone, life had to resume apace, and potterers who aspired to continue their shuffling became lazy – something you never, ever wanted to be.

My pottering pleasure has been tainted, therefore, by a sneaking guilt that trails me like a mangy dog. I've had to keep throwing it tidbits of productivity to stop it snapping at my heels. Even sitting here I can feel it stalking me, as if the enjoyment of coolamon making is momentarily bestowed upon me by an extraordinarily magnanimous part of myself, and is liable to be snatched away at any moment. I have three long winter months to do *whatever* I want, *whatever* my heart desires, I remind myself. I'm not sure if I believe it.

Fire grumbles with hunger and I nestle a log within the coals. Shy, fire hangs back at first, before leaping around it with fierce licks.

"You're a bit high maintenance, aren't you?" I joke.

Tending to this small being helps to absolve the nagging feeling that I should be somewhere else, doing something more useful. Fire is my pet, my responsibility. My lifeline.

*

The thin fingers of the sun are waving goodbye as the feeding flocks complete their supper alms round. It is a subdued dusk chorus. I look around to survey the results of my day. Looking like a miniature dragon boat, my bangalow bucket sits fat and full with water and cord. A shelf inside my shelter is a nature museum, adorned with shells, stones and bones, while underneath I've stashed candles, toilet paper and small tools. Whittled wooden hooks lashed to the main shelter frame hang with drying bunches of lomandra for basket weaving, and a hat rack fashioned from a many-forked branch sports my weathered Akubra and felt hat. I fiddle with the string loops of my most exciting addition: cobbled together from an old blanket and a branch, a shelter door that rolls up and down like a retractable awning. No more freezing nose in bed.

I should be pleased but instead I'm flat, restless. I poke at the remains of my morning fire, the coals cold and crumbly. While it's not a feeling I have had to contend with much in my life, the scratchy yearning in the pit of my stomach is unmistakeable.

Loneliness.

What is it about this time of day that takes solitude and twists it into loneliness? It's as if a primal instinct kicks in right on dusk, and I'm back out on the prairie searching wildly for my tribe before the lions can claim me. This afternoon it's sharper, clutching tight at my guts and gnawing on them. How dare it! I've been hanging out to be alone for the last six months, and loneliness thinks it can just waltz in and stay for dinner.

The lone currawong bookends the day, pausing on the upward inflection as if waiting for an answer to its question. Not a breath of wind has moved through the forest all day. If it was still when I woke, it is positively statuesque now, a collective ear pricked and listening.

"Wheeeeeeee!" I yell defiantly, as I jump up and perform a little stamp and twirl, needing to prove that I have not turned to stone.

I busy myself with fire preparations, trying to ignore the gut twist. After I have exhausted all fussing, I sit as close to the fire as I can without burning myself. Cold currents tremor down my limbs. How long before Chloe returns, I wonder? How many kilometres between me and the next human? *Come on, you're finally alone by your fire. Enjoy it, for God's sake.*

The dark from outside is creeping in. I poke my head out the entrance and cast a quick glance around, glad to be able to roll down my blanket door. I'm in for the night.

Wetting some loose strands of native hibiscus on my tongue, I draw up my trousers and begin rolling them back and forth across my thigh like the women in Arnhem land showed me, adding in strands as necessary to make string. They would all be up there now, sitting around a fire together, the bright-eyed kids draping themselves over any available lap. I could be there too, but, no, this is where I want to be. At least I think I do. The back and forth action soothes me, the shivers slowly subsiding. A shaft of milky light lands on the crown of my head, the almost-full moon a single round eye looking in through the smoke hole. Good old Grandmother Moon, peeking in to check on me. Reminding me that I'm not alone.

It's not being alone that worries me, but the company I keep sometimes when I am alone: the characters who come out to play in the empty rooms of solitude, the shadow walkers within.

This *is* where I want to be, though. Here, with the moon on my shoulder and fire at my side. The last dregs of loneliness scatter under the moon's gaze, and I smile up into her face. I watch as she dips below the chimney lip, then I put my head down and keep rolling.

2.

With a gasp, I lower myself into the envelope of icy water banked by fallen logs in Snake Creek and rub handfuls of small pebbles over my skin, an attempt to peel away a week's worth of charcoal and grime. A few minutes is all I can bear. On a log, I catch shards of sunlight filtering through the trees. My skin tingles with a thousand pinpricks. I'm glad I made myself go in. I feel alive.

I wade upstream to check on the turtle trap hidden behind a clump of lomandra. The construction was a group effort during our trapping workshop in autumn. It's mostly still intact, a semi-circle of closely spaced sticks, driven a foot deep into the mud to prevent the turtle from digging its way out, and rising half a foot above the surface so it can't climb over. A few days ago I baited it with some offal, propping the door open with a small stick, which I hoped the turtle I had seen sunning itself on a nearby log would dislodge on its way in. The beauty of this trap is that it's non-lethal, the turtle swimming around in the enclosure while the trapper deliberates whether turtle soup is on the menu, or whether it's too cute to eat. I'm not faced with that dilemma today – the meat is gone, and the door closed. I suspect the bait stick is too close to the door, allowing the munchkin to grab the prize and back out of there, licking its lips.

Back along the bank, I notice five-leaf water vine, the native grape that we made into jam during summer. Maybe this could be the material to make my kitchen basket with? Closing my eyes and holding one leaf, I extend my awareness into it, asking if it would like to be transformed into a basket. I remember back to shelter building, when my efforts at gathering materials in an intentional manner felt contrived and perfunctory. Nothing has sprouted lips and talked to me yet, but I enjoy the ritual of it now. If nothing else, it makes the world around me, and by extension me as well, more alive and imaginative. The leaf offers no resistance. I pull on the vine, coiling it around my elbow and thumb like a rope, feeling a bit Tarzan-like, as if I'm about to swing out over the creek.

I settle into a grassy spot by the creek instead and strip leaves from eight of the sturdiest lengths to be the warp for a simple woven basket. Laying them crossways, I attempt to secure them at the base with two thin strands. The first weaver snaps at the leaf node. It's definitely not cane.

Over and under, over and under. My hands soon learn the amount of give the vine can offer, gently persuading it to bend without breaking. I relax into the weaver's mantra. The burble of the creek washes over me, a river stone caressed by the shallow rapids. I am absorbed deeper and deeper in the task until all movement – hands, fingers, thoughts – merge into one action. And yet as I am sucked into a single point, so too do I expand out in wider and wider circles, catching distant birdsong, small movements of cloud.

Over and under, over and under. It's like shelter building, the same experience of being so physically engrossed in a project that my awareness enters my hands, bypassing my conscious mind and communicating with the materials so that I intuitively know how they want to move.

Over and under, over and under. Time warps and weaves in on itself, marked only by leopard spots of light moving across my body. We have structured our world to avoid the time-consuming tasks of simple living. If this is how it feels to be consumed by time, then I'm willing to be eaten alive. I'm relishing these days of repetition, the over-and-under involved in creating house and home. I feel as if I've stepped into the "chop wood, carry water" koan, glimpsing the joy that follows when path and practice are synonymous – when life is meditation and meditation is life.

Yesterday I started on my "couch", lashing branches together to form an A-frame backrest, which I wedged against one of the shelter poles. A flat basket for drying tinder hangs from a rafter above the end of my bed. Behind it is a small bookshelf, which holds select texts: *Women Who Run with the Wolves*, Bill Plotkin's *Soulcraft*, a Robert Johnston dream interpretation manual, Tom Brown Jr's *Awakening the Spirits*, *The Tibetan Book of Living and Dying*, a bird-ID book and my journal. My kitchen is also in the throes of primitive redecoration. I've dug a hole in the ground at the back for perishables and have hung three wooden shelves with hibiscus cordage along the wall of one side, filling them with tins and glass jars of grains and legumes. My shelter is starting to look seriously homely.

Over and under, over and under. The sun flickers on my back. This is so lovely down here; I really should be enjoying this more. I wonder what time it is. Butterflies suddenly take flight in my belly, flapping around desperately in search of a solid perch.

My mind latches onto future home-making projects. A blady grass mat for my backrest, a large basket for my clothes. Mulling over this list is comforting, soothing, a familiar old blanket. I know how to do this. *Doing*, that is. The plans protect me, distract me, are buying me time.

Over and under, over and under. A family of wrens dances in close, the male so blue it makes the sky look pastel. Flicking his tail feather from side to side, he watches over his harem foraging in the grass. My weaving hands pause as I view the visitors.

Hurry up, you need to get this done so you can move on to the other baskets, and then the bowl, and the spoons. You haven't got all day.

The wrens suddenly scatter as if frightened by the thought. My fingers stiffen, quickening. The lengthening shadow of a tree looks like it's waving me a disingenuous greeting. Adrenalin courses through my body. Small lines furrow my forehead and my awareness retracts back from my hands to my mind.

And what is this homemaker business, anyway? Baskets aren't going to keep you alive. I thought you wanted to be a tracker? A skills guru? An awareness ninja? You've hardly even started night walking. This is your one opportunity to apply yourself to something extraordinary.

Extraordinary. The word catches like a burr in my throat. Skills and spaciousness, everythingness and nothingness. I want them all. How can I? I double over in a rasping cough as saliva dribbles down my airway. Slow down, I know what my real work is – feeling and following my heart. And right now I want to sit by the creek and weave a basket.

Do you really? Or is this just another project to tick off the list? Maybe what you actually want is to sit in the hammock all winter. Look at you beavering away like you've done all your life. Nothing's changed. You're too scared to really follow your heart.

A currawong flies to a low perch, looking at me from the corner of its eye. It reminds me of the day I ran from a mountaintop, currawongs flocking around me like prison wardens escorting me to the gate.

After my trip to tracker school, I bought sacks of rice and lentils, and asked Dad to drop me at a forest hut on the edge of the Barrington Tops national park for thirty days of solitude. Rather than dreamily wandering through the forest, drinking in my own company with the thirst of a desert pilgrim, as I'd envisaged, I found that solitude was a fierce magnifying glass, bringing every nuance of my being into accentuated focus, blowing up every internal freckle, every blemish. Its stare was penetrating – everywhere I turned, there it was, or rather, there *I* was, in my face. I tried to outpace the voices of fear and judgment and doubt, hauling myself up a vicious five-day mountain climb in scorching heat, the only thing slowing me down a tiger snake camouflaged on the trail. Perhaps if I had stayed long enough, I would have found a friend in myself, but back then my company was too stark, too sharp. The relentless harassment had me scuttling back to civilisation after seventeen days.

Get a grip, I tell myself. You're not on the mountain now. You're older and wiser. Trust in what your heart wants to do.

But maybe it's true, maybe I'm not following my heart. I suddenly feel as if I have sand in my eyes and can't see which is the face of truth and which is that of the charlatan. How can it be this hard? Okay, I'll just get this basket done and *then* I'll get back to the flow, I reason, trying desperately to placate both sides of me.

I pick up the pace, my face red with the knowledge that I am being seduced again by the false promise that there is a magic point in the future when enough will be enough, when I will tick the right number of boxes to give me permission to slow down. The two weavers whip against my legs as I fling them over each other.

Over and under. Gotta keep going. *Over and under.* Justify your existence.

Over and under. When this is finished. *Over and under.* Then I'll have time.

One of the weavers breaks.

Oh, look what happens when you rush. You've come all this way out to the bush, pushed everyone away to get your precious time alone, and you still can't rest. You will never find peace.

"Stop!" I yell and throw the basket on the ground. "I don't believe you. You're an imposter." The face of the judge steps out from the shadows, and it's the pursed-lipped woman with coiffed blue hair from my dreams, shaking her head in stern disapproval. I turn and run, birds scattering. Faster and faster, anywhere but here, anywhere but in my head. Tripping on a tree root, I fall face down, furious tears staining my face. The wrinkled fingers of my stalker wrap around my throat in triumph. It's no use: I've tried all year to ignore the judge, to tell her to pack her bags and leave, but there's no escape. I lie limp on the ground as silent tears fall.

3.

Perched atop my sit spot, I am listening, my entire body receiving sound as if it's covered in tiny ears, a giant sensory organ. When I drop the string that connects the sounds to their sources, they become just frequency, just sensation: minor chords and cascading harmonies piano-tinkling down my spine. As if pushed from behind, I lurch forward. Moments later the sound arrives: a wave, slowly gathering momentum before crashing over me. I hold my breath until it passes. I open my eyes to dozens of white ibis flying north in a V-formation.

The white-cheeked honeyeaters hold silent momentarily before exploding in a kerfuffle of squawks nearby. While there's nothing unusual about that, this outburst seems particularly serious. Maybe I should investigate. Walking to the other end of the log, I jump down and creep up behind a thicket.

Craning my head into the low branches of a shrub, I see a grey butcherbird looking decidedly guilty. "Caught red-handed," I grin. I've had a grudge against butcherbirds ever since one of them swiped my budgerigar when I was a kid. The bird flashes me an annoyed glance and takes off. Moving on from my summer frenzy of naming and labelling sit spot inhabitants, I'm more interested now in relationships – between birds, between birds and the forest, between birds and myself. Sound is the key to this study. According to Niko, all songbirds have five calls: companion contact, song, juvenile begging, aggression (usually male territorial disputes) and alarm. Identifying them is the cornerstone of coming to know the forest through the eyes and ears of the birds. Every event sends out a concentric ripple of presence, like a pebble thrown into a pond. I tune into bird radio every morning, then keep one antenna up and tracking throughout the day, sparking up when a disturbance breaks the still waters. It's like having a cricket match on in the background, the mumble of the commentator a distant nasal hum until the hullabaloo of a wicket snaps me back to attention.

A slight breeze stirs the tops of the trees, a wax museum come to life. I sling my water bottle over my shoulder in its new string-net holder and wander south, following a red clay trail out of camp. Nuggetty black stringybarks wave me on like royal guards. A wedge-tailed eagle circles above, panning for its breakfast. Overnight, patersonia lilies have thrown down a bedspread of purple to complement the mauve pea-like flowering vine that's climbing over rocks.

I come to the first fork. I remember this one, and take the right. The path divides again. They will keep peeling away like this, branching further from the original node, like a family tree becoming more distantly related. Both trails beckon with an equal mix of anticipation and trepidation. I wait until I feel a movement in my feet. They guide me left, picking up the trail that begins to ascend the yellowing backbone of the sandstone ridge.

With my binge of home making subsiding, I've taken to hiking out in larger concentric circles each day, pushing the boundaries of my backyard. I now fill my pockets with dried fruit and nuts, knowing I won't be able to resist the lure of the undiscovered around the next corner. Rather than setting an agenda, I let curiosity be my navigator and just wander. The focused bushwalks of my earlier years, shouldering a heavy pack from points A to B, bear little resemblance to these meanders. When bushwalking, there is a right way and a wrong way, a track to be followed or deviated from. When wandering, deviation *is* the trail, "lost" a relative concept known in shades of discomfort and excitement. It's more of an exploration. And just like a good explorer, I return home to fill in the blank spaces on my map with the trails taken, treasures found, features noted.

It's starting to look like a map in a fantasy novel. There are the "goodlands" (grasstree stalk heaven, native raspberry avenue, clay cutting, far waterhole), the "badlands" (wild dog quarry, eerie night spot, quicksand swamp, blueberry clearfell), the creeks and features that demarcate them, the trails that cross and connect them. There are features known by events (mudfight river bend, vision quest site, powerful owl meeting), by who dwells there (death-adder trail, thornbill dormitory, eastern-grey kangaroo lay). There are those close by and well known (shelters, sit spot, power tree, big-toe tree, swimming hole) and those farther away and little known (paperbark-Ent swamp, full-moon sandstone boulders, bangalow-palm fairy glen). Day by day I am colouring in the spaces between and beyond, trying to connect the dots into a coherent whole, make the landscape familiar and known. It's a way of befriending the land, building relationships and assigning meaning. I like to think I'm mapping the story of the land, but it's as much my story that I reference: my impressions, my tracks, my landmarks. I map the land as much to know myself as to know it.

Fresh bandicoot prints cross my path. I look around, half expecting to see a small furry mound goading me, like the White Rabbit, to follow it. The tracks lead me to a critter crossroads, the full extent of rush-hour traffic laid out on a sandy thoroughfare. I squat for a closer look.

Tracking. If birds are the spoken language, tracks are the written word. They are the hieroglyphs of the land itself, an ancient code inscribed on the Earth's slate. Very few are committed enough to decipher it, but I've met one who is.

Tom Brown Jr is the founder and head honcho of the tracker school where Ryan and I studied. The first time I saw him, he was sucking down a cigarette in between slurps of a takeaway coffee. Pacing through camp like a disgruntled bear, his giant sun-browned arms protruding from a muscle tee, piercing blue eyes brooding and intense, Tom defied any stereotype his often doe-eyed students tried to project onto him.

"If you think you're going to sit under a tree with an old man and chew the fat of the land then you've come to the wrong place." Dozens of shoulders slumped.

Brought up by Baptist parents in the conservative 1950s backwater of semi-rural New Jersey, Tom is an odd cross between hick and shaman. As told in his autobiography, *The Tracker*, at seven years of age he was playing by a creek behind his house when Stalking Wolf, one of the last great trackers of the southern Lipan Apache, stumbled upon Tom – apparently fulfilling a vision, and bringing to an end a 63-year solo walk across the Americas. Over the next decade, Tom and Stalking Wolf's grandson Rick were tutored in the ways of the woods, in between cheeseburgers and school. As a young adult, Tom gained notoriety for his work in law enforcement, tracking murderers and lost children. He became an unwilling guru, with hundreds of eager apprentices knocking at his door.

Decades later, his reluctance is still palpable. Tom sneered, challenged and pleaded with us to learn the ways of the earth as he crushed a disposable water bottle with one hand and tossed it over his shoulder. There is a less-than-subtle apocalyptic tone to his invitation, and I met more than one can-filled bunker-owning acolyte.

On the morning we were to start tracking lessons, camp was jumpy. Tom seemed even more intense, if that was possible. He entered the Taj (the primitive teaching shed) quietly, outwardly subdued but crackling with energy. Narrowing his eyes, he spun around to face us.

"Did any of you see the tracks this morning of the deer that walked up to the flintknapping pit and grazed on the new shoots of the blueberry?" He eyed the crowd, shocked, as if in disbelief at our ignorance. "He looked left, sniffed the ground twice, before walking right over the tracks of the raccoon that passed through the oak thicket an hour or so before.

"And how many of you noticed the tracks of the feral cat, a large male that stalked along the far edge of the Taj? Perhaps it was after the mice, two of them, that scampered along this

MY YEAR WITHOUT MATCHES

podium." Silence. "After today, I promise you'll never see the ground in the same way again. Follow me."

We filed along track after track, identifying the compression shapes paws and hooves make in the sand by deer, raccoon, dog, cat, fox, coyote, rabbit, bird and mouse. Tom moved into increasingly more difficult terrain, locating new tracks with an air of boredom. He saved the best for last – the trail of a mouse in pine needles. The skeptic in me spluttered. With a tired sigh, Tom directed me to where pollen on the leaf had been removed, leaving the perfect compression shape of the left hind foot of a mouse. I gaped. He rolled his eyes.

And that was just kindergarten stuff. The real deal was the ability to read the "micro and macro pressure releases" – tracking at the level of an individual grain of sand. This is where the practical science of tracking transformed into art, where the "who, when and where" questions sharpened to "How tall? How heavy? Moving how quickly? Bladder full or empty? Emotional state?" As if to lend weight to this seemingly unbelievable ability, Tom banned us from reading the tracks of our classmates. "An invasion of privacy," he claimed. After hours of sketching my thumbprint in a cup of sand I was too cross-eyed to contemplate any recreational private-eye behaviour.

As the training unfolded, we found ourselves tracking fox prints across packed gravel, deer prints in pine needles by moonlight. Our fingers held one end of the string, and at the other end was the animal we tracked. Sometimes you could sense it, as if the string pulled taut when the animal moved, jerked sideways as it changed direction. One day, struggling to find a deer print in pine needles, I stood back to take a break and the entire line of tracks lit up in front of me with neon brightness. It was then I understood what Tom meant by tracking being a window into the soul of the land itself. And why he had warned us that once you start tracking, you can never stop.

"I have given you the key, but only dirt time will unlock that door," he sniggered. "I can tell you now, only two percent of you will ever pick up that key. The majority will walk away today full of good intentions that will fade to dust when you return to your domestic lives."

I promised myself that I wouldn't let this ancient knowledge die in my hands.

On my belly now, my nose centimetres from the track of a swamp wallaby, I strain to remember the words to describe the micro landscape features of the track. *Cliff, dome, crest.* When Tom was a kid in training, his dirt time apparently formed calluses on his ribs. Mine are soft. I notice a smooth hill outside the print. *Ridge.* My gaze follows the change in direction it indicates, connecting the dots to nibbled blades of grass, the tattered ends still green. The string tugs in my fingers.

The idea with the second half of the year is that we choose an area of study to focus on. I've decided on tracking and trapping. For a real survival skill, I'm going to have a much better chance of trapping than hunting, and you have to track to be able to trap. If I commit to eating meat only from wild animals, that will give me a real incentive.

My mind buzzes and whirrs with plans – where I'll put my tracking box, what kind of trap I'll start with, how many hours a day I'll spend with my nose in the dirt. It's all a bit exciting really, six whole months of tracking and trapping.

Hang on, slow down. *I thought your project was following the heart rather than mastering any one skill?* Yes, well, there's time for it all. What could be more wild than reading the tracks of animals? This is quite possibly the only opportunity I'll have to learn one of the most sacred and ancient arts of all time.

And, anyway, I *am* doing the heart business, checking in throughout the day with how I'm feeling. Just like bird radio, though, the more I tune in, the louder the signal gets, and it's not always music I want to hear. Following Malcolm's suggestion, I've been getting up and moving when difficult emotions arise.

"Emotion is just energy in motion," he said. "Dance to the soundtrack of your heart."

Numerous dance floors have been added to my map. No-one can hear or see me, the bush the only witness to my shake, rattle and roll. The more I give physical shape to the emotions rather than trying to analyse or ignore them, the more it opens new frontiers of feeling. I can sense it loosening the screws of my heart, reconfiguring the nuts and bolts of my make-up.

It's a kind of tracking through my internal landscape, the wild places and sharp edges I find on the land mirroring the ones I am discovering within. I'm following the well-trodden pathways of habitual thought and feeling; discovering new patterns in the changing weather of emotion, where the trails of fear, anger, grief and joy intersect, and where they diverge, where I lose them and find myself adrift in a wilderness.

I rest my cheek on the sand, the raised edges of the tracks looking like tiny ripples. I think back to last night's dreams. A tiger quoll, fierce and cat-like, plays around my legs. A young female lion pads up to me and stares deeply into my eyes. I'm a little scared, as the longer I meet her gaze, the more I realise we are one and the same. I woke with the feeling of her warrior strength lying beside me, wild and soft.

*

A red-necked wallaby lopes out to feed. Facing the opposite direction, he hasn't seen or smelt me yet. As slowly as possible, I rise into a push-up position, gradually coming into a crouching stalk. The wallaby puts his head up, twitches his nose and turns his ears. I freeze. Slowing my step to a virtually imperceptible motion, I scatter my gaze. Just as I near the ten-foot mark, a yellow robin flies in to let out a single tweet above the wallaby. The wallaby doesn't even bother to double-check, thumping away milliseconds after the subtle alarm.

The more I notice in this forest, the more I realise I must miss. There are layers of relationship that I can only guess at, understandings and agreements that I am not privy to. They blur species boundaries, make a mockery of linear food chains, create fissures in distinct lines of kinship. Like the webs of white root fungus that hold the forest together beneath the surface, so too are there hidden webs above, feathery and fine. They are inside me too, these mysteries, secret alliances whose operations underpin the entire system from subterranean depths. They tell me more about what I don't know, than what I do. I am trying to find a way to weave myself into this fabric, form my bonds, make my allies. I am trying to make visible the invisible.

*

At dusk I walk past Snake Creek until the soil leaches to sand, and gums give way to thickets of banksia, garnia and melaleuca. A runaway pine tree from the plantation nearby has sprung up on the edge of the swamp. I climb to the highest point, where five branches fan out in a star, and nestle in. The low sun glows on my left cheek. I burrow my arms up the opposite sleeves of my jumper and rest my head back against a branch, staring up into the twilight.

It's good to be out of camp. The others, Chloe included, returned like a flock of noisy white cockatoos a few days ago. We gathered inside Ryan's teepee, loud voices squawking in my ears, questions prodding me like sharp spears. I scrambled to bundle up and fit back together the pieces of me that lay scattered over the land, in order to present some vague semblance of myself. Unlike the others, I had no holiday snapshots at the ready. My words sounded crass and clunky, betraying the subtleties of something I don't yet understand myself, something that exists only in the daily movement of my limbs through space.

I didn't realise how raw I was until rubbed. Like the winter trees, I am stripped of bark, in the middle of a shedding process that needs the privacy of darkness.

The sun is threatening to slip behind the western cliffs. It thickens in the middle, spreads like butter across the tops of the far stringybarks and waits. Just before it gives up, the ivory eye of the moon rises in the east to meet its gaze. The solstice always feels too soon, but perhaps it is time. I sway gently in my nest, a fulcrum between the light and dark.

4.

Three men fling mud in the faces of three women. A gang of men, the ringleader a bully I know, kicks in the flimsy sheet walls I have erected in an attempt to carve out a bedroom space for myself. A woman is tortured and gagged as a warning of what will happen if she continues to stand up to them. I wake, heart pounding, to blackness. Rubbing my throat, I bring my knees close to my chest.

A strange clicking is coming from outside. I silence it by pulling the blanket up, my cold ears appreciating the gesture. Mangled lines from a half-remembered poem play on loop, "What will you do with your one wild life, your one precious day?" They take on a childish singsong tone, mocking, taunting. Stay under the blankets, that's what I plan to do.

I eventually pull on the woollens I left on the dirt next to my swag last night and roll up the door to another exquisite misty morning. My belly growls. I couldn't be bothered making dinner last night. I step out for a pee. Overnight, ants have carpeted their mound with yellow wattle flowers. Why, I wonder? Attracting insects? Sandbags for rain? It looks like an Indian funeral wreath of tiny marigolds.

The clicking begins again. I feel like something is watching me, the hairs on my neck prickling. A *whoosh* of feathers against moist air. I spin around to find a raven perched on top of my chimney, jet-black beady eyes staring directly into mine. The clicking turns guttural, whirring and slurring. Its language is lost on me. Corvids such as ravens, crows and magpies don't adhere to the standard five calls of the songbirds. Their language is complex, resisting all attempts to map and translate it. Perhaps there are no corresponding words.

I walk over to the kitchen to contemplate food. Black wings follow me.

"What do you want?"

The raven clicks and whirrs.

Kneeling to set kindling, I freeze when I notice a dog print at least as large as my hand etched in the sand. I look behind me, half expecting to see yellow eyes staring out from behind a tree. I search for more prints. Another lies closer to my shelter, the toe mounds dug in as if straining forward, sniffing or salivating, perhaps. I've heard dingos howling from the western ridge lately, so it may have been one of them. If I were a better tracker, I could date the prints.

Maybe they're my prints, I think, and guffaw. I feel half-wolf at the moment, skulking around camp, the hooded coat I sewed from an old woollen blanket hung loosely around my bony shoulders. My skin hasn't seen water in more than a week and is wolf-grey, clogged with dirt. I'm certainly hairy enough.

The raven cocks its head and continues staring at me. What is this, freak-out-Claire day, or something? As if I needed that. I'm freaking myself out enough these days. I throw an arm up in its direction, barely raising more than a ruffle of feathers.

As I steel myself for the hand-drill, my fingers are so cold I almost have to prise them open to support the stalk.

Good luck getting one out of me today, the invisible fire warns. A familiar cavern of dread opens up.

I yelp at the squeeze of my blisters. There is a strange pleasure in the intensity of pain this morning. It reminds me I'm alive. I push my palms harder against the stalk, steadying myself as nausea sweeps over me. My eyes bunch up tight in focus as I drill. There's barely enough dust to fill the notch before my arms seize up.

"Fuck you!" I yell and hurl my kit at the nearest tree, holding out my bleeding palms towards where the sticks lie. "What more do you want from me?"

I pummel a coal out of my bow-drill kit and shove it under my kindling. Fire nibbles at the offering, wilfully slow. I force-feed it twigs until it has no choice but to explode in a fireball.

I heat porridge leftovers and brew a billy of tea. The sun cresting the canopy is beaming ice rather than warmth. I should go down to my sit spot or work on my tracking box, but I can't be bothered. Be useful then, make something. I forage for some good-sized coals with the wattle-stick tongs I made yesterday, and transport them to the bowl cavity I've been burning out of a thick branch. I hold the coals down with the tongs, blowing on them just enough to keep them red but not flaming. I'm already eating and stirring with coal-burnt spoons, and this bowl will complete the set.

I jump at a high-pitched squeal in the distance. For a second I think it's a voice calling me out of a dream. Is it a bird? It sounds a bit like Nikki. I shrink back against the kitchen wall.

I've been asserting my boundaries with canine territorialism since the others got back. Wary and defensive, I offer no excuses for my self-imposed isolation. I'm not fit for human company even if I wanted it. I am empty of routine, sleeping odd hours and padding the trails alone at any time of the day or night. I wake alert, ears pricked and heart pounding. My companion is the moon, my comfort the sharp rub of splintered log against my naked body as I seek contact with the sun. My feet grow increasingly confident as I rove further afield, playing on narrow logs and scaling branches, watching mists roll in on dusk from the high perch of my sunset tree. Inside my lair at night I lick my wounds, gnaw on the bones of the day, sucking out the marrow and scratching it in my journal with dirty fingernails.

*

The moon rises full. I pace restlessly, procrastinating about fire lighting. I've been wandering downstream by the creek all afternoon. This land is full of edges, carved up and piecemeal. Where once I turned up my nose at them, I now find myself drawn to them, to the frayed borders where the wild butts up against the tame. I find myself lingering along the messy lines where bands of wattle break the back of disused paddocks, loitering in groves of chainsawn offcuts where airless soil grows thick with weeds. This land is wild in the way I need it to be. Not in the way that hangs immortalised in picture frames on walls, but like a half-domesticated animal, fierce and defensive, unshod. It doesn't try to be anything it's not. I like that about it.

A dingo howls in the distance. That is one edge I have been as yet unwilling to cross. I've been wanting to further extend my night wanders, but my fear of dogs has prevented me. On my jogging loop, I recently caught glimpse of a huge black one slinking into the bushes on the edge of a quarry about three kilometres away.

It howls again, this time louder, as if in challenge. I pace. I feel reckless. What the heck: if you can't beat 'em, join 'em.

I set off with a stick in hand, crossing Snake Creek with a quick step, and begin the trail to the quarry. I will myself not to hum, not wanting to distract myself from the sounds of the night, from the band of tension building around my chest. The moon is still low and barely casts a glow under the tree line where I walk. I haven't brought a torch.

As I near the quarry I slow, not sure whether I should stomp, to make my presence known, or creep in. Bushes rustle behind me and I spin around. Creeping is useless. This is not my turf. I'm sure I've already been spotted by multiple sets of eyes, ears and noses. I stride in, feigning confidence, scanning for any sign of movement before planting myself atop the most exposed mound in the centre. Trees take on grotesque shapes, contorted faces appearing in the branches and leaves. Was that a snarl? They're winning.

Dragging myself up to standing, I let out a blood-curdling howl. The forest freezes. I break into it again with another long howl. Shapes shifts uneasily around me. Cackling like a mad-woman, I jog back to my shelter.

*

The stick I've been whittling all morning is growing too thin to grip. I set it down amidst the carpet of shavings and stare out into the bush. The wolf is hungry again. Good. Lunch is something to look forward to, something to do. It's a welcome marker in the absence of any other, giving my day shape and structure.

I savour a little longer the anticipation of eating by scraping a final layer of charcoal from the coal-burnt wooden bowl with the edge of a rock. A smear of olive oil shines it up, ready for use. I spoon in leftover rice and dhal and set it on my breakfast bar. A moth flutters in to perch on the edge, its Persian-carpet wings faintly humming. Morning, too, teeters precariously on the edge.

My stomach growls but I resist picking up the spoon, knowing the full bowl is all that stands between me and the long empty afternoon, the stark and uncompromising sun that I shrink from, guilty in the knowledge that I have turned down the precious invitation it offered me hours earlier, yet again missing the oppor-tunity to fully taste the nectar of life. Night is undemanding. I am at home in the shadows of night, but the afternoon gives me nowhere to hide. It's a daily midlife crisis, which I have come to expect, the idealistic dreams of the morning crashing into the cold reality of the limits of this day, this life.

The comfort of food overrides my reluctance, and I bury myself in the contents of the bowl until the last spoonful of rice hangs in the air in front of me. I bring it to my mouth with resig-nation, mentally writing off another day, whittled away, another day in which I have been a mere visitor to my life, rather than a participant in it.

The day falls prey to a constricting stillness, every scratch and murmur in perfect syncopation, as if orchestrated. There is only one note of discord. Me. I sink further into the leaf litter, wanting to hide. A grey fantail lands near me, and it's unusual to see it so close to the ground. For a second, my heart lifts at this seeming gesture of generosity. I extend one hand towards it. It flies away. Of course it wasn't visiting, I chastise myself. What am I to this forest? Nothing, worth only the energy expenditure of an occasional alarm call. All my talk of connection is just anthropocentrism, a gross bid for social standing in a world that is entirely indifferent to me. The forest doesn't care whether I spend the year curled up in a ball, whining, or become a master tracker. It's been going about its business long before I got here and will continue long after I return.

Return to what, exactly? I used to be so certain about life, about who I was and what I wanted. Things were constant, stable: right or wrong, good or bad. Who is this creature that changes as quickly as the weather? I can't decide what to do with my day, let alone my life. The foundations are now just shifting sands under my feet.

I pad back into the kitchen, sniffing for more food. I grab the milk-powder tin and shovel spoonfuls into my mouth, scrape at the sides of the empty peanut butter jar. My eyes dart around manically for something else, anything to dull the sharp clawing. I find a half-packet of dates and polish them off. Within minutes my belly begins to bloat. It's a welcome distraction. I crawl off to nurse the ache in the sun.

Behind me fire pops indignantly, begging me to feed it. Well, I won't. See how *you* like being cold. The grey fantail flits up the top of the canopy, fanning its tail feathers back and forth as if in triumph. *Catch me if you can.* Its wings lift in a sudden breeze. Branches sway in graceful unison, belittling me with their seamless choreography. I should get up and move. Instead, I slump my head onto the cold earth, arms wrapped around my middle. I don't want to dance. For a while it felt great, like I was unburdening myself of heavy coats. It wouldn't be too long, I thought, until I shook myself free of all the extraneous bulk I carried. Now it seems like every time I dance, I stir up more and more gunk. I have no idea how deep the well is, but the waters are growing more and more murky.

The bush closes in, leaves reflecting back at me a thousand sparkles of sunlight. They shimmer mercilessly, so beautiful that it hurts. The whole forest is wrapped in an air of self-satisfied contentment. I want it to give me a sign – something, anything – but it won't. It just exists. Nothing more. A cruel Zen master whacks me over the back again and again with a truth too stark. Is this all? Is this enough?

The Buddha said if we saw the perfection of the world, we would throw our heads back and laugh at the sky. I see perfection everywhere, but my head hangs low. A hundred yards away, I can see the empty hammock and half-made tracking box. I lie between them, paralysed, my dreams sinking into the sand. What am I so scared of? Of making wrong decisions. Of failing. I can't do doing and I can't do not-doing. I can't do anything and I can't do nothing. Tears spring to my eyes. I'm flinging mud in my own face day after day. The spaces in between sound grow and pulse with emotions, overlapping and collapsing into each other. They're sucking me in, dragging me down into a whirlpool. Craving, emptiness, doubt, anger, judgment, confusion, fear, all blend together until indistinguishable. I sink further into the quicksand.

I've got to get out of here. Jumping to my feet, I crash through the bush to where my bike is parked under a tree. Wind pushes my steel-wool hair back at sharp angles from my face as I careen down the hill, going anywhere but here. The wheels lurch between pot holes and wash-aways, but I don't brake. I approach the bridge at speed. Three single planks of wood are spaced at car-tyre width. I tunnel my vision and mount a single plank smoothly. I'm halfway across when the handlebars wobble. The front wheel drops, catching between the planks. The bike squeals to a standstill, tipping violently to one side. I fly off the seat and over the edge. I fall as if in slow motion, watching the water gums above get smaller and further away, until I smash the surface with my back.

I sink quickly to the bottom, my head knocking hard against a flat rock. I momentarily black out. The cold creek infiltrates my wool layers, filling my many pockets and pinning me under. I'm aware this is happening but can't seem to motivate my limbs into action. They do so on their own time, suddenly flailing with a violence that heaves me up onto the bank. I splutter and cough, my hand reaching instinctively for the rapidly swelling lump on the back of my head. What just happened? For a few moments, I can't quite piece it together. There is no sequence of events, just an awareness that I'm very cold, and night is coming.

I need fire.

Shaking, I take the back path to my shelter. My fingers struggle to unpeel sodden clothes. I stand naked and stunned, shivering so hard I think my teeth might shatter. The coals in the fireplace are black. I look around in the hope that matches will miraculously appear. The cold drips ice through my bones. *I need fire*. Squatting, I scratch blueing fingers into the mound, blowing hopefully. Nothing. Against reason, I blow again, my face centimetres from the coals. A small red light shines a tiny spark. I pick my way to it with shaking hands. I whisper another breath. A blackened banksia cone lights up a window of red from deep within. My heart leaps.

I blow again and the light grows. *Fire*. I can't believe it. It's been here all the time, holding out for me, softly smouldering. It is the light of a single candle on a windowsill to a lost traveller on a dark night. One is all I need. I sprinkle it with bracken fern. It pulses and glows in time with my breath.

I've heard about the banksia cone carrying fire for a tribe across long distances, wrapped in lichen and mosses and paperbark to stay alight. There's life in the ashes waiting for us to find them. The old ways are coming back.

"Thank you, thank you, thank you," I mouth to fire as it bursts into flame. I blanket it with sticks. Wrapping a shawl around me, I curl up on my grass mat and fall into a deep sleep.

5.

"You're right where you need to be," Malcolm says with certainty, which is not the response I was expecting after the sorry tale I've just told him.

"Where, in the puddle on the floor, or the fireball of anger, or with the maniac dancing on the log?"

Malcolm laughs. I giggle too. It's good to smile.

I shift my position on the front step of Kate and Sam's shack. I'm glad Skype doesn't have enough reception for video, if my black fingernails are any indication of the rest of my appearance.

"But Malcolm, I just feel like I'm going backwards. I thought the more I danced, the more I listened to my heart, the clearer I would become. I'm overwhelmed. It's all just too hard, and possibly pointless."

"Claire, you're in the process of waking up your emotional body. As you tune into your feelings, all the emotional material from your life that has been unexpressed is cracking open and seeking release. As your awareness expands, so too does your capacity to feel. It can be joy, compassion and peace, but also grief, anger and suffering. As you chew through the undigested emotions from your past, the veil between you and your truth will lift."

"That's the problem," I say. "I'll have an inspiration to do something and then doubts will jump in, and I'll question the whole thing and wonder what is actually motivating me, and then get paranoid I'm making the wrong decision."

Skype crackles, and I press the headphones to my ears.

"The power of the feminine comes from responding to creative impulses as they arise, not from what you think you should be doing. Try catching the first impulse and going with it before your mind can jump in."

I sigh. "It all sounds so easy talking to you, but as soon as I'm on my own, I just feel swamped and lose trust and feel like I'm ... failing, I guess." My voice cracks. "No matter what I do, it's never quite enough."

"That's a very valuable realisation. Do you see how that belief has been driving you all these years?"

Malcolm hesitates, as if unsure whether to elaborate.

"Claire, you have chosen one of the most powerful environments for healing. By nature, the forest is in constant flow. When you immerse yourself in that fluidity, the parts of you that are stuck will quickly seek to shift."

I'm struck by the image. It makes sense. The more I saturate myself in the rhythm of the forest, wandering and listening, the more the feelings arise, seemingly without a trigger. I've been judging myself for being out of sync, but perhaps I really am in the flow.

"But you're resisting it," Malcolm continues. "Your identity is crumbling around you, and the old you is clinging on, terrified of letting go."

A sensation of vertigo comes over me, as if I'm leaning out over a great height. It's true. I am scared.

"You're dismantling your core operating system. It isn't going to be easy. Transformation generally isn't. Just keep leaning in to your sharp places."

Leaning? I think I've been impaling myself on mine.

Malcolm thinks for a few seconds, his tone softening.

"Spend time near water. Watch how it moves, what its qualities are. Let it teach you what you need to know."

"Water. Yeah, okay," I say, happy for any suggestions.

"Claire, your boat has well and truly left the harbour. I know there's no land in sight yet, but, as best you can, trust where the current is taking you and let go."

With the clunk of the virtual phone, I take my first deep breath in weeks, my lungs expanding in relief that I'm not completely stuffing up. Gratitude for this cyber-elder pools in my eyes. I wish I could carry him around in my pocket.

*

I rest my back against a tree across from the swimming hole and bury my feet in the sandy bank. The water is still, bar the kaleidoscope of overlapping ripples where insects alight. A dragonfly hovers above the glassy surface, its image reflected back in pieces. A tea-tree branch submerged in the shallows releases a pungent scent of decay.

The billabong looks entirely different here at the neck, the wide banks tapering to a narrow channel, bunching the water in fistfuls before releasing them downstream in a mirror image of the place upriver where it funnels in. It's like a giant heart, the trickling creek at either end the valves that pump life-giving waters in and out, the wide atrium accepting all that comes, warming the waters before sending them on their way.

How long does water rest here for? Minutes, days, weeks? It must be patient. On the far side where the bank curls in on itself, dust and stamens collect on the surface. But still there is no jostling movement, no unnecessary rapids. Water waits, knowing the time for change will come, when the rains will flush it clean again. Right now, water rests content in the task of holding so still that the blue-green arc of the swamp-mahogany leaves is reflected perfectly.

Downstream, the current skimming over stones tinkles a beckoning. Stripping off, I step in ankle-deep at the creek mouth. Tensing at the cold, I falter and grab onto to a clump of reeds. *Allow*, the water gurgles. I try to relax as it inches itself in painful increments over my thighs. *Allow*, water urges. *Allow, allow, allow.* I dissolve the rest of my body in the water until I'm floating. Water cradles me with strong and gentle arms, spinning me slowly on the spot three times as if to loosen my grip on direction. Reeds tickle my back. Suspended webs hang centimetres above my nose. With half-closed eyes I let myself go ragdoll limp, drifting like a leaf on the surface. Currents dance around me, shifting my limbs to their flow. There is purpose and volition in their movement, but they follow no leader, responding in the moment to the obstacles and openings presented to them. The cold evaporates the more I surrender to it, the more I, too, become viscous and fluid, another trusting passenger on the journey back to the sea.

Afterwards, as I walk back to my shelter, I still feel like I'm swimming, my limbs light and jellied, my thoughts brief and passing. There is nothing but sensation, sun on goosepimpling skin, bare feet navigating the gravel trail. And then something shifts, slows, drops. I'm aware that I'm walking but don't seem to be making any ground. The forest around me morphs, distorts, becomes brighter and closer. It's like I've walked into a painting, no longer a two-dimensional landscape but a place of depth and colour and feeling. Trees that I have walked past every day jump out at me with individual detail – the birthmarks of burls, bark curling over like thick eyelashes. They stretch their long-armed branches towards me in greeting. I stop, open-mouthed. Look at this forest. Look at these trees! Not just biological systems but living, breathing beings – each with its own personality and presence – sentient creatures reaching tall towards the sky and gently swaying. My limbs involuntarily begin to move with them, frolicking in the watery playground. I look back on the pain of the last weeks and months, my lifetime even, with almost disbelief. So stilted, so rigid – I get it now. I've been splashing around in dirty puddles, and all the time the river of life was flowing around me. All I had to was let go of the bank.

I wander up to the edge of the quarry. The sun glints off the exposed scars of quartz. It is perhaps the most beautiful thing I have ever seen. I throw back my head and laugh at the sky.

*

Ryan lifts the lid on the camp oven, a strong smell of cinnamon escaping with the steam.

"I see you've prepared something special," I smile, knowing I am in for Ryan's infamous one-pot wonder: baked vegetables with cinnamon and raisins.

"Dessert and dinner in one; you can't go past it," Ryan grins back.

This afternoon I found a note poking out from a tree near the entrance to my shelter, which read "dinner?" My acceptance was given with a tiny cairn of rocks near Ryan's shelter trail. This is the first dinner I've shared with Ryan – well, with anyone – all winter. It was a serious relief not to have to think about fire this afternoon. I stretch out on the wooden floor and look up at the apex of the teepee.

"You've finished thatching?" I say incredulously, seeing that the tarp has been removed.

"Yeah!" he smiles and shakes his head. "Seven months later."

He certainly seems chipper, more like the Ryan I'd first met in the breakfast queue at the tracker school, but he has done ever since he told me he was leaving after he returned from the Northern Territory. I assume tonight is our goodbye. I'm feeling a bit regretful that I haven't spent more time with him, but then again ... I've been busy.

"So ... you've had a time of it lately?" Ryan prods.

"You could say that," I laugh.

"D'ya reckon you're done yet?"

"Hmm, not sure. For a time I hope. Wouldn't mind a bit of a breather. How 'bout you?"

"Well, that's kinda why I invited you over, apart from wanting to hang out, of course. Ever since I decided to leave, I've been having a great time. For the first week or so all I did was sit around and read and look at the bush, except this time without the guilty feeling that I should be doing something useful, you know?"

"Ha, yeah, I know."

"I was seeing everything in a way I hadn't before. It was all so beautiful. Every moment was precious, but not in a pressured way, just poignant or something.

"One morning I found some horse tracks and started following them, and ended up miles and miles from camp in someone's backyard. It was hilarious. But, the thing was, I wasn't trying to track, I was just having fun."

I'm envious. A few days after my tree-inspired insight, I found myself slipping back into the old thought patterns, judging myself for the fall. I've tried everything I can to get the flow back again – lie in my hammock, dance, swim, but the more I want it, the more elusive it becomes. It might have something to do with a seemingly innocent list that I made during my brief enlightenment phase. Optimistically titled "Things I Am Inspired To Do", the list nevertheless took on a taskmaster quality – goading me to place neat little red ticks next to the entries. *Tracking. Trapping. Stag watch. Night stalking. Hide tanning.* I watched, dismayed, as the trees shrank their heads back inside their bark shells.

"So, what's your secret, Zen master?" I say.

"Quitting! I had to quit, to let go of the pressure to be here in a particular way before I could really *be* here ... And that's why I've decided to stay."

"What?" I jump up and smother him with a hug.

"It's crazy, isn't it," Ryan says. "All of us running around trying to get somewhere, and the place we really want to get to is right under our noses ..."

"... and can only be found when we stop trying to find it," I say, finishing his sentence.

"Yeah. When we quit all the bullshit – the judgments, the self-doubt, the striving."

"So laziness as a spiritual practice, then?" I say, grinning.

"Something like that," Ryan laughs.

He turns to retrieve two wooden bowls from a shelf.

"Oh, and Nikki and I are back together again. Just so you know. But that's not the reason I'm staying."

"No, of course it isn't," I grin.

"You ready for it?" asks Ryan, lifting up a raisin-dotted sweet potato.

I nod. "You have no idea how ready."

*

As I walk back home in the dark, my mind contemplates the conundrum: how do I quit without giving up? If it was something I could just knuckle down and get done, then I would, but my usual tools – discipline, determination, willpower – are as good as useless here. This is not something that can be done, only allowed. It will arise only through *not-doing.* Through *undoing.* Through grace. I feel like Alice falling down the rabbit hole, scratching my head over a ridiculous riddle.

Once I'm tucked up in bed, I hunch over my journal, trying to work it out.

My pen pauses as I feel the magnitude of the shift I'm asking myself to make. I can sense myself on the edge of a threshold, yearning to step over and yet terrified of what I might need to sacrifice in order to live for even one moment in that glorious spaciousness, that vast open plain where everything is possible and where freedom is sweet on my tongue. Instead of answers, my pen offers a single question.

Can I give up an inch of the striving, without giving up the gifts of my longing, the ache that drives me onwards?

*

The next morning I head to the creek.

At snake bend I sit and wait for the trickle of the current over rocks to smooth and slow my thoughts. The earth under me is solid and still, seemingly opposed to the free-flowing river bumping up next to it. But isn't this part of the river too? Without the banks, water would spill everywhere, losing momentum. It's the very structure of the bank that directs and focuses water, gathering and channelling its power. A piece of debris teeters back and forth on a snag, the current massaging it free. Water is no passive receiver in this process, though. The push and pull it exerts simultaneously shapes the banks, carving out its chosen course.

Perhaps the bank is like the mind – able to shape the flow of creative energy into a form that can manifest its potential. If the bank were to try and take over, straightening the twists and turns of water's natural course, creating dams and causeways to *control* the flow, the river would lose vitality and stagnate. When they work together, each respecting the function of the other, they gain the ability to swell together into a large and powerful river.

Goals and intentions could be similar, a goal like a bank without a river, rigid and dry, gripping on to a premeditated route and outcome. An intention, however, is softened by water, flowing with the double-backs and S-bends of life; it allows the changes wrought by tributaries and fallen logs, all the while holding firm in its desire to move steadily downstream. I've been too long on the parched bank. I need to give up the effort of moving towards a goal, and dive into my intention of living in flow with my heart.

Releasing the contemplation, I watch as currents swirl and eddy over each other with ease. A burst of bubbles suddenly appears on the surface, shortly followed by another. A turtle, perhaps? A silky fur back appears. Could it be? Oh my God, it is – a platypus! I try to contain my shivery excitement. It dives down to nuzzle the bottom with its bill, and I crane my neck. It surfaces, this time closer to me. It's a smaller one, and even more outrageously cute, than I remember ever seeing. When the platypus was first taken to Europe, the scientists thought it too odd to be true and declared it a hoax. I'm not surprised. In what strange mood did the Earth dream up this oily little creature? I drop a few giggly tears at the crazy beauty of it; it is slippery and silent as it disappears again.

*

Tonight, time has stopped, and whenever I wake from an epic dream, I feel like hours must have passed. I don't mind. It's a deliciously dark-chocolate night to hang out in. I picture what is around me, the laden tinder basket, the seaweed hanging from the roof stiff as bootlaces, the timber bowl caked with egg and sweet potato. My shelter shivers and creaks in a breeze. I imagine the hairs of the thatch standing up like goosebumps. Poor thing, it's probably cold.

The smallest ember is still glowing in the firepit. I roll out of bed and scramble for some tinder. The coal fattens.

Now? Fire yawns. *You're insatiable.*

It's true. I don't feel like I would ever tire of these fireside nights in my cocoon. I'm naked, and my toes are starting to cool. Tiny pebbles dig into my knees. I rub my hands over my ribs and lower back. I can feel the curve of my spine arching over to meet fire.

Won't you indulge me again, darling? My lips almost kiss the coal as I blow.

Feeding fire the most succulent tiny twigs, I tease it slowly into flame. My shelter groans in satisfaction as its frosty toes thaw too. Fire begs for more. My lungs are life-giving bellows. Both shelter and fire are breathing with me, the grass of the shelter like gills filtering smoke, the three of us forming part of some larger, universal breath.

Switching on my head torch, I pull down the book of Australian animal wisdom a friend sent me recently and flick to the platypus page. *Platypus represents the true essence of women's sacred wisdom,* it reads. *The ability to trust blindly in one's inner direction and move as one with the creative ebbs and flows of Mother Earth. Both male and female platypus are born with venomous spurs on their hind legs, but as they grow, the females lose their spurs. Symbolically, the females learn to trust their Dreaming and the protection they receive through their sense of self-worth and connection to Spirit.*

I close the book and imagine my new friend, its little heart beating away in a burrow not unlike my own. I picture myself entering its watery world, at home in the dark, cold undercurrents. Right now, I don't need to be anything in this life but the smallness and fullness of this gal sitting by her fire, listening to the rise and fall and movements of her own breath, her own heart. Just this.

*

That night I dream again. I am at a party and wander outside to find my grandmother lying on the bride's chaise longue. Behind her are my family of Aboriginal women from Arnhem land. I'm annoyed that I have been inside at the party, when I could have been out here. My grandmother and I cry out to each other and tenderly embrace. She is close to death, and I'm both grateful and sad that I have this precious time with her. In the moonlight she teaches me a song and dance. I can't believe it has taken me all these years to learn it. I wonder how many other songs and dances I have missed.

6.

"Your sleeping bags and matches are wet. You dropped your knife somewhere on the trail. And the temperature at dusk is hovering barely above zero. You have exactly one hour to get fire," Kate looks at her watch, "Starting ... now!"

I spring into a jog and head west, plucking seed heads of whiskey grass and stuffing them into my pocket. Chloe crashes off to my right towards the ridge. It's our first group activity since autumn. I was a bit reluctant to join in, but when I heard what the challenge was, I couldn't resist. I've become very reliant on well-dried wild tobacco and lantana, and my treasured collection of carefully selected grasstree, mullein and golden-rod stalks. I'm dubious about our chances. Casuarina and banksia are the best potential boards, provided we can find dead and dry accessible branches. Anything on the ground would be too wet.

I have been setting my own little fire missions lately (apart from the usual hand-drill ones, of course). A few times after heavy rain, and once *in* pouring rain, I challenged myself to collect that night's tinder bundle. I fished around under the skirts of grasstrees for the petticoat of dry needles, plucked dry stamens from the underbelly of banksia flowers where the water didn't run, and fossicked for dry inner bark of swamp mahogany and stringybark. The key to success was unlimited time: a slow treasure hunt. I reckon I learnt more about those plants in that test than in a whole year of taking from them in fair weather. There were surprise treasures too – a bandicoot nest and a bush laden with ripe sour currents. I've also experimented with wattle cord for the string of my bow-drill. Wrapping it around the spindle about five times, I had to keep the bow tilted downwards so the string didn't rub on itself. After much puffing and multiple cord snaps, I did manage a coal.

Hearing a break, I giggle to see Ryan falling halfway out of a banksia. With a hooked stick I reach up and snap off a dead casuarina branch. The timber is usually a bit too hard for me, but with five of us it could be okay.

Back at the Gunyah, Chloe and Dan are setting the kindling teepee. Ryan races in, throws the banksia branch on the ground, empties his pockets of rocks and starts percussively chipping two together. I'll leave that one to him. My brief attempt at flintknapping, in the US, resulted in six stitches on the back of my hand, at an expensive hospital.

"Yay, Nik," I yell, as Nikki runs in, lathered in sweat, a beautifully straight grasstree stalk from the heath in hand.

"Where are we up to?" she says, breathless.

"Here, try notching this," Dan says, handing her a crudely hacked banksia branch.

I shed my jumper and start mashing stringybark between my palms.

"Halfway," Kate calls. Balanced on her knee, Bella gurgles and grins at the spectacle.

"Okay, let's do it," says Nikki.

We place our hands on the stalk and pause to set the intention. Ryan starts, struggling to find purchase with the roughly made notch. Finally it burns in and the first whiff of smoke appears.

"Woohoo!" Dan exclaims.

We pass it around the circle, the smoke building until the branch suddenly splits in two.

"Boards, we need more boards," Nikki says.

Ryan races into the bush. I grab the rock he abandoned and start trying to carve a notch in a natural fork in a banksia.

"Fifteen minutes," Kate warns.

"Okay, I think this one's good to go," I say.

Ryan sprints in just as smoke is gusting out.

"Last one," Chloe says, gritting her teeth.

Ryan strips his shirt off to take over, his pecs rippling as he leans into the stalk and whips his arms back and forth. Nikki holds the board down, smoke enveloping her.

"We're almost there," Nikki urges. I can feel the coal close, aching to burst. Sweat drips from Ryan's forehead. What a goddamn sexy act of creation this is. I can't believe I hadn't seen it before. The joining of the long straight stalk in the notch opening; the slow warm-up, the building of friction, heat and pressure; the knowing of when to pull back and when to give, the blending of finesse and brute strength. It's the original dance between the masculine and the feminine. The universe making love to itself right here. It's positively blushworthy. Ryan grits his teeth and grunts with effort.

"I think we've got one," Dan yells. Panting, Ryan gently takes the coal and tips it into Nikki's awaiting tinder bundle. We fall silent as she blows on it, midwifing it into flame.

"Fucking beauty," Dan says.

"Time's up," says Kate, coming over to celebrate with us.

Putting on a billy of tea, we settle in cross-legged around our truly homemade fire. I'm surprised how cosy it feels to be in the group again. Maybe I'm ready to come out of hibernation. The bush certainly is. The butcherbirds are starting the day with a new amorous-sounding song. I've seen my first goanna, been bitten again by my first ant and my first mosquito. My low-level snake alert system has switched back on since the death adder was spotted again near the kitchen. A myriad of yellow pea-related flowers are lighting up shrubs one by one, while delicate carpets of white, purple and pink sprinkle the forest floor. All the wattles are coming out. It's like unwrapping a new present every day, and I'm never sure which gift will have chosen to unveil itself from its khaki camouflage overnight.

This morning I went wandering along the creek and savoured the crunch of the first ripe dianella berry. I felt ripe this morning too, my heart soft as ice-cream on a hot day, swirled through with nostalgia, both melancholic and sweet. It ran down the sticky fingers of the early morning light, pooling at my feet as I stood transfixed, watching the feeding flocks drum up business.

Another sign that spring is knocking came earlier today, when I was waiting for Ryan on the side of the trail and found myself stepping out of the sun and into the shade. I liked that I noticed the significance of it. It reminded me of a story a friend told me, how when he was walking with his family under the awnings of the sidewalk in early summer in New York City, someone stopped them and said, "You guys must be Australian; you're the only ones walking in the shade." Now *that* is awareness.

*

The boil of the billy is rattling the lid when a car engine rumbles up the trail. Sam gets out, looking grave.

"Everything okay?" Kate says.

"Well, no, not really," Sam says, kissing Bella on the forehead and settling on the ground next to Kate. He turns to all of us.

"I just had a visit from Terri."

"Oh?" Ryan says. Yesterday, Ryan helped her and a local handyman shift her water tank. Terri and her kids have become part of our extended tribe, often delivering us a roadkill roo with the weekly bread delivery. On a particularly frosty morning recently, my pre-breakfast wander took me up their driveway. I peeked in the window to see the three of them curled up on the couch, eating pancakes and reading. They beckoned me inside with broad smiles. It was like stumbling upon a gingerbread house in the middle of the woods.

Sam sighs before continuing. "Terri just told me that yesterday she found Lily hiding in the car. She said that the handyman had taken her behind the shed, pulled down his pants and asked her to touch him."

"What the ...?" Dan trails off. We gasp.

"She's pretty sure nothing else happened but wanted to know if Ryan noticed anything."

"No ... nothing," Ryan stumbles, looking shocked. "After we moved the tank, I left him to it. I can't believe it."

"Oh my God," said Chloe.

"Has Terri contacted the police?" Kate asks.

"She just did this morning, yes."

Nikki starts crying softly. "Why do people do things like that? I don't understand."

"I just can't believe it. He seemed so normal," Ryan says. He can't stop shaking his head.

Bella is squawking and Kate shushes her onto the boob. "Thank God it wasn't worse. What's the stat – something like one in three women over their lifetimes?"

"Yeah, and it's not just women either," says Dan.

"It's just another symptom of a sick society," Ryan says. "Another form of disrespect."

"Disconnection, it all comes back to disconnection," Kate says grimly, smoothing Bella's forehead.

My face has become hot and I can't think of anything to say.

"There's no excuse; it's just crap," says Nikki, drilling a stick into the ground. "I hope the police follow it up."

"If it's any consolation, Lily seemed her normal self when I was up there, pulling me into a game of tips," Sam says.

"Yeah, but it's the whole culture of it," says Chloe coming back with mugs and honey. "And you never know where things like that get buried."

I look at the ground, feeling strangely frozen.

"Are you okay, Dunny?" Dan asks me, pouring the tea.

"I've never told anyone this before," I say, breathing in and out slowly. "When I was about four or five, a family friend used to do that to me. I did touch him. I don't think it went any further. I don't feel anger or anything, really. I'm not sure why I felt the need to share it now, but there it is."

Dan goes quiet and looks at the ground, clenching and

unclenching his fists, then looks up at me with lips gripped tight and a knowing flash in his eyes.

Nikki comes over and takes my hand. I can see her slender fingers lying in mine but can't seem to feel them. I shrug to assure them I'm fine. It does feel a little strange to have said it. Not a huge relief, just like something has been turned inside out.

*

A rock face edges out to meet the first branch of a blackbutt tree. I nestle myself into the crook, the cool breeze of the approaching front watering my eyes, and rest my cheek against a milky white limb. In the last few days since our fire circle, I've been mooching around in a strange fog, my wanders stilted and colourless. I can't even be bothered with my sit spot. Rather than the urgency of thought that usually pushes my hand across the page of my journal, I'm drawing only doodles in the margins. The mountains and valleys of my moods have levelled out into a featureless plateau.

I mentally add this climbing tree to the ones tagged on my ever-expanding adventure map. I currently have three favourites – the grandmother fig, the sunrise/sunset pine and a particularly comfortable camphor laurel on the edge of the paddock. I visit them often. There's something about being off the ground that is inherently calming, as if the physical act of gaining height allows me to see everything as a higher, wiser self. The tigers of the mind can be growling below on the savannah but I am safe above, just another monkey on a branch. As a child, I would regularly climb the four massive Moreton Bay fig trees whose marauding roots broke the ceramic water pipes around the house. I always made sure to leave a gift for the fairies in the tree hollows. There was one rule if you climbed trees with me – once amongst the whispering leaves, secrets must be whispered and only truth told.

"What secrets do you have for me today?" I ask the tree.

Wisha wisha wisha, the leaves reply. *Something is lost that must be found.* That night I dream. I am one of two female national park rangers for a remote northern hemisphere fjord, a land of ice and vast mountains. We are patrolling an area that is in danger of being vandalised by men in a four-wheel drive. I remark that it's the edges that are always under attack and need protection. We receive advice – just do what you're doing, no need to amp up the effort. I pull out a map and realise I'm standing on the edge of a massive icy area that I haven't yet explored. I know that when the time comes, I will have to enter it.

*

"How ya doin'?" Kate asks when she sees me on The Block a few days later.

"Hmm, okay, I guess," I say. She tilts her head and looks at me quizzically. I can't give her any more information because I don't know myself. Terri and the kids came up last night to cook up the bat they had found dead in their house that morning. Lily seemed fine, crawling onto my lap and making up songs about bat stew. Everyone seems to have gone back to normal. Except me.

"You've had a big winter. Maybe you need to take a break," she says.

I remember back to what Chloe said about things getting buried. This year does seem to be acting like a poultice – drawing all the toxins to the surface. It's been one thing after another. Maybe I'm just tired.

A couple of days later I ask Dan to drop me at an isolated national park campsite by the beach. Despite the crystal blue waters lapping gently around my ankles, my restlessness amplifies. A tightness grips my abdomen, restricting my breath. It's impossible to sit. I walk kilometres to the nearest shop to buy a newspaper but can't focus on the words. I fixate on why I didn't buy chocolate. I walk all the way back to get a family-sized block and wolf it down in a matter of minutes. There is the weight of someone sitting on my chest, but I have no idea who it is or how to shake it.

One afternoon, I attempt to climb a rocky headland, struggling to find toeholds in the smooth face of the lava blocks. I lick my salt-encrusted lips as an easterly blast whistles in my ears and whips my cheeks. From the top, seemingly endless white sand disappears into sea mist to the north. In the other direction, another vast stretch of coastline is broken only by the form of a single fisherman. I slump against a rock, gazing blankly to sea, barely lifting my eyes when a humpback whale launches its bulk out of the water in a spectacular breach.

A teenage girl bursts onto the headland with a delighted cry, having just caught the whale's display. She is barefoot, dressed in a maroon woollen wraparound dress tied at the waist with a colourful embroidered belt. On her wrist is a plaited leather strap. Dark ringlets fall over white cheeks. Not seeing me, the girl throws her arms out wide as if embracing the sea, her mouth open in rapture. She turns abruptly, perhaps remembering herself. I get up and follow her, just far enough behind to remain unseen. Three younger siblings, similarly crowned in curls, join her, the smallest boy pulling her hand back towards the start of the trail. Around the bend a woman appears swathed in an alpaca-wool wrap, long dark hair falling like silken seaweed down her back. She moves as if directed by the flow of her hair towards her brood. She looks like Selkie, the folkloric seal woman who I'd just been reading about in *Women Who Run with the Wolves*. In the tale, Selkie leaves her underwater home to marry a lonely fisherman and bear his son. Instead of letting her return after seven summers, as promised, her husband hides her seal skin. Selkie grows dry and brittle. When her son finds the hidden pelt, Selkie makes the excruciating decision to leave him and return home, in order to save her own life.

I crouch in the bushes, watching the mother. She smiles broadly as her children run towards her. She has a wholly human face and yet it could also be the face of a goddess, the archetypal feminine in flesh and blood. It sparks a familiar yearning. During town missions I scan the faces of women, watching their features and mannerisms, searching for that which is universal. I catch glimpses of it in a smile, in the way a woman turns and takes the hand of a child. I saw it once between the lines on one wrinkled face, heard it in the methodical tapping of her shoes as she sat on a park bench amidst roses and looked out onto a river. The expression changes but the essence remains the same. The life of a woman so ordinary – and yet within that, or perhaps because of it, is the extraordinary.

A male figure walks calmly towards the mother, taking her hand. He looks vaguely familiar. He turns to face me. I do know him – it's my first boyfriend from primary school. How I adored this boy, worshipped him with the intensity of first love. The scene takes on an unreal quality, as if I have walked into a movie that I auditioned for but didn't get the part. I watch them drive away with the eyes of the girl who was unceremoniously dumped in the school playground.

That night I can't bear the thought of being alone. I wander the beach, begging for scraps of conversation from the fishermen, grateful if they care to swap platitudes with me. I stalk the caravan park at dusk, staring through cracks in awnings and porthole windows at couples etched in sunken seats, eating mashed potato and drinking beer. Right now I want to be them, heavy-set with routine, telling the same joke day after day about the bream running hotter than the missus. The belt of tension wrapped around my chest pulls in tighter. Cadging a ride to the pub, I order a large meatlovers pizza and a bottle of wine, and set myself down in front of the television. Halfway through the bottle, I stumble outside and shove a few coins into the public phone.

"Hey, guess who?" Despite six months of almost no contact, my close friend Amie miraculously answers her phone. I pour the story out to her.

"... and now I'm not sure what's wrong with me, Ames. I'm just flat and empty and have no idea why. The judge is so loud in my ear. I just constantly feel like I'm failing."

"Whoa, whoa ... just back up a bit to that thing about your family friend. That's pretty big stuff. Are you sure you don't have any feelings about that?" Amie says.

I pause, about to assure her it really isn't that big a deal, when something rumbles within. I begin shaking. A flood of tears surges up through my chest, erupting with earthquake intensity. I squat on the phonebooth floor, my body racked with sobs, vaguely listening to Amie's soothing sounds encouraging them out. I pull myself together enough to persuade her that I'm okay, hang up the phone, get a lift back to my tent and, the following day, to The Block.

*

Back home, the earthquake continues to heave and pitch the ground under me. I move between shelter and forest in a blur of tears. Day after day, I ride waves of grief. Like a flood, the waves rise out of nowhere and subside just as fast, leaving no trace of story, just clear puddles, in their wake. I am in the caught in the eye of a storm, and all I can do is let it pick me up and toss me, while I wait for it to pass.

Instead, the storm grows, changing direction, bringing with it fierce gusts of hot wind. Grief turns into red-hot anger that spits and froths. It simmers inside me, a lava threatening to break the surface. I strangle the sound that wants to come out, scared, but it rises in my throat and chest. There is no stopping it. I wail. I howl.

I scratch and hiss and claw, animated by an alien energy that has overtaken my body. I screech. I kick and punch the air, as if trying to beat an assailant back, desperately trying to create space around me. The waves come in sets, my voice rising in crescendo as each one breaks. I don't know who or what this is. My body is a stranger to me, a repository of secrets that it is no longer willing to conceal. I am embarrassed for it. I try to reason with it, distract it, get on with other things. Instead, another seam of steaming anger builds. I curl up on the ground tighter and tighter, trying to squeeze it out.

Whatever you resist, persists. Malcolm's words float in. *Emotion is just energy in motion.*

Let the emotion be your soundtrack, and let your body do the rest.

I begin to soften, my shoulders dropping, cheekbones heavy against the dirt. I imperceptibly drop further, sinking into the earth, allowing it to envelop me. My plates of armour crack and crumble. A wave of exhaustion ripples through me, and I give my all to the solid bones of the ground beneath me. Fear and dread flood my veins like mercury, holding me in a cold metallic embrace, sharp fingernails clawing at my skin. The judge walks along my back, pinning me down with her heels, looking for a fight. I offer no resistance. She trembles, and I sense gaps in her form, empty spaces, black holes so vast that nothing could ever fill them. A pulsing heat fills my limbs. It draws me up on my hands, my knees, picks up my feet, marching them on the spot.

The stamp of my feet deepens, my thighs burning as I drive hot stakes of anger into the earth. My head and neck begin to loosen, roll and wobble, and when my spine gives in, my entire body surrenders to the moves of a fierce choreographer. My eyes close, all thoughts lost to the volition of a body possessed by the pure white heat of emotion. My form twists and flickers like flame, reaching out hungrily, spiralling and writhing. I stretch and contort into ever-changing shapes, strung out on wires of staccato energy. Tears mix with sweat as I wheel and turn, careening through space as if I'm a bird riding the winds of a storm front.

As I rise and fall, I become aware of a pattern to the emotions, a sense that they are arising with the urgency of a breath held underwater for a time longer than my life, larger than my experience. Faces of women flash in front of me: those of my mother, grandmother and others unknown. What if this is not just my pain? My limbs respond with a fresh burst of energy as if in agreement. That's right, it isn't just my dirty laundry – I'm doing the washing for a line of women who came before me. I don't know who, and it doesn't matter. I just know with sudden clarity that this rage is more than just mine. It is rage for all the ways our wings have been clipped, our wild places burnt, tamed and cut down. It is a grief for all the ways we have been led in the opposite direction of our real selves, lost in the thickets of others' expectations. It is the culmination of years of simmering resentment at being kept running on the treadmill of ambition and striving. It is a rebellion against the abuse of the collective soul. It has waited, collecting, until such time as it could be released, my body now a channel to transmute some measure of oppression into this raw material, to play a role in some larger healing.

Gradually, in a time measured only by the depth of my tracks in the sand, the wind gusts abate. My arms circle slowly, lifting on the in-breath, and dropping on the out. A spring of grief bubbles up and douses the last flames of fire with tears, the mourning needing no words, no explanation. It soon quells to quietness and slowly, slowly, to stillness. To peace. I lie on the ground, scoured and cleansed like a storm-ravaged beach.

When I eventually open my eyes and look around, the forest springs out at me with technicolour vividness. It, too, feels washed clean, luminous and alive. I nuzzle the powdery petals of a flannel flower, tickle my cheek on a melaleuca blossom. A swamp wallaby lopes out onto the path in front of me, feeding on the grassy verge. It's the first time I have seen more than the disappearing tail of one. I breathe in the full-bodied warmth of it.

Dragging my swag outside, I watch as the moon slips between silently shifting clouds. Night fliers follow their trajectories. Moonshadow and moonshine dance across my face. I drift in and out of sleep. In a dream, I search for my grandmother's precious moonstone necklace. Have the stones been lost? I must find them. I wake to find the moon is a stone pendant suspended over me; the stars are millions of shards shattered from the stone. Leaves above rustle and whisper. *Something lost must be found.*

The powerful owl hoots nearby. My eyes snap open. I suddenly know what I must find. My power.

*

The next day, my hunt begins.

I walk, one foot in front of the other, along the forest trails, but travel backwards, back through the days, months and years of my life – searching for where I lost my power, scanning for signs of it dropped or hidden in some crevice. The land guides me through the contours of my stories: the tributaries, saddles and ridges, the sheer rock walls and dead ends. I let the memories rise and fall on the breath of the wind, surfacing spontaneously like the bubbles on the creek I walk beside. Starting as a trickle, they pour forth in the wide-open catchment of my attention.

I come across snapshots frozen in time, where I played nice, smiled pretty, placated, pretended. Moments when I busied myself, turned my back on the moon, on a friend, on my heart, in pursuit of some false treasure. I'm a huntress on the trail of inadequacy, of failure, sniffing out where it seeded, where it first took root. I turn the soil, unearthing the times when my feelings were bulldozed by others, when I learnt to take the wheel myself and ride roughshod over whimsy, over weakness, over what I really desired, over what I deemed inappropriate. I remember when I willingly strapped the goals of others to my back and lugged them with tenacity along paths that were not of my choosing. My pursuit continues at night, tracking back through years of journals, my dreams taking me to muddy schoolyards and classroom, faces long forgotten. It's a recapitulation, piecing together patterns, seeing the compression shapes of my life's wanderings. Each memory is a moonstone dropped, which I now collect again, reclaiming it from where it had been lodged, threading it back around my neck and cutting the cord that tied it to the past.

The next day, I continue, following my life's footprints as they grew, into offices and boardrooms, kitchen tables and bedrooms, backtracking for where my jewels were pirated, squandered, or carelessly dropped through holes in my pockets. As I walk, the land is my confidante and my canvas, the dots and dashes that I mark with a stick painting the passage of my life into a long snake.

Pretty soon, I know I'm not alone. There is a presence walking alongside me. She is calm, steadfast, compassionate. She falls in step easily, knows the path well. She has been there before, was there all along. She was there when I peddled my original power on the street for the best price and bought a cheap imitation. She was there when I tried to outrun her, when I didn't have time to play. She was there when I gave away my sealskin, and it was she who retrieved it. She has always been there, unchanging, essential. With her as my companion, the painting changes, the dots not just holes where I lost myself, but necessary landmarks by which I can now find myself again. She reminds me that the same path on which I lost my power is the very one that allows me to find it, to know it by its absence, to make a fierce promise never to let it go again.

On the final day of my hunt, a storm threatens. I scratch in the last few landmarks before the clouds break. I watch the splash of raindrops make rivers of my dots and dashes, like a fresh memory laid on the earth, washing the canvas clean.

As the gentle rain falls, I send a question out into the forest. Is there anything else I need to know? I let my body be my radar, my feet the steering wheel. They guide me upwards towards the boulders, where a grove of old casuarinas stand in a circle. *Wisha wisha wisha.* They whisper as I step into the centre. *Wisha wisha wisha.* I look up. A pair of tawny frogmouths huddles together in a tree fork, the grey mottle of their feathers almost indistinct from the bark. Suddenly one opens its eyes, turning its head in my direction. The heat from the glare of its firebrand eyes nearly throws me backwards. I hold its gaze, though, both of us unblinking. *Who are you?* It demands to know. *Who are you* not *to be powerful? What arrogance! Claim what is rightfully yours and be on your way.*

The storm circles around again. I look down at my bare brown feet, the ligaments strong and supple, raised like a sinewy runner's. A clap of thunder sends down a fresh deluge, and I begin to dance, slowly at first and then furiously, as the rain turns into a waterfall. Stripping off layers, I dance naked, hair slapping against my face, until I lose sense of where I begin and end. Until I am just skin, just water, just tracks in the sand.

*

On dusk at my shelter, I fetch my firestick from its hook and settle in beside the board. The habitual tension is already straining my neck, the performance anxiety stiffening my jaw. I pause.

No, there is another way. Where does power come from? What would water do?

My blindfold hangs on the rafters overhead. I reach up for it, and tie it around my eyes. I begin to spin the stalk slowly, focusing on the sensation of it moving from fingertip to fingertip, evenly, steadily. My shoulders relax into the rhythm. As my arms tire, I take deep breaths, visualising free-flowing water in a river. A fresh burst of energy floods in. I hear the sweet sound of biting through glaze, wood grinding on wood, becoming dust. I drop to a fast, fluid stroke, power coursing through my core and down into my arms. I'm barely puffing. I could keep going, but I sense it. I remove my blindfold to find an ember glowing at my feet.

Snuggled around my fire that night, I am not alone. There is a solid beating entity inside me, so alive with feeling that it aches. It is my hub, my sun, my compass. It sends shivers of delight up and through my back and arms. It talks. I ask it questions and it answers. I feel like I've just discovered a best friend, one that has always been there, waiting for me to notice it. It is not perfect nor always amiable. It is a relationship like any other, with all its pushes and pulls, its arguments and intimacy. It is not grand, just extraordinarily ordinary.

I reach out to my journal lying open on the blanket. Today needs only one line.

Now I have my heart.

SPRING

*

Don't ask what the world needs.
Ask what makes you come alive, and go do it.
Because what the world needs is people
who have come alive.

HAROLD THURMAN

*

THE SACRED ORDER OF SURVIVAL:

1. Shelter
2. Water
3. Fire
4. Food

1.

Wallaby bullets out of the scrub towards us, its body tense and hunched. Beach sand sprays up into my face from the force of its tail thump. I catch one raspy breath and the distinct smell of terror. We are invisible to wallaby, its crazed eyes fixed on the last spear of amber sun angling into the choppy waves. Dingo is seconds behind and faster, gums peeled back in a hungry snarl. It pulls up ankle-deep, watching wallaby struggle against the relentless waves. Wallaby turns to face its hunter.

"Should we do something?" Nikki asks. We rise, our knives sandy and slack by our sides, abandoning the half-skinned shark we've been crouched over. Ryan extends an answer in the form of one silently raised arm, but we all know the question was rhetorical. There is nothing to do but watch death dance.

Dingo lunges, taking a sharp nip at wallaby's back leg. Wallaby tries heroically to fend it off with a tail swipe but instead falls under a surge of whitewater. Wallaby springs back up like a boxer from the count. It falters, looking desperately from side to side for escape routes. Dingo lunges in for another go, again just a nip, the incoming wave again taking wallaby to the ocean floor, and this time it takes longer to surface. Dingo dances around its prey, pawing and taunting it like a cat. With sinking dread I realise this is going to be no quick execution, but the cruellest of deaths by a thousand cuts, dingo calculating precisely the least amount of energy expenditure necessary to aid wallaby's inevitable fall. I can't bear to watch but am simultaneously transfixed. Excruciating minutes pass, a thin red gruel lapping at the wallaby, now swaying on its haunches. Dingo waits with a slack jaw, its hanging tongue dripping with saliva. Just as the dark is about to rob us of the final scene, the wallaby lifts its head above the waves one last time, the muscles in its neck bulging from the strain. Even when it hits the sand, water gushing up its red nostrils and into its lungs, its tail continues to thump the shallows in death throes, slower and slower. With a final swipe, a wave rolls its lifeless body towards the waiting fangs of the dog. Dingo wastes no time now, seizing it by the scruff of the neck like a kitten and dragging it silently into the shadows of the banksia scrub.

The onshore wind blows in a wintery dusk. I walk shaky-legged back to our camp, leaving the other two staring as the waves make red frothy chalk outlines on the shore. The half-skinned wobbe-gong in my hand flaps open like the loose sole of a shoe, and is just as tough. Washed up, or discarded by fishermen, it took us a couple of hours to get it this far, its hide more exoskeleton than skin. The others return, spin up a fire and quietly cuddle together. Ryan tenses slightly as Nikki leans in. I enter the cast of light tentatively, not quite trusting the sudden easy warmth of flame and company, and my own pull towards it, as if I'm expecting it to turn around and bite me. But tonight I'm relieved to have a buffer against the rawness of the hungry night. I take a seat across from the couple, flick open my knife and begin to sharpen the barbs on my fish spear. The spear's probably more for aesthetics than anything else. Thwarted by big seas and inexperience, our two-day fishing trip has so far amounted to three pippies. I perched for what seemed like hours on a slippery rock in the rain with my newly carved fish spear, thrusting it in towards the tail of the fish to account for the refrac-tion of water, like I'd been told to do. The one and only fish, that is. To claim that it was the one that got away would be a gross exag-geration. Ryan and Nik's fishing line met with equal success.

I rotate my spear over the coals to harden the barbs. The bubbling beans and rice gradually revive us from our shocked quiet, our vicarious brush with death fast becoming a thing of legend, as Nikki and Ryan replay it scene by scene. Rubbing a smooth beach stone over the spear, I compress and further harden the wood fibres. I touch my finger to the point. It's sharp, alright. Now it just needs a fish intent on suicide to prove it.

"Community-minded, fun, sporty, enthusiastic, obsessed with fairness." Ryan and Nikki are in full campfire mode now, playing the "How would you describe me to a friend?" game. "Afraid of weakness," Ryan adds, as an afterthought. Nikki looks up at him questioningly before continuing to peel the outer skin from the roots of a bungwall fern. She lays a long white rhizome on the coals, and it sizzles on contact.

My thoughts stray back to wallaby, its limbs being torn apart and scattered, with every voracious bite becoming less plump wallaby and more empty carcass, flesh disappearing inside dingo. Right now wallaby is *literally* turning into dingo. Its flesh is already stewing in digestive juices, feeding dingo cells, dingo blood, wallaby visible only as a spring in dingo's step and meat on its bones. But hang on – doesn't that mean that dingo is becoming wallaby as well? Where does dingo start and wallaby finish? How can anything claim to be one thing when it is a product of many? Even my body – how much of it can I claim as mine and how much is the oats I ate for breakfast, the microbial soil workers that nourished it, the hands that tended it? My mind spins with the implications, dingo dissolving into wallaby and back again. Nothing is fixed, nothing ever solid. It's all just energy being recycled; energy exchanged, bartered or borrowed; life force moving in and out in constant flow.

Still, poor wallaby. I, too, feel like I've been in the grip of nature's tooth and claw, something brutal but beautiful happening to me. I'm also dingo, emerging from a long hibernation, skin loose on my bones, with an empty belly. I am ... bloody hungry, actually.

"Practical yet philosophical," Nikki says, pausing to look at Ryan. "Gentle yet strong, open yet guarded." Ryan looks up from his whittling.

"Confident yet unsure," I finish.

They turn to me.

"A deep thinker," Nikki starts. "Determined. Wise."

Ryan narrows his eyes. "Authentic. Charismatic ... Hard on herself."

"Takes one to know one," I smile back.

My belly growls loudly. I stir the pot of rice and beans, wishing it was wallaby. The thought crosses my mind to rob dingo of its dinner, but I remember its ribs lined up like monkey bars, much like mine. Not withstanding all the walking, dancing and fire making I've been doing, I have been fasting one day a week and shivering the rest of my body fat away. My no-store-bought meat policy (apart from the extra-large meatlovers pizza at the pub) has amounted to my cut of two roadkill roos and one roadkill possum, three whelk, and a thigh of Terri's chicken, which I helped to kill and prepare. I rarely enjoy the fasting day but love the lightness I wake up with the next morning. It makes me feel animal-like, lithe and lizardy, able to slip and slide unseen between spaces, flexible both inside and out. And the spartan diet has meant that for the first time in years I'm not bloated at the end of every day.

But it's spring now. The famine is over, it's time to feast. Time to be fed from the fat of the land.

Time to hunt.

*

BMX bandits on the beat, Ryan and I once back at home set off on our bikes with cordage, knives and peanut butter, laughing as we remember Dan getting pulled over by the cops and trying to explain why he had rope, garbage bags and gloves in the back of his van. "Roadkill kit" apparently didn't fly so well. It's easy to forget this life is far from normal.

Ryan follows my lead through the mud puddles of the heath, to the trail of my shortcut jogging loop a few kilometres away. I've been eyeing off this spot for a few months as a potential trapping site, the wallabies all channelled into a few obvious entry points on the grassy fence-line. We fashion the simplest of snares with green parachute cord, propping it open at wallaby head height with a couple of twigs and tying it to the wire. Practising the double noose knot Ryan showed me, I set a few more by myself. I'm a little concerned about how I am almost excited as I lay death row. It's the first time that I really feel I might be capable of feeding myself in the bush, even without a knife.

The T-bar snare ramps up the technology significantly. I take Ryan's lead, setting two sharpened and notched ten-inch sticks into the ground and fixing a looped cord to a slightly smaller T-bar stick, which we bait with peanut butter. It takes us a good ten minutes and several false springs to balance the T-bar in the notches, while pulling down a wattle sapling to attach it to. The snare will theoretically lure an animal to stick its head through the looped cord, which, when pressure is exerted upon it, tightens and triggers the sapling to snap back, essentially hanging the animal.

"So, how ya going with that book?" Ryan asks, rubbing the back of his knife against the notch to make it more sensitive (as if it wasn't already hard enough to set).

"Well, you'll be pleased to know that five months in, he's only just finishing his shelter."

Ryan raises an eyebrow and smiles.

I've been finding it hard to put down *Solitude*, the journal of Bob Kull, a one-legged American guy who spent a year alone on a remote Patagonian island. His experience so far is uncannily similar to mine (albeit on a different scale). Impatient about all the things he wants to do, he is rushing around trying to finish his shelter so he can properly "start" his experience, all the while admonishing himself for not sitting still long enough to soak in the light of the passing storms, as he thought he would. Instead of a firestick to throw around, he throws around the cat given to him by sailors, then becomes dismayed by his callous behaviour and guiltily feeds it his few treats. He is also shocked by his four-seasons-in-a-day emotions, the way he seems to be growing less rather than more equanimous, storms of rage and grief rolling in regularly. I sense icebergs ahead, as he plans and replans all the things he wants to do in the remaining months: scientific research, explorations of the remote archipelago, meditation, staring into the sea, ridding himself of fear and delusion, getting clear on his life vision ... the all-too-familiar list. A few months ahead of him, I want to tell him that it's okay, that it's all perfect, and he should just weather the storms as best he can.

At the creek that afternoon, I weave native grape vine through the holes in our group eel trap, baiting the narrow end of the funnel with a chunk of stinky wobbegong. It seems too simple. I can't imagine that a creature as adept as an eel, able to schlep across land to the next waterhole, could not swim backwards out of such a trap. It's too large an evolutionary oversight. But, hey, we've all got our weaknesses. The proof will either be thrashing around tomorrow or not. I lower the trap into the deep hole next to the big-toe tree, tying it off to a sapling.

Up to my knees in cold mud, I jump at the screech overhead and grab a clump of lomandra for balance. I look up to catch the white jet stream of the channel-billed cuckoo, the first one returning for the season. My heart flies up to greet it as it peels upwards on the breeze. "Hello, up there," I call. "Welcome back."

"Welcome back, spring," I'm tempted to call, but don't, knowing that to another observer, the crown of spring returning could just as easily be given to the shining bronze cuckoo – the first time its male called from deep within a frosty forest thicket in August, stirring dreams of nests and mates. Or earlier still to some who pay close attention: the rose robin's first faint chirp from high in the canopy, one glassy day in mid-July. The seasons are subjective, the word itself too neat to reflect the overlapping and incremental waves of change that accompany the Earth's rotation. For every dependable thing – migratory birds, the spawning of mullet – others resist expectations, rail against routine. You can't count on trees. Eucalypt flowering is capricious and arrhythmic, budding some years and not others, responding to water and other mysterious personal preferences. There are no distinct lines, no four-season scores, no party of leaves released en masse to signal the turning of the page. There is just a movement back and forth across an invisible line, a warm breeze on cheeks followed by a cold snap, a brave rustle from the burrow and a scurry back within. Assume nothing, this land tells me. Keep your ears pricked, it demands. Hone your skills if you want to survive. I am in awe of those who can and have. I follow the call of the cuckoo out to the open heath. The sun beats down and I step into the shade.

*

"A hide is a commitment," Sam says, holding up the hairy shell of someone else's feast. I'm still stuck on the last thing he said, though – that every animal has enough brains to tan its own hide. Including us, he says, answering my question, although I wonder how he's so sure. The whole equation has me boggled. It's poetic, I guess, in a weird way. I'm struggling to picture by what kind of accidental or experimental process the link was discovered, which kooky caveman found that if you smear the brains of a dead animal into its own skin, and then smoke it, you get soft and durable leather.

The invitation to prove the theory right or wrong is in front of me, a deer skin bartered from a nearby venison farm. Pulling on some gloves, I gingerly extract the hide from the ash solution it has been soaking in for the last few days, the alkaline bath helping to loosen the fibres. It's bloated and swollen like a tongue, bits of flesh still hanging from it.

"I've already got mine," says Nikki, holding up the stiff shark skin.

Flies descend quickly as I scrape the meat still attached to the hide onto the ground. Transferring the hide to a workhorse beam, I ready myself for the graining process – removing the hair, epidermis and grain layer from one side of the skin. I copy Ryan, leaning my belly against the wet edge of the hide to stop it slipping from the beam. Gripping the scraper firmly in both hands, I bear my weight down and into the hide. The tool glides over it, as if I had merely wiped it with a tissue.

"This time with feeling," Dan laughs. With a mock grunt, I dig the scraper in further and push down. A peeling of snotty stuff comes loose in one long string. Wow, this is going to need some serious elbow grease. Luckily I have a bit more now than I used to.

"Okay, ten thousand more of those and I'll have done one side," I say, wishing I was joking. Why did I think this bush skill would somehow be different to all the others, which require brute strength, skill, perseverance and practicality? I'm glad I've got a metal scraper and not the traditional rib bone to work with.

Scrape, scrape, scrape. Shift hide across beam. Discard snot. *Scrape, scrape, scrape.* I settle into a rhythm, soon finding myself in that sweet spot of monotonous motion. A holiday from my brain is what it feels like.

Deja vu washes over me again, and this time the sense is stronger. Even the dull ache in my shoulders feels familiar. It's like a lineage coming alive in my hands. Nothing else could be as right as working this skin, learning how to clothe and warm myself. Why don't they teach this stuff in schools?

"Howdy, partners, how y'all goin' on ma buckskin moccasins?" Chloe says, returning from a break. Ryan shakes his head at her accent. We've all been talking in our best midwestern drawls all morning, channelling the mountain man I've been telling them about – the guy I bought a deer-antler knife from in the US, who told me he had never sat on a toilet. My throaty laugh feels rusty, but refreshingly so.

"So, part-timer, how does it feel to be leaving?" Nikki asks, Chloe smiling at the nickname she used to flinch from. Her part-time status is about to go to zero-time in a few days, when she permanently moves into Niko's bush palace in the hills, a couple of hours south.

"I don't know … sad, exciting, scary." Chloe says, as she scrapes, obviously relieved to have finally made the decision.

Prising off a long string of grain, I catch a glimpse of the fibres underneath – a matrix of small protein strands twisted together like DNA. I scrape over the same spot and look closer. Every strand is woven randomly but connected to every other strand, each patch as unique as a fingerprint. This is what skin really looks like, so flexible and yet so strong. How incredible. This animal could have had a shell or armour, but life repeatedly chose, over millions of years, to remain soft and vulnerable, to sense the world rather than defend against it, receive rather than repel.

I glance over at Nikki. The permanent worry line in the middle of her forehead has gone. She looks younger. The others do too. We scrape silently side by side, the dull sound of metal dragging heavily against wood, shearing off skin, cleaving off layers. Something has been working us too, stripping back the layers, scraping away our defences, paring us back to reveal glimpses of our essential nature underneath. Making us soft, making us supple. Strong.

"Yep, you won't be far behind me – only three months to go," Chloe says. My cheerfulness sinks like a stone in water. Leaving? No! I don't want to. *I can't.* I'm surprised by the fierceness of my response, the sense that there is more I came here to do. I keep scraping.

2.

K nee-deep in club rushes on the shortcut to the traps, I am tempted to stop. The sun is tickling the tops of the banksias, and I can hear a bowerbird in the scrub nearby. The image I woke up with returns – an animal flailing around in the snare. I keep wading, up along the sandy heath, past the dog tracks, past sunset tree and butcherbird straight. My belly clenches tighter as I approach trap bend. I can immediately see the T-bar is empty, as is the second snare. The first is hidden in grass. I creep forward. The noose hangs limply in two broken pieces, the grass underneath trodden and bent. A chew-through. Close call. I'm both relieved and disappointed. I replace the broken cord with a new one, remembering to smudge it with ash from my pocket to disguise the scent.

There are another couple of traps down the trail to check on now. A few days ago I decided to set a Paiute and a figure four – both deadfall traps involving a heavy object, such as a rock, leaning precariously over a trigger stick, waiting to crush a small creature. They looked so much simpler in my notebook than in reality, although if trapping was easy, Davy Crockett wouldn't have been such a hero and Ludwig Leichhardt might have survived. Whittling the appropriate notches at exactly the right angles, despite this being the beginner's standard in small game traps, was itself a Rubik's Cube. Getting both traps to balance against their bait sticks was like walking a tightrope.

The figure four is still holding, but the Paiute has been triggered, a puff of grey-brown fur collected on one edge of the rock. Phew, another near miss. Or maybe with traps, the gap between close call and catch is bigger than it looks. I wonder what will bridge it?

Harvesting a strand of settlers flax, I divide it in two and squat back on my feet to weave it into a short string. Attaching it to a tiny toggle stick, I attempt to balance it against an equally thin horizontal trigger stick held up by a rock. Just when I have exhausted every remaining expletive, my knuckles grazed and bleeding from the number of times I trap my fingers, it holds.

The day is unfolding as blue as the ocean and as endless. Wet grasstree needles decorate my legs with long calligraphy strokes as I wend my way back. I shiver, partly in delight and partly recoiling from the cold touch. The green rounds of geebung fruit litter the ground, the bush-food all-day sucker. I pocket some and pop two in my mouth, rolling them around my tongue to crack and spit out the bitter shell, before holding on to the sweet, fleshy coating of the seed.

I don't actually want to go back to camp. Hides are on a brains-hunting hiatus, and I could do with a break anyway – my shoulders from scraping and the rest of me from social stimulation. My head is dull and cloudy, the same tired-but-wired feeling that used to be my default in the city. I'm amazed at how hard it used to be to drag myself out of the concrete jungle, even when I wanted to. When I would finally overcome the inertia, it would take about forty-eight hours in the mountain air for me to defrag and my atrophied senses to re-engage. I take a deep lungful of the cool morning air and splash my face from a puddle, feeling my clarity returning.

Besides, I need to save myself for Chloe's farewell party tonight. My stomach flip flops. Why am I feeling so strange about it? We haven't spent vast quantities of time together this year. I've been a bit short with her during the last week, but I'm not sure why. Chloe's last day on The Block – imagine if it was mine.

Wandering down to my sit spot, I reach into my pocket for my breakfast of dried fruit and nuts. Around me the shelter builders are at full tilt: grey fantails twittering to each other as they fly in and out of crannies in tree trunks, emerging with beaks full of silken spiderweb, yellow-throated scrubwrens gathering moss and weaving it into tear-shaped hanging bowers. The polite society of winter birds and well-organised feeding flocks have collapsed into a chaotic free-for-all, the northern migrants back in full cacophonous swing, yelling over each other across the breakfast table. Regent bowerbirds swoop and flutter in a game of catch and kiss around me. A skink pops its head through a hole in the log, perching on tiny fingers as if on the starting blocks. The delicate cream curls of the hakea flower brush against my cheek, yet another spiky thing finally showing its softer side. What the sandstone country lacks in lush greenery, it makes up for in abundance of flowers. The mountain devils disappointed the eastern spinebills for mere weeks, the last flowering barely brown before they burst forth again on the top ridge. Yellow is most definitely the fashion of the season. I challenge myself to describe the different shades – the midday sun of the glory peas, the avenues of buttercup bossias, the egg and bacon of the heath shrub.

I got a bit of a shock recently when, on Niko's suggestion, I tried to draw some common birds from memory. How far does the yellow on a yellow robin extend down its belly? Where exactly is the white on the tail feathers of a currawong? On the belly of a magpie? Apart from the obvious features, I kept literally drawing blanks. So much for telling individual birds apart. Instead of a boon, my familiarity has become a blinker. What I was seeing was a label, a template based on the hundreds of birds I had seen. It was humbling to discover how deep the ruts of my visual senses are, how regularly my eyes run on autopilot. I'd see more if I looked at them with my eyes closed. Since then, I've been making an effort to see things as they *really* are.

A kookaburra flies in on cue, offering itself as a life model. It perches on a branch, bobbing its head as if in agreement with some invisible presence on the ground. I note the stretch of its Zorro mask, the ring around its eye, the grey-green of its legs and feet, the sky-blue markings on its wings. A fan of tail feathers exposes an arrow-shaped painting of rusty stripes and spots. Look at it now – it's hooting with laughter, but stumbling and brash, like a young lad learning to whistle, practising over and over again. I can't help but laugh, both at it and with it and just because I can. My bird book tells me that according to Aboriginal legend, the kookaburra's laughter is a signal for the sky people to light the great fires that illuminate and warm the Earth by day. To imitate the laugh is taboo, for the sky people may take offence and plunge the Earth back into darkness. Oops, too late. They seem to have forgiven my transgression this morning, as the sky remains bright.

I hop down from my throne to examine some fresh pademelon tracks. My sit spot is somewhat of a moveable feast these days. I used to have to wait at least twenty minutes for the birds to get over the shock of my presence and settle back to their natural baseline, but they seem accustomed to me now. I'll often sit for only ten or fifteen minutes, just long enough to plug in, before wandering off in pursuit of some curiosity. Although I spiral out in wider and wider circles from my sit spot, it remains home base, an invisible string tethering me to it from wherever I roam.

Spying an old fence post, I follow it up and along a line of lichen-covered boulders to where it disappears in the middle of a reed-choked swamp. A row of gnarled she-oaks hangs over the edge, the breeze rustling through it like tinsel. It sure feels like this place hasn't had many visitors for a good while; it's a little bit *Picnic at Hanging Rock*. It's amazing how quickly the land changes. Snatching the binos from around my neck, I'm in time to see a grassbird dancing on top of the garnia. A new bird! Today, I'm going to *really* sketch it. My eyes snap a hundred photos in a matter of seconds, from every angle. The rusty red of the wing feathers, the small white smudge near the eye.

I lean against a heart-shaped granite boulder, and watch as storm clouds stir up the blue, stirring leaves around my ankles, stirring my thoughts within. The sounds of the wild are everywhere and moving in everything – in the fresh crunch of gum leaves underfoot, in the *tizz tizz* of the grassbird. All of it, me, gloriously untameable and free.

The grassbird flits away. I tip my head and let my senses expand out, drinking the morning in, dissolving into the sea of blue-green leaves above. A sudden blur of dizziness has me reaching for the rock to sit on and resting with my eyes closed. When I open them a few minutes later, a mouse the colour of leaf litter skips across the rock face not metres from me: an antechinus! It stops, its long pointed nose sniffing, the mushroom pink of the inside of its ear tracking for sound. It hops closer, a miniature rabbit. Closer still ... a ruler length from my feet. Oh, you little magical burr of fur, I see you. I wonder what you are seeing? My toes do look a lot like brown rocks. My God, it isn't – it is! – sniffing my big toe, tickling me with its whiskers. I let out a held smile as he scurries away.

How can Chloe bear to leave? I can hardly stand the thought of leaving in a few months. Leaving is the wrong word. It feels like abandoning. Who will sketch the birds? Who will warm my shelter? It will grow cold and lonely. My heart aches at the thought.

*

As I approach the Gunyah, Dan fiddles to connect his iPod with the battery-operated speakers on a camp table outside. He's decided Chloe's send-off is going to be a daggy disco. I wince as Cyndi Lauper blasts, and wait for him to adjust the volume.

"Had a fight with a lawnmower?" I say, borrowing Dad's standard haircut joke. Dan looks up and grins, his head now bald except for a monkish fringe at the back.

Nikki is stringing up some bush-style bunting along the guttering, Ryan lighting a fire in the clearing. I sit my plate of geebung and dianella berries down amongst the more traditional party food. Kate and Sam are away visiting family but sent up some macadamia-and-riberry swirl jam for making fairy bread.

"Where's the keynote?" I ask.

"Dunno. Eloped, maybe?" says Dan, crunching into a corn chip.

"Here she comes," I say, as Chloe's figure appears down the trail. I see she has her city civvies on – blue jeans and Blundstone boots, a white embroidered top and hoop earrings, her hair pulled back in a loose knot.

"Daaa, da-da-da," sings Dan, running to offer his arm as if walking her down the aisle. Chloe slaps at him playfully.

"Jealous?" she says, twisting his arm into a hug.

I busy myself with organising bowls and cups, trying to ignore the churning in my belly. Why do I feel so hurt?

We gather for a grevillea-steeped tonic water toast.

"To Chloe and her twitcher – may they live happily feathered after," says Dan, tipping his glass. As Chloe and I clunk glasses, I catch her eye. She looks a little sad. I look away.

An doof-style Irish jig is on, and Ryan has launched into an impeccable Michael Flatley impersonation. We look at one another incredulously.

"You think you know someone ..." Nikki says, laughing.

Chloe nibbles tentatively on some popcorn and looks down at her watch. She must be like me. I hate goodbyes. I'd much prefer to just disappear.

"Okay, I'm off," she suddenly announces, picking up her backpack.

"What – already? But you haven't even had a dance," Dan protests.

I stand at the end of the hug line-up. Why am I so nervous?

"Well, I guess this is it," says Chloe, shrugging her arms out to me.

"Well, at least you'll have twenty-four-hour access to a bird encyclopedia," I say, masking the emotion in my throat. Chloe laughs awkwardly. We embrace. I have the sense she wants to hold it longer, but I pull away. Turning to leave, Chloe spins back around and grabs my hands. My heart thumps.

"You know, Claire, it's like Claudia said: why we think we're doing something generally never turns out to be the reason."

I resist the urge to retract my hands and instead relax my hands in hers, lifting my head to meet her gaze. Her moist eyes are

MY YEAR WITHOUT MATCHES

more grey than blue tonight, and flecked with green. Strands of her ponytail have fallen out and curve around her heart-shaped face. Her lips press together in a slight smile, questioning and soft. How many times have I looked at her face this year and not seen it? I haven't wanted to. I've been clinging on to an image of the person I wanted her to be, rather than the one right in front of me, full of optimism, hope and uncertainty. No wonder I feel abandoned whenever I look for the Chloe of the past, who isn't there anymore. She presses my hands in hers to signal release, but this time it is me who clings on. It's time to really see her. Chloe's eyes widen slightly. I soften mine into wide-angle vision. There she is, the Chloe I remember. Underneath, she is still the same, just like me, searching for happiness, for connection, freedom. For truth.

"Take care," I blurt out.

"You too," she says. Like a runaway bride, she disappears down the track with a wave. The Block suddenly feels empty, as if a chunk of the past that has taken up so much space has left with her. High on sugar and the lightness of a burden lifted, I dance with the others as if wonderfully drunk, unable to stop moving under the stars, unable to think of a reason why I shouldn't be madly in love with everything and everyone.

226

3.

"Brain milkshake, anyone?" Ryan offers, holding out a frothing pink bowl that looks scarily like a strawberry smoothie. I take a whiff and gag. Urrggh. Who needs the smell of roasted coffee at breakfast when you can inhale sheep's brains, instead? My hide is thirsty for it, though, sucking it up in great gulps. I look up at the line of cirrus clouds creeping in. Not now, I tell them sternly. I'm not in the mood for an all-nighter. Once brain-soaked, the hides have to be continuously stretched until they're completely dry in order for the brain juices to fully infiltrate the fibres. Too hot, and they'll dry before they've properly softened, too wet and they won't dry at all. It looked promising this morning from the eagle's nest pine, clear pink light spreading a broad smile across the eastern horizon, the dew a dusting of icing sugar on the fresh red shoots of the gums.

I make sure I've got snacks close by before retrieving my demanding charge from the brain soup. Flecks of brain juice splash up in my face as I throw it over the wringing beam lashed between two trees. Folding it into a donut shape, I feed a smooth stick through the hole and twist it hard in opposing directions, washerwoman-style. The hide bubbles and gurgles as it releases rivers of pink juice onto the ground and up my arms. It's stiff with raised wrinkles when I unwrap it, and I have to dig my knees in to stretch out the creases. My hide is already a completely different beast since the brain bath. Its current incarnation is a cross between a chamois, plasticine and a rubber mat. Nikki grabs the other side of it and pulls against me, both of us leaning out to lend our weight to the stretch, slowly spinning the hide clockwise, pulling and stretching it like a pizza base.

"Work it, baby, work it," Ryan jokes, looking up from where he is rubbing his hide in fast bursts over a smooth log, like he's using a rag to polish a boot, the hide almost doubling in size.

"So, what's news on the possum front?" I ask Nikki.

"You wouldn't believe it – he's completely disappeared," she says incredulously.

"What – since the stick?"

"Yep, since the stick."

"Wow, that's wacky ... just goes to show ..."

Nik nods in amazed agreement. "Possum magic, eh?"

Nikki and I have both been graced by overly familiar possums around our shelters in the last few months. The cute neighbour factor wore off as their nightly raids on our food supplies grew more brazen. Even more annoying was the complete disregard the marauders showed for our attempts to scare them off, my possum barely bothering to scamper a few feet off the ground when I launched out of my shelter brandishing a knife and yelling obscenities, Nikki's going so far as to steal bread out of her hand. So far they have correctly called our bluffs. The night one broke into my macadamia butter jar, the last of my cuddly possum sentimentality disappeared. After much talk of ethics and practicalities, Nikki and I decided that it was time to tan these possums' hides. While my talk of trap setting has so far amounted to just that, a week or so ago Nikki walked into the forest with the clear intention of finding a killing stick, whittled the one she found into shape, sat it next to her sharpened knife, cooked dinner, then sat in (trepidatious) wait. For the first time in weeks, that night and every night since, the possum was a no-show.

I've heard that Native Americans never go out explicitly to hunt, only ever "taking their arrows for a walk". The whole idea of mental camouflage doesn't seem so far-fetched now. It's similar with birds. When my thoughts are quiet, I scarcely raise a flutter as I walk, as if my humanness has disappeared, and along with it all the usual inter-species rules, as I saw with the antechinus toe-nibbling incident. But when my mind is full of argument, I can just as easily scatter a flock of wrens from fifty yards away.

I had a wren moment recently. Hanging out at my shelter, I couldn't work out why I had started to feel jumpy. Ten minutes later Dan revved up the main drag. He's been spending at least as much time off The Block as on, doing odd jobs at Terri's and hanging out at Kate and Sam's. When I saw him that night he was defensive, as if picking up on my judgment without my saying anything. It's been increasingly like that with the whole group – we know exactly how the others are feeling, even if it's left unsaid. There's nowhere to hide here. You're naked, whether you like it or not. It'd be impossible to stay this sensitive in the city – I'd short-circuit. The city, where I'll be in less than three months. Where has the time gone? And just three of us left (well, three and a half, if you count Dan). How sad that just as I'm ready to come out of hibernation and play, I'm left mostly on my own with a couple who are in constant relationship turmoil. I'm afraid my prediction might be right – it'll all end in tears.

"Any news on the traps?" Nik asks. I don't answer immediately, too busy abrading my hide across a blunt dovetail edge cut into a stump. Any kid-glove treatment I offered the hide is long gone. In fact, it seems to enjoy the fiercest beating I can give it, palms of soft suede already appearing.

"Nope, none since the chew-through," I say, puffing, thinking back to my lacklustre check on the traps this morning. They had seemed saggy, but in no particular physical way. It was more as if they had lost their trap-ness, and were now just a collection of string and sticks tied together. It's getting harder to motivate myself for the morning trap loop, as I'm already assuming I'll find them empty. Maybe I should take them down, though the thought of that saddens me.

*

The clouds recede. After discovering more ways to stretch and bend a hide than there are yoga poses in an ashram, by mid-afternoon I hold it against my cheek and detect not the faintest moisture.

"It's dry!" I call excitedly, wrapping it around me and catwalking a *Clan of the Cave Bear* strapless dress (albeit with a wicked split up the side). I can't take my hands off it; it has such a deliciously velvety texture, I could almost eat it. Another successful recipe in the ancient book of bush alchemy – take one hairy stink bomb of a hide, add ash, elbow grease, brains, more elbow grease and voila, a frock fit for Cinderella at a primitive ball.

"Wilma Flintstone, eat your heart out," says Ryan, with a wolf whistle. "You'd just better hope it doesn't rain, you'll turn back into a pumpkin." He's right, the recipe isn't quite complete. Unless smoked, my primitive prom dress will turn back into a stiff board at the first hint of water.

Ryan starts digging out three small pits for the smoking. I sit nearby, my back resting against a tree, using sinew we saved from the Achilles tendon of the roadkill roo to sew up some holes that stretched open during the softening process.

"You gonna quest?" Ryan asks, between shovelfuls, referring to Kate's recent suggestion of another group vision quest.

"Nope, not me." I answer, a little defensively. "Not feeling called to it."

"I'm going to," Ryan offers.

"Same," adds Nik.

"Really? You feel like questing again?" I say, with a strain in my voice.

"Yeah, may as well now while I've got the time. Who knows what'll happen back out in the unreal world," Ryan says, glancing over at Nik.

The decision that felt so clear a few days ago suddenly feels a bit shaky. Maybe I should quest – up the ante a bit before the end of the year.

We've been over this a million times, I remind myself. My edge is in learning how *not* to push myself – following my heart, remember? I know how powerful the quest is. I've been there. It's not something you do just because your mates are. The argument is persuasive enough to calm me. Good. The last thing I need is another crisis.

Bob Kull is in the midst of a crisis, though, in *Solitude*. His exploratory boating forays have all been lead-ups to a glacier trip eighty miles away. As the time draws closer, his excitement is turning into a freak-out about the boat breaking down or some other catastrophe stranding him in an icy wilderness. He is stymied and can't work out whether he is stubbornly pushing forward on some unnecessary hero's mission, or whether his fear and resistance are justified human concerns for the real risks – and that underneath he really wants to do it. *You're already doing it, Bob*, I want to tell him. *You don't have to go.* But I can tell he won't be satisfied unless he does.

I watch enviously as Ryan barely raises a puff to produce his coal. I don't need a man; I've got a hand-drill. It provides all the on-again, off-again, love-hate relationship drama I need. It might be off for a while now, the sheep brains having softened the calluses that have taken most of the year to harden.

After lighting a fire the size of a dinner plate in his pit, Ryan passes me a lit stick. Once a coal base is established, I throw in green leaves and sawdust, plumes of thick smoke rising up into the hide, which I've loosely sewn together and suspended over the pit. I peg it down with rocks at the base. It fills like a balloon, smoke wisping out from between the joins. Paranoid about it catching fire, I shovel in more sawdust, and the smoke evaporates. Damn. Nothing to do but collect more kindling and start over. Ryan has pinned his hide to an op-shop denim skirt to get some distance between it and the fire. He sits back, laughing, as I cluck around my pit. Of course, always Mr Practicality. Eventually, the coals are smoking again and I can relax.

As the light fades, so too does our conversation, lapsing into the spaces between the languid pinging of the yellow-faced honeyeaters, between distant screeches of white cockatoos returning to roost. Venus rises and Nikki nestles some eggs on the coals to cook. I rest against a tree, absorbed by the stain spreading like a slow-burning grassfire across my hide, in hues of smoky summer suns, darkening at the edges.

*

This morning all I need is a grass mat just big enough for a caterpillar like me to curl upon, a paperbark roof just sturdy enough to keep me dry, and a fire just large enough to warm my toes. My small movements are habitual: feed the flames, look out at the trampolining of raindrops on banksia leaves, and back to the book.

Poor Bob is still sweating the glacier question, tormented by a voice telling him he is failing – that after nine months of solitude, he *should* have cultivated either the clarity to know what he wants to do, or the equanimity to let any well-intentioned plans go. Ouch, I know how he feels. We're both questing beasts, although my glaciers are comparatively risk-free. It's painful to read how harsh he is being on himself. You wouldn't inflict such harshness on your enemy, so why do we do it to ourselves?

I think back to my most recent conversation with Malcolm. He explained that, as children, we often absorb the message that love is conditional upon our doing something that gains others' approval. The inner critic moves in to help us meet that perceived need. The problem is, the critic gets so comfortable in our psyche that it continues to bark orders at us long after it has worn out its welcome. I have a sense it's not just the critic at work with Bob, though. I think he really does want to go to the glacier, but it's getting all knotted up with his self-worth struggle.

My recent glacier was an overnight adventure on my bike into a state forest. What looked straightforward on the topographic map ended up being an absolute mission – I became lost and had to push my bike through deep sand for kilometres. When I finally limped it home, I crawled into my hammock, every muscle and bone unable to offer any resistance, thoughts too tired to even surface. I dropped into a kind of meditation, highly alert and yet deeply relaxed. Everything was amplified, softened, the single hum of a passing insect so vivid, so singular, and yet melting into a swelling sea of sound. My heart felt blown open. Did I have to push myself to the limit in order to experience this? I wondered. Or was it just another case of the critic pushing me onwards? I was too tired to expect answers, but they arose unbidden. There are many faces of the feminine, many voices within me, which all need expression. I followed the calling of the adventurer, the one who wants to explore, be tested, ford streams and scale mountains. And now I experience the one whose great heights are known only in pure receptivity and total surrender. Both are aspects of this complex being.

My fasting belly rumbles and I run my hands over my ribs. Bob is talking again about his fresh fish. It's been ages since I've eaten meat. I'm pretty sure I'm low in iron, often dizzy when I stand up. I really should go and check the traps but can't stop turning the pages. Yesterday I got there to discover that I'd left my knife at home. Carelessness. That is *not* the behaviour of a hunter, I chastised myself. Neither is this mid-morning lie-in. It's yet another sign that I'm being half-arsed about the whole trap thing. Part of it is jitters about coming across a half-strangled wallaby and having to finish it off with my own hands. Mostly, though, it's because the whole idea has slipped back into the realm of fantasy. I'm a helpless white girl in the bush, remember? Not someone with the boldness and skill to feed myself, to assert some measure of independence from consumer society. The thought of taking the traps down triggers an ache of disappointment. It's something I really wanted out of this year. There's been the bird on the beach and the snake and roadkill, but this is different. This is *my* mission. I want to know in all its visceral intensity what it means to take life, to be wholly responsibility for the meat on my plate. And not just any meat. I want to taste the flesh and blood of this country. To animate my body with the animate energy of this land.

I think back to Nikki's possum stick and the idea of intention.

Maybe it's like it is with fire: you have to want it more than anything, and then let go of the trying. Take your arrows for a walk,
but with an empty belly.

Dog-earing Bob's book, I jump up into a squat, my hands raised
like paws in front of my chest. I look left. I look right. I nuzzle the
back of my hand with my nose. I hop forward onto my paws, my feet
following in a single jump. I lean down until my hair falls on the
ground and I nibble some grass. I poke my head back up and tip my
ears again. With a giant leap I bound forward, legs like springs,
feeling the weight of my invisible tail hitting the ground behind me.

My belly growls again. I rest my knuckles on the ground in
front of me.

Wallaby family, I am hungry. My tribe is hungry. I send messages
silently. *I know it's a big ask, but if you feel able to sacrifice one of your
mob, I will do my best to honour its life.*

But I totally understand if you don't want to, I add, as an afterthought.

*

Threading my knife onto my belt, I head for the traps, a bit light-
headed from fasting. Rain is sprinkling on Snake Creek when I
rock-hop across, sprinkling in the pools of wallaby tracks in the
sand. I follow them through the forest to the heath, past sunrise
tree, taking a left onto trap trail. It's quiet, with none of the usual
thumps of disappearing wildlife. A willie wagtail hooks in front of
me, landing on the wire above the first snare and swinging his tail
from side to side. I approach slowly. Something has changed. A
faded brown rope is sticking out of the grass. How did that get
there? The rope is rusty and discoloured and ... furry. I stiffen. It
looks like a tail. I must be imagining it. I avert my gaze and walk
on, calmly checking the other traps. They're all empty. My heart
leaps into my throat. It *was* a tail. Holy crap, it's a whole wallaby.
Please be dead. I crouch down and poke it. It doesn't flinch. It

takes two hands to roll it face up. Its eyes are milky, a noose pulled tightly around its neck. I scan for blood, but there's none. It's starting to stiffen.

I killed a wallaby. Oh my God, what do I do? *Come on, this is your wallaby. You asked for this, remember?* Cut the noose off, that's right. Drag it under the fence. It's dead, it's fucking dead, and I killed it! Okay, calm down. I notice a pouch and my heart jumps. I peer in. Thank God, it's empty. I burst into tears, wailing like a mourning mother. "I'm so sorry," I blubber.

She's starting to bloat, so I need to get her home. I edge my forearms under her body and strain to lift. Her head twists unnaturally to one side, leaning against my breast and staring at me with drunken eyes. I cringe and look away. I don't want to do this. *You have to.* I juggle her until she's cradled in my arms like a baby. Her mouth is open, the tongue lolling over my left arm. My right hand supports the rear, her tail arching over and bouncing in time with my step. The dead weight is so real. "I'm sorry, thank you" – I sob this mantra over and over as I walk, half-blinded by tears and rain. My arms begin to ache. I can't believe this is the same three kilometres I just walked. My forearms go numb, and I hug the wallaby in closer to lessen the weight. It's like I'm hugging a child. It *is* someone's child. "I'm sorry, thank you." My sobs subside into a soft cooing. I sing the lullaby my grandmother used to croon to me for the rest of the way home. By the time I reach the Gunyah and let out the loudest cooee I can muster, my arms are about to break.

"Oh my God, you're joking. The snare?" Ryan calls out, jogging towards me with Nikki next to him. I nod. Thank Christ they're here. Seeing the belly, Ryan starts flinging a rope over the top beam, Nikki helping me lower the wallaby to the ground.

"You okay?" she asks. I nod.

Following Ryan's lead, I split open the skin between the ankle tendons, my own Achilles tingling in empathy. Feeding a rope through the incisions, Ryan pulls the rope until she is hanging upside down by the legs at head height. Blood starts a consistent drip from her mouth.

"Watch out!" Ryan calls, as a split breaks open and she swings towards us.

"Urrggh," I say, ducking. I watch as Ryan attaches her again.

The others hang back to allow me the first cut. Her fur is still glistening from the rain.

"Thank you, girl. Thank you so much," I whisper, stroking her side.

Pinching to raise the skin near the bumhole with my left hand, I inch the point of my knife in until it pierces the surface. Don't cut through the sphincter, please. I screw up my nose, even though all I can smell so far is grass. The skin tears opens, like cloth ripping. Ryan and Nikki join me. *Snip, snip*, following an imagined dot-to-dot along the inside of the legs and arms, taking her apart at the seams.

Nikki starts up a dirge-like hum, slow and meandering. It helps to keep my hands steady as I nip away at the flesh holding the skin. I turn over her paws. The fingers are long and dainty, charcoal towards the tips, with dark nails. I spread them out on my palm, mimicking the way she would press them into the earth in a slow lope.

"Let's keep them for tracking," Nikki says.

The wallaby is naked to the waist, the hide hanging over her head, as if she's been caught in the middle of undressing. Her bare legs are pink and muscly. Grabbing fistfuls of separated skin, Nikki and I pull down hard. It doesn't budge. We are almost swinging off it before the fat layers finally release their grip and the hide slides off with a suction slurp. Ryan helps to catch it, guiding it over the forearms and head as if unzipping the wallaby from a tight jumpsuit. Gloves of furred feet, paws and head are all that are left.

I brace myself for the next step – gutting. I circle her a few times, working my way up to the first cut, this time through the fat, revealing the first shocking glimpse of bright red blood. This is where she really comes unstitched, underwear and all. I slice as shallowly as I can. Snaking intestines bulge from the cavity. They are lumpy with pockets of greenery, dinner from last night, perhaps ingested moments before she was snared. I hope she died quickly. It looked like it, from the tight grab of the noose.

The first rank whiff of bodily fluids hits my nostrils with a wallop. I gag and look longingly at Ryan.

"It's all yours, Ms Macbeth," Ryan says, stepping aside. It's just blood. This is you too, remember, just turned inside out. I turn away to take a deep breath and steel myself, then turn back and squelch my hand inside, fishing for the esophagus. I feel something like a corrugated pipe – that must be it. I pull it, the dripping throat of the wallaby lengthening as if choking.

"Okay, your turn," I grimace. Ryan relents just in time to catch the guts, a writhing bag of giant worms.

"Gross," I squeal and jump on the spot as they land with a splat on hessian bags. I've been trying not to be disgusted but *this* is the definition of the word.

"Well, you don't get much more real than this," I say, wiping my forehead with the back of my bloodied forearm, "Hung, drawn and nearly quartered."

"They don't show you this on the polystyrene packaging, do they?" Nik says wryly.

There's a slight green tinge to some of the meat on the back. I admonish myself for not checking on the traps earlier. Ryan starts a fire to get the coal base going.

"Sorry, matey," I say, as I lever my knife between hip bones, "They didn't teach me butchering in school."

It's hardly quartering, more like a salvage operation. Still, we manage to collect the backstrap, most of the leg meat, the sinew for sewing, the paws for tracking practice, the tail for soup and the liver for tonight's entree.

"What should we do with the guts?" Nikki asks.

"Well, we could make sausages ... or a water pouch from the stomach?" Nikki makes a face. "Condoms?" I smile. I let Ryan saw off the head and bag it up, along with the intestines, for Jessie. Now would be a choice moment to have instant hot water.

I'm starting to feel nauseated, partly from lack of food, and partly from the sight of the carcass swinging from the beam. This wallaby was happily feeding on grass tips alongside its siblings a day ago, looking forward to easy summer days, to perhaps its first joey. What a sacrifice. How will I ever repay it?

I start chopping up the meat for the stew.

"You've forgotten something," Ryan says. "The rule of your first successful hunt."

"What's that?" I ask dubiously.

"You have to eat the heart."

It's easily recognisable, a neat pink nugget amongst the off-cuts. It fits like a slippery shell in my hand, a small fist enclosed within mine. I turn it over. It's harder than I imagined. I lay it on the coals. It sizzles, quickly darkening in colour. I turn it until the coals no longer stick, the sign that it's cooked through. I slice a corner off and take a nibble. It's chewy and grassy, rich and dense. My appetite surges back. I bring it to my mouth and bite it in two. Almost instantaneously my lethargy disappears, as if my cells are already pulsing with new blood. I finish the second half in a few mouthfuls, my cheeks flushing red. Sitting back, I rest my hand over the place where the heart sits in my stomach, just centimetres from the surface. It pulses gently. I feel full, but not like I've eaten a heavy steak, just deeply sated. Nourished.

I look over at Nikki stirring the stew pot, her curls falling down over her face. How beautiful. Sensing my gaze, she looks up and smiles. That is how I repay the wallaby – by living a good life, a life of integrity and love, of service and meaning. This is what I owe everything that has given up its life for mine. It all seems so obvious, the responsibility of being alive and being fed by others, by the air and water and soil microbes. I have to live honourably, not because of some moral code I've come up with, but in order to honour life itself.

I send wallaby my last silent thanks for her sacrifice, for the opportunity she gave me to attend to death, and, therefore, to life. This is perhaps the best gift I've ever been offered.

4.

Nikki appears like a puff of smoke, a restless shadow in the willowy pre-dawn. Her wobble is almost imperceptible, a slight weave to her walk. I see that under her shawl she is wearing the same clothes she left in, one pant leg half-rolled, her feet bare. She glances once more back into the mist, then turns to lift her eyes to mine as she enters the sphere of firelight. Before she has gathered together words or gestures, before she has fully realised she is no longer out there in the shell-shocked silence of her vigil, her gaze takes me out there with her, into the excruciating rawness and emptiness, the beauty and terror of the moment-to-moment meeting of herself. I falter at the intensity of her presence, struggling to remember her as Nikki.

My hug brings her some of the way back, and I help her down by the fire. She sits and slowly extends her palms towards the flames. A small smile curls her lips upwards, as if she's holding a secret, committing it to memory before the whirlwind of speech threatens to blow it away. Ryan wanders in next, soft and steadfast. They embrace wordlessly. Dan waits until the precipice of dawn to appear, perhaps relishing the last few moments of peace. Or perhaps he just slept in.

They sit quietly, staring at the flames, eyes wide, as if seeing fire for the first time. Small whispers of conversation emerge, scatters of laughter. Ryan gulps greedily at the bowl of miso soup

Kate hands him, which revives him enough after a few minutes so that he notices the new hide top I'm wearing. He winks at me in approval. I grin. I have had fun playing primitive seamstress in the last few days. It was nerve-racking cutting into the hide with just a newspaper pattern to guide me. I left the naturally frilled edge to hang asymmetrically on one side and laced up the other with a thin ribbon of hide. I wore the top during my last visit to the quest area to check on the others' marker boxes. They were my favourite times of the day, out there bobbing around in their bubble. By day four it was like riding waves of silence.

I hadn't felt bad for not questing until now, when the results of my four days seem like a poor substitute for the internal handiwork they've been doing. I feel like a spiritual dole bludger, hitching a free ride on their enlightened coat-tails.

Stop the judgment. My task here is not to be the hardcore spiritual survivalist, it's to follow my heart, which clearly did not want to quest. I have been enjoying my buckwheat pancakes immensely. Besides, I console myself, I've got something brewing of my own, something I *want* to do. A wandering walkabout. A quest of my own design.

It's about time I set the terms and conditions for it. How long should I go for? What will I take? Maybe no food. Or just nuts and an apple? Two days might be enough; no, definitely three. *Come on, this might be your last chance to do something spectacular.* Just look at these questers – nothing gambled, nothing gained.

Whoa back, slow down. What do I *really* want out of this quest? I look around at the others, their faces still completely stripped of any masks. This is what I want. To live every day from such a place of connectedness, of grace. I know that getting to this place has probably been one of the hardest things they will ever do, every morning waking and wondering how they would get through another sun cycle, at least once packing their belongings and standing on the edge of their circle with tears streaming down their faces. But they stayed. "Ask yourself," Kate suggested to them for when things got tough, "how bad do you really want it?" My answer to that is with the longing of a lioness.

The smooth suede of my hide top brushes against my belly. Its softness didn't happen through my sitting around wishing for it. It took elbow grease, tenacity, determination and patience. Perhaps this is the equation necessary for transformation. So, back to those walkabout quest terms. As I wrestle with the details, inspiration gives me the finger and promptly slips out the back door.

Dawn has long made invisible tracks back into the forest. Nikki and Ryan spoon each other by the fire. I start chopping zucchini for their first meal. By the time I have grated three beetroot and half my knuckles into the salad bowl, the terms of my contract have been decided. It is to be a wandering survival quest, taking only water and a knife, catching food opportunistically, leaving in four days and returning on the fifth morning. With a heavy heart, I sign my name in scribbly gum ink on the dotted line.

*

"Another slice please, extra cream," I say to the waitress. She looks at me questioningly. "Actually, make that two slices and a latte."

Like every other this morning this week, I woke with a sense of impending doom. The thought of yet another day on The Block, killing time before my quest, was more than I could bear. I caught a ride to town with Terri.

The waitress watches as I shovel the chocolate caramel slice into my mouth, the sugar and caffeine overriding one edge with their own – much more pleasant – spacey one.

The clock on the cafe wall ticks loudly. It's still another couple of hours 'til I have to meet Terri. I trawl the streets, making up stories about the lives of the people I pass: the teenage pram pushers, the shop assistants on lunchtime errands, the wrinkled women in shapeless floral dresses and orthopedic shoes gossiping outside the bakery. Few acknowledge me. I fantasise about being taken home by one of them, wrapped in their patchwork quilt and fed chicken soup. I would tell them my plan, and they would laugh and tell me not to be silly, to stay with them instead.

Schoolkids overtake me, bags thumping against their backs as they race to be the first home. Mum waits by the gate, chatting to the mum next door. They all look so goddamn smug in their safe routines – the afternoon raid on the fridge, the TV cartoons, dinner at six, Dad home soon. Isn't that kind of complacency why I left? I left to find a simple life in the bush, but maybe what I need is the simplicity of a sun-filled verandah with a couch and a dog and a good book, a toy on the shelf for my nieces and nephew, a trellis of climbing beans, a candle on the windowsill for me to light at dusk.

Why do I seem to want such conflicting things in life? It's all so confusing.

I run into the library and pound out an email.

What are the most effective practices for change? For connection with the mystery, for cultivating wisdom and clarity? Does transformation necessitate sacrifice? Is harder better? How do we know when we need to push through resistance, and when to allow ourselves to just be? How do we follow our hearts?

I type in the names of six of my wisest women friends.

Tomorrow morning at first light, I walk out into the wilderness for four days and nights seeking answers to these questions, seeking a way to be most awake and alive in this world. I am scared and confused. Please hold me in your hearts.

PS Reply by post.

With a sigh I click *send*, knowing their replies will come too late to help me on my quest.

I trudge back up the street. An unusual woman walks towards me. Her hair is pulled back in a low bun, tight ringlets escaping to frame her round face. She looks at me intently with dark eyes, hesitates, and then gently touches my arm. I stop.

"This is going to sound strange, but I'm a clairvoyant, and I just had a flash of you sitting in a cave, like one of those Indian sadhus. I'm not sure why, but I felt like I needed to tell you."

"Oh, okay. That's ... thanks," I stumble.

I'm silent on the way back to The Block.

Terri drops me off at the bridge.

"Good luck," she says, "I'll be thinking of you."

I feel sick as I squeeze out a goodbye, knowing she is the last person I will see for another five days. I've already left a note at the kitchen, telling everyone not to expect me for a few days. My steps up the path are leaden, my belly a tight ball of tension. A willy-willy gusts around my ankles. I swallow back the sense that I'm an abandoned child, lost in the woods.

Ryan swings out of his shelter path and onto the trail. His walk is measured and smooth, still floating on quest cloud nine. Damn. There's no point hiding, he's seen me.

"Hey, heard you're heading out," he says, walking towards me.

"Yep, sparrow's fart tomorrow. My turn for the sledgehammer," I say, attempting lightness.

"How ya feeling?" he asks, his face calmly inquisitive.

"A bit scared, you know, the usual resistance, I guess," I say, the word "resistance" slamming into my chest like a demolition ball.

"Do you really want to do it?"

Don't go there, Ryan, I plead silently, as the lump in my throat threatens to choke me. I look down and roll loose stones under my boot.

"'Cause you don't have to, you know. There's nothing to prove here."

I double over, exploding with a loud sob.

Ryan pulls me up, my head collapsing onto his chest. "Shh," he says, smoothing down my hair.

"I ... just can't do it, Ryan. I don't know ... what I need to do ..." I stammer out between sobs. "You did ... you did it."

"Yeah, but I had to quit first."

I collapse in a fresh bout of tears. "I thought I wanted to ... I just don't know ... who I am anymore."

Ryan cups my face in his hands so that I'm forced to look at him.

"Claire, listen to me," he says, more serious than I have ever seen him. "Your presence is stunning. If you could only see how beautiful you are when you're just being yourself. You change people just by being you."

For a second it is my grandmother and not Ryan standing in front of me. *Thank you for being you.*

Like a knife piercing the fog, I suddenly see myself through Ryan's eyes, through my grandmother's, the perfection already there, waiting for me realise it. I don't need a sledgehammer. All I need to do is blow with the gentlest of breaths.

"I quit," I say quietly. "I quit, I quit, I quit, *I quit!*" I yell, throwing up my arms.

"I quit." I laugh this time. Ryan takes my hands and spins me around, spins until we both collapse onto our backs, a pair of silly quitters, wise fools, lying on the gravel, howling with laughter, the kookaburras picking up our refrain and running with it 'til day's end.

5.

wake at first light with a stabbing fear, forgetting I had quit. The remembrance spreads through me like bush honey, sweet and runny. I spring out of bed to greet the day, looking around to see what I missed during last week's self-absorption. Like magical beanstalks, the new grasstree flowers have grown at least a foot.

"*Eee-choong!*" A rufous whistler flits in to show me it has returned for the summer.

"I'm back tooooo," I sing in reply.

Jumping up on the log, I'm a gymnast on the beam, scissor kicking and toes pointing, chest puffed out and arms lifted in finale. Wattlebirds hiccup in applause. Bowing, I take a running leap from the log up the trunk of the scribbly gum, returning as a barefoot Charlie Chaplin, with a stick cane and bark hat, tapping in the dirt. I'm a pole dancer around a tree, gyrating to the hoot of the kookaburra. I'm a jazz ballerina, hands circling in dramatic twirling waves. The day is mine, all mine, to do whatsoever my heart desires.

I stop and tip my face to the rising sun. So, then, what do I want to do with this day? My breathing is the slow swell of the sea.

Turning, I walk back into my shelter and calmly begin to fill a small pack – water bottle, rolled blanket, sandals, fire-kit, bandage, an apple, nuts and a sweet potato. Winking at the Wild Woman, I duck under my doorway, pad down my shelter trail, past the empty

Gunyah and out of camp. If my pack is light, my plans are even lighter. All I know is I'm walking. Wandering. Perhaps overnight, perhaps longer. I don't know, and I don't want to. Right now, I just want to feel my feet moving across the earth, before the doubts and the plans can catch me, before I try to pin them down with meaning. I would probably have made the same tracks had this been my official Wandering Quest. But it is not that. How glad I am not to be *that* woman on the trail today. I'm a little nervous, a little excited, but keep my thoughts firmly on the step of one foot in front of the other, in the appreciation of waking birdsong and the open horizon ahead.

Snake Creek has been flushed clean by spring rains, the water jostling around my shins as I cross. Out on the heath track, my feet veer south-west. I hesitate slightly but continue. The faint tyre tracks peter out at the broken fence, as I knew they would. From here on in there are no tracks, just kilometres of seemingly identical ridges, sandstone clefts and rainforest gullies of the wilderness reserve. I rarely venture here, the land of lost borders on my adventure map. Looking back in the direction I came from, I snap a twig from a shrub as I step into the unfamiliar, as much a farewell as an announcement of my presence on new country. The rising sun is a steady friend as I walk, notwithstanding the vagaries of weaving between grasstrees and granite boulders, ducking under tea-tree thickets and vines.

I climb incidentally, sneaking sideways up to the ridge. After many false summits, by mid-afternoon I end up on a wide rock of granite, looking out over a deep valley to a twin cliff in the west. I feel like I've been here before. In fact, I'm sure I remember this rock. It can't be. Oh my God, it is – there's the ring of stones from our fire. I've walked back to the exact place where Nikki, Chloe and I spent autumn equinox.

It looks like no-one has been up here since. I take off my pack and stretch. Pardalotes contact-call in the forest canopy. Clouds throw moving shadows across the granite. The winter coats of blackbutt are strewn messily over the rocks, as if shed in a moment of passion. It's more beautiful than I remember, quieter and older.

The Block seems a universe away. A single raven launches itself across the valley, its cawing slow and mournful. The rustle of leaves above invites rather than interrupts the stillness. I realise I'm holding my breath. If I was wearing a watch, I'd check that the second hand was still ticking. I can imagine time losing its way up here, slipping between cracks in the rocks, in the spaces between birdsong, minutes turning into days and years into minutes. What's six years to this mountain, or 60,000 years, for that matter? Barely more than a rippling and crumbling of stone. In some ways it feels like yesterday that I was up here; in others, it feels much longer than the six months, the image I have of myself then as someone years younger. I had just finished my shelter and was itching to be alone. And here I am, solo, just as I wanted. Maybe just as the land wanted too.

Come on, every mystic needs a roof.

I haul my sore feet up and look around for a site. The sun quickly slips as I stack rib-bone sticks along the sides of a long pole, which I snap between the fork of a tree and wedge against a rock. I hum as I work, orioles rolling their *r*s through the valley. It's already starting to feel homely – it's amazing what a few sticks thrown together can do. The shelter looks a bit like the skeleton of a beached whale. It's going to be more psychological protection than anything. I would need at least half a metre of leaf litter to keep me dry, let alone warm, and that's clearly not going to happen on this ridge. Still, better some than none. Propping up a latticework of wattle against the ribs, I collect what leaves I can find and tip them on, topping it off with a patchwork quilt of bark. Stuffing a mattress of leaves inside, two scorpions scuttle out. Not my perfect idea of bed mates.

The sun is still a couple of handspans away from the cliffs. The fireplace has held one sacred fire and tonight will hold another.

Despite the waning light, I take my time, choosing each stick carefully, turning it over in my hands as I summon the qualities of each direction. I don't have to imagine or make them up now. I know them as scents and sounds, as friends with personalities – the sly southerly creeping in on cirrus clouds and huddling me close to the hearth, the north-east sunrise warming my cold face in winter, the burnt-out smell of summer's westerly. I bed them down like compass bearings on the rock, the foundation upon which all else stands. Circling the fireplace I set the kindling, not so much holding a question as extending a prayer down through my arms and into each stick.

The sun flings out its last net for the day, catching the bent backs of the tussock grass and staining them gold, like the webs of the golden-orb spider above. I cast my own net, an upturned hat catching the fine powder of stringybark crushed between my palms, the stamens of spent banksia flowers. I mix the ingredients like a cake batter, holding them to my cheek to check for moisture, before sprinkling them into the bracken-fern bowl. I pull the icing on the cake from my pocket – the head of a bulrush flower that I collected on the way – and pluck the fluff to line the heart of the bundle.

The hand-drill stalk held upright between my palms is another directional marker, pointing up where the four directions dissolve into the limitless, into the endless circular turnings of the stars and seasons and all other mysteries. A coal slips out like the fifth child.

With my face centimetres from the tiny glow, I feel as if I could be looking into the eye of the big bang moments before the explosion, swirling with the same creative potential, aroused by the same evolutionary drive for life, for being. Perhaps it was this very force that brought me out to the forest, the same one that wills me now to transfer the smoking coal into the bundle, to hold it above my head as if in offering, and give it three long, steady breaths of life. It flickers for a moment, then roars into flame. Shadows skip and sway through the forest. The fire is unusually bright, lighting up the white backs of the trees, the rocks. A burning stick arches itself in ecstasy, moments before collapse.

Prying out some early coals, I place them in the nook of a small hollow branch, cover them with green gum leaves and stick the branch inside the shelter. Smoke fissures the bark. Panicked scuttles and scratches reveal themselves as lines of bugs in mass exodus. I hope the scorpions are amongst them. Squeezing myself inside, the crackle of the fire lulls me to sleep.

In my dream, the fire has gone out. I'm desperately trying to restart it, but the coals are too small. Wild dogs inch closer as they see my futile struggle. I want to run away but instead run towards the pack. To my surprise they scatter. I realise they are much smaller than I thought, no threat at all. One dog morphs into a young man, tall and steady. We find a dead chicken and eat it together, my hunger finally sated.

*

I wake and can only guess at the hour. The kingdom of night insects gives me clues. There is a point at which its symphony changes, seesawing back and forth like a DJ merging tracks, signalling the liminal time, when it is no longer night but not yet morning. I catch it now as the insects pause, as if recalibrating, soon settling into a new syncopated rhythm, like fingers thrumming on a table. I shift my sore hips and poke my head out of the shelter. A yellow crescent moon has risen. My heart stirs and thumps awake. It has its own rhythm too, its own language, which I have been learning when sleep abandons me to the forest's twitching hour.

I shiver under the blanket. I get up and feed the coals into flames, rubbing my legs together like a cricket's and curling them around the fire. When the hair on my arms stands to attention, I sit up and cast a nervous glance around. I'm being watched; I can feel it. Across the valley, stars rest motionless on the treetops. The insect song quietens. The whole forest is tense, waiting, listening. Time and space roll up tighter and tighter, sucked into a single sizzling point. My ears ring with the building pressure. It releases in a furious flapping of ghost-white wings coming towards me, closer and closer, until they stop, hovering at my eye level with an almost imperceptible beat. I stare into two unblinking marble eyes, barely having time to register their presence before they vanish. I stumble to my feet, scanning the branches for signs of the visitor. Did I imagine it? Seconds later it's back, just as swift and silent, but closer this time, holding my gaze with the intensity of a lover. And, then again, gone, banking abruptly to one side, it takes off across the valley, a white speck slipping behind the black curtain of the cliffs.

Holy crap, was that a white-throated nightjar? It must have been. I've been hoping to see one all year. But what exactly ... was *that*?

I sit, gaping, on the granite outcrop. Looking out in the direction of the disappearing bird, I can suddenly see myself from the vantage of the invisible wings – a young woman, poised at the edge of a fire, on the edge of a vast escarpment, on the edge of time.

In that moment I am neither myself nor the bird, but both. I am the white-winged bird, the woman here now and the one from six months ago. I am the rock I sit on, the valley below and the sky above. I am scorpion and crow and fire and moon. I am as timeless and eternal as the mountain range itself, the molten fires that pushed them upwards, and the Dreaming that created them.

In that second I understand that, rather than sharing an interaction, the bird and I are part of one coordinated action, one continuous dance happening not between us, but through us. We are expressions of a planet that is alive and responsive, a sentient universe dreaming itself into being moment by moment, every movement both spontaneous and perfectly choreographed.

*

I wake in time to see the sun rise burgundy, like a plum ready for picking. It washes me in shades of pink. My sweet potato lies forgotten in the coals. Chipping off the charred skin, I munch on the pulp as I descend. The valley is hot and heavy, as if gravity grasps more firmly as I move nearer to sea level. I swing into camp just long enough to restock my bag with apples, water and sweet potatoes.

As my walkabout continues, so too does the dance of the land. I am the black cockatoo calling at dusk, the frogs in full symphony in the reeds. I am the tallest of trees swaying in unison and the kangaroos at rest. I am the brown falcon who plucks a koel from its nest and thrashes it to death on the ground, and the one who watches wide-eyed, who moves in to snap the koel's collarbone and sever the wings, fanning them out to marvel at the kaleidoscope of spotted dots and wrapping them in paperbark for safe-keeping.

As I walk, I collect stones in my hands, carry them for so long and leave them some place else. I imagine them as stitches that I sew across the country. My needle runs up and over the spine of the ridge, zigzags back and forth between valley, swamp and gully; between tussock grass and forest. Stone by stone I am sewing the land together, embedding myself deeper in its fabric. The land wills me to walk it as much as I want to walk it, my steps not a burden but a balm, each footstep another thread knitting the broken pieces together, fastening the patches into a whole.

I walk that day and most of the next, resting for the night on the edge of a forest clearing.

And, as surely as my wander started, so does it finish. I walked a figure eight over the land, looping west to east and back again to this bellybutton in the middle, the bulging billabong where I float under the crown of thorns of a currawong's nest.

Above me, the clouds are like hands dancing, reminding me that I never dance alone, that the Earth is constantly extending an invitation, beckoning me to join it in conscious creation, the one happening right now in the millions of ways to move and be moved. It's my call whether I resist the dance, or allow myself to flow with it, like wings over a valley.

6.

A fresh rain shower blows in sideways, and I hop on the spot to warm up. It's been wild weather lately – the wettest spring in history, I'm told. I've been re-enacting *The Wind in the Willows* by the creek, just "messing about in boats" like Ratty: stream floating, sunbaking, playing across logs, pottering along the edge. It's the anticipation of floods that magnetises me down here. I mark out the rise and fall of the current with a planted stick, keep tabs on the muddy water line on hanging branches. I love a good flood. As a kid, a flood didn't just mean a holiday from school, it meant a general strike for the whole workaday family world. Out would come the tiddly-winks, the cake tins and the rock 'n' roll vinyl. For a few wonderful days, we were pirates on our own island. Now, with the ground saturated and the rain continuing, we are being flooded in with glorious regularity.

This morning the current has slowed enough for a group exercise. I'm struggling to convince myself it's a good thing. I wait until the last possible moment before I strip to underwear and tie a blindfold around my forehead.

"Why do we do this again?" Dan asks, shivering next to me.

It's the swimming rule, I remind myself. I never regret it.

"Ask me again at the end," I say, as I pull my blindfold down.

The four of us chain up, each placing a hand on the shoulder in front. Dan takes the first turn to be our collective eyes. Stepping out, I immediately crash into Ryan, Nikki's toenail taking the skin off my heel.

"Ouch," I exclaim and am hushed to silence.

We stand and sway until our hips move in alignment, before trying again, our legs and arms gradually falling into centipede coordination down the main trail. At the water's edge, we wait to hear the sound of Kate beating a drum at the bridge before we separate.

Within minutes, the comforting sound of other footsteps fade in the inevitable blind scatter. Without a tether, I slowly begin to step across the dampened leaf litter, focusing on the placement of each foot, the inwards roll of its ball when it confirms safe ground. I'm glad of my recent blindfold practice, my body now familiar enough with sight restriction for my awareness to drop quickly from head to foot, the surface of my skin assuming responsibility for movement.

Soon, even my awareness of the rain disappears in my concentration on the next step, in the touch of spiderweb, fern, tree root. The intermittent drumbeat is a welcome marker. I know the creek is close when the feathery brush of bracken fern gives way to clumps of lomandra, then sand, and then finally water, ice cubes running all over me. I gasp, swimming out blindly in a breaststroke. I bounce between the creek banks like a tenpin bowling ball. Imagining the bridge at the end throws off my focus, and I lunge out too quickly, bumping my head on a branch. I centre myself with some deep breaths before entering the creek again, my right hand periodically scanning at head height for obstacles. Beginnings and endings blur as, step by step, stroke by stroke, I search for the path of least resistance.

The drum sounds again, reminding me to find the others. I squeal as an arm grabs mine. It's Nikki's. Huddled like sardines, we wait at the choke of the creek until the other two bump up against us, shrieking with laughter as we pull one another's blindfolds free. It's only then that my shivers resume, and I'm amazed to find that an hour has passed with scarcely a thought to the cold.

"You gonna help paint some signs this arvo?" Nikki asks, as we walk back. "There's some food prep needs doing too."

I tense. The "open weekend" is less than a week away, an invitation to friends, family and neighbours to check out just what kind of rock we've been hiding under. The word's out and I'm slightly concerned about locals turning up with eskies full of beer. I'm already feeling protective of my shelter, picturing kids swinging off the beams and jumping into the hearth. I left my invites until last week, hoping it would be too late for most of my mob. Ryan's braver than me – his whole family are flying in from Colorado.

"Yeah, a bit later," I say evasively. The blindfold walk has me all dreamy and spacious and I'm itching to get out for a wander.

I head to the paddocks, wanting to be where big sky meets big trees. The breeze caresses me like the creek currents, the clouds breaking up enough to allow handfuls of warm sun to rest on my back. These days are like a continuous game of hopscotch, each square a different element that I jump between on whim. I'm getting better at knowing which one I need in any moment: the warmth of fire, the fluidity of water, the freedom of air on my limbs as I walk, or the stillness of lying on the earth. My emotions rock-hop a similar elemental pattern, sometimes fiery and passionate, other times sad, reflective or high-spirited, ever-changing and seasonal.

Two wedge-tailed eagles flush out the top of a flooded gum and make overlapping circles above. A pair of white-naped honeyeaters squawk, as they launch from a shrub and descend in spirals around each other. Two lizards play ring-a-ring o' roses around a tree. Two red ants are in mock battle, two dollarbirds gossiping on a branch. It's a veritable Noah's Ark. I just don't buy the science that says animals only ever expend energy for survival purposes. From my observations, there are most definitely frivolous, rambunctious and playful antics on display.

Skipping into the clearing, I wend my way through blady grass, rolling against trees rubbed smooth by cattle, pulling back weeds to uncover wildflowers and sticky sundews. In the middle of a stand of pines, a circle of field mushrooms has sprouted, their gills pink and fleshy. I fill my bangalow-palm backpack with enough for dinner. A wallaby feeds close by. He watches me for a while then lowers his head to the grass. I inch towards him with eyes downcast, pretending to be absorbed in mushroom picking. His tail is not three metres from me before he makes a few lazy hops in the other direction. My smile turns into a muffled yawn, tiredness from my late-night date with Bob Kull.

His glacier mission was a success! I'm so glad. After months of torment, on one unusually calm morning, he packed supplies and extra petrol, gave Cat an especially tender pat, and before he could change his mind, turned his rudder east. The fear was real. Any mistake – a map blown overboard, the engine spluttering to a halt – could be fatal. He gave up trying to remember the maze of icy corridors his passage took. The way back was not now. He just needed to get there. And get there he did, just in time to witness a numinous blue light emanating from a mountainous frozen waterfall. Bathed in the luminescence, time slowed to a glacial stillness. He wondered whether he had unwittingly steered himself into a dream: so beautiful, so hypnotic, the light lured him closer. Just as I was beginning to worry that he would be seduced by the blue, his face frozen in awe for eternity, he shook himself free of the trance, remembered that this was not a place to stay overnight, and started the motor for home.

Still swimming in the afterglow of the light, as his little boat chugged back through the waters towards the island he would soon be leaving, Bob looked back at the months of worry. They were worth it for one glimpse of the glacier. Heeding the call of the wild had gifted him a glimpse of the light that would always be with him. His fears had to be met, resistances confronted, emotions navigated. The endless questioning and self-judgment were a ridiculous waste of time and yet also provided the energetic tension that propelled him out there. But there also would have been no great failure if he had not gone. There was no right or wrong, just one decision or another, both with their lessons. Must he have reached the glacier to finally find contentment? Perhaps the adventurer needed space before the homebody and monk could visit. Or perhaps he felt like he had finally earnt his right to just enjoy himself. Still, I'm relieved that he went, and relieved that he returned. It's lovely to read about his finally being relaxed, petting Cat playfully, puttering around in his boat, watching the light change as summer beckons. He doesn't fight the wind now but lets it shapeshift him, indoors and out.

I sink against a tree trunk, watching weebills twitter in the wattle, and the rise of the escarpment in the distance. The wallaby swishes its tail, as native bees murmur among the sweet gum blossoms. Mosquitoes halo my head but don't land, granting me grace enough to stretch out long. Ah, this glorious moment, when there is nowhere I am trying to get to, nothing I should be doing. I'm just here. Sounds and smells heighten and vibrate. The whole idea of getting up and launching myself towards some imagined future, clambering to be something other than just one of many beings enjoying this spring day, suddenly strikes me as ludicrous. There really *is* only this moment, tumbling into the next and the next. Is anything worth rushing for? I doubt it. If it had taken me all year to build my shelter with this awareness, it would have been time well spent. Poor old rushing, it only ever wants to taste more of life, but by its very nature, misses it.

A few days ago, I found a note from Terri under a rock at my shelter trailhead. *Claire, I kept meaning to say to you, after your overnight wander you came back really honest, with a joy shining through. As though you have complete trust and no fear of your truth – how awesome.*

In this moment she's right – it is awesome. Of course beingness isn't what I feared. Life hasn't ground to a stagnant halt. I haven't dissolved into a puddle of apathy. Rather than a vacuum, not-doing is a state of being that exists within everything, the centre of stillness in any action. Just like the roos in the paddock – eating when hungry, resting when hot – vision unfolds from moment to moment. It's the motivation that shifts, from the fear of not being enough to one of fullness overflowing.

A piece of blue sky flutters down to land on a tuft of whiskey grass, clinging to it as it sways. I remember this one: it was a sweltering summer morning and I was waiting in the preschool carpark for Mum. As she fiddled to unstrap my baby sister, a butterfly as blue as my dress flew down to land on my arm. I didn't flinch or make a noise, only my eyes widening in surprise. So blue, and scalloped like curtains at the edges. No-one else saw it and I didn't tell. It was for me. A gift, a secret. I held it close to me all day, that feeling of butterfly on my skin. And now it visits again, for a few seconds, letting go on the updraft and soon swallowed again by the sky.

*

I jog back to my shelter as the clouds burst open again. From a distance I probably look naked, the top made of deer hide almost as tanned as my own, and just as smoky. I'm acutely aware of it against me as I run, that and the whiskey grass drying on my chest.

The hand-drill offers me a welcome coal. The bundle is taking a bit more encouragement, moisture pouring out in plumes of smoke. I squat to nurture it. A green branch lies close to the door of my shelter, snapped in two like a broken bone. The eucalyptus oil is pungent in my nose. I can smell more rain coming too. It won't be long, ten minutes perhaps. And it won't be too much longer before the summer rains wash me out of here for good. I won't get to see the branch wither and dry, becoming kindling. The wind gusts in and I cradle the bundle to me, lavishing it with a deep breath. The coal draws more of the tinder to it, glowing fat and full.

Cupping the bundle with both hands, I tip my head back and pull it back and forth near my lips, my strong breaths spreading heat fast. The flames are timid in the humidity and I keep blowing until the kindling catches.

I sit back to watch it grow.

Stay, fire coos. *We have such little time left together, stay here and let me warm you today.*

Another rainy afternoon in my shelter. There can't be many left. I wonder if I would tire of them. I move my hand over the fire, as if wanting to stroke it. I remember back to when I first arrived, feeling like I was intruding on the land, apologetic for my presence. Now I think the land might miss me when I'm gone. Who else is going to appreciate the efforts of the latest pea to flower, to gape in awe at the intricacy of a nest? Who else is going to offer up a fire in thanks?

Settling into my couch, I pick up my latest project – a bag for my firesticks made from the hide of the wallaby. I smooth the leather out over my knee. It's only half as thick as the deer's, and yet unbreakably strong. Despite the smoking, it only stained to a weak tea-coloured tan. The bag looks a bit like a medieval boot, folded over at the top and fastened with a leather drawstring. It's all that's left of the wallaby now, except for what lives on in me. Drawing the sinew through my mouth, I thread the needle and begin looping it over a small bone, the drawstring fastener. I'm really going to look the part soon, cave-woman top and wallaby firestick bag.

Hanging the finished bag on my hat hook, I pull the string that holds a bundle of letters together, responses from my wise women, postmarked from around the world. I shuffle them like cards, enjoying the feel of the paper, the knowledge of the words they contain.

Guru Janey Pops has some difficult spiritual tasks for you, writes my friend Jane from Broken Hill.

Your presence is soon required in the pizza parlour – someone in the shop will be affected by your energy, and it will make them question their life.

Your presence is soon required in the cinema. The inspiration from the film will set you thinking about new ideas relevant to your work in the world. Get my drift? Jane quips in mock sternness. I giggle, imagining her wagging one finger at me.

Keep honouring the deep feminine voice within, Terry writes, having just returned from a week-long solo walk in the Snowy Mountains. *Bring her flowers, take her to the movies, let her lounge around in her jammies all morning, take her to galleries, to cafes, let her play and be joyful.*

Ruth's letter is typed in small font from a cafe in Sweden, where she has been studying bodywork. *Do not trust your mind when critical self-doubt is in the driving seat!* she implores. *We are seeking to bring the end of suffering, and this we can only do with kindness. This need not dumb us down or promote procrastination or complacency. On the contrary, loving acceptance helps us work with whatever is present so we can liberate ourselves more easily from what holds us back in life.* Enclosed is the Buddha's Eightfold Path for further reading.

I was surprised to receive the next letter, assuming that my friend Colleen was still in South America studying plants but she must have returned. *It's early here. I've been up since 2.30am baking cakes for a group of pollination ecologists,* she writes in a loosely looping print. *My journey has led me to understand that our whole life is the quest. Whether making biscuits, fasting, picking up kindling – all is sacred.*

It is our attitude that determines whether our life is full of suffering or happiness. If our quest in life is to be centred, clear and aligned to a purpose greater than self, then with conscious awareness we can bring the divine into mindful daily practices, however great or small. With this embodiment of spirit, all of life can become a prayer, full of life and love.

I unfold the next letter carefully, worried the handmade Indian paper that Emma wrote on, at the end of her three months in a Burmese Buddhist monastery, might tear.

You're right – it's been all about learning to "do" nothing! I struggled with that so much, coming to see just how strongly the habitually conditioned ego wants to "do". I constantly felt like I needed to push myself and that nothing I could do would be enough – which I discovered completely inhibits the possibility of really being in the moment. The most amazing thing about retreat for me was uncovering the layers of striving. Even when I thought I had learnt to see them and let go, they would appear on a more subtle level, sometimes requiring Sayadaw to point them out to me quite bluntly. One thing I have learnt more deeply this year is that the path is *the goal. I still have many doubts and fears, but trying to get to a point where all my problems are solved is really missing the point – there is no destination – just life giving us more grist for the mill, more opportunities to practise acceptance and awareness, and let go of expectations of how things should be.*

A Rumi poem falls out and onto the dust. Tonight it seems even more poignant. I pin it up on the runner next to Wild Woman.

Very little grows on jagged rock.
Be ground. Be crumbled.
So wild flowers will come up
Where you are.
You have been stony for too many years.
Try something different. Surrender.

7.

"How'dya do that?" I ask through clenched teeth, desperately trying to inch my way up the slippery stem of a bangalow. Nikki clambers up the palm next door as if her fingers were claws, resting in a squat just shy of the fronds.

"If you need a break, press the soles of your feet into the trunk and sit back on your ankles," she calls down.

I look up at her incredulously.

Rest? Every muscle is screaming just to maintain my hard-won two metres.

"Wrap your hands around the back of the trunk, straighten your arms, and use the tension to just kind of walk up."

"Easier said than done, spiderwoman," I say, moments before gravity wins out and I plop back into the mud. So much for the bush ninja. I think I'll stick to trees with branches.

Pulling the machete from her belt, Nikki begins to chop just below the first leaf sheath, our sacrificial palm struggling to survive amidst more dominant neighbours. I can't believe she can do that and stay up there. The leaf eventually falls with a *whoosh*. I move in for the groundwork, straddling it to machete off the head and separate the two-foot length of palm heart. Nik slides down next to me, graceful as Batman down his bat pole.

"Okay, now show me your foot glue," I joke.

"Don't forget I only just got hand-drill a few weeks ago," Nikki says, trying to make me feel better.

True, Nik *had* only just spun her first hand-drill coal mere weeks short of the end of the year, but that's only because of her neck injury. Hacking off the fronds to use in a shelter demonstration, Nikki gives the remains of the trunk a pat of thanks. I'm relieved that in a recent check on the paperbark I wounded at the start of the year, I found it alive and well.

"Come on," she says with a smile, shrugging it off. "This won't feed the masses."

The masses. Kate has just informed us that as part of the open-weekend proceedings, we each have thirty minutes to talk about what we've learnt from our individual focus areas of the last six months. What am I going to say? Should I tell them about the tracks that grief, fear and anger leave across the body? Explain the art of wandering? Talk about fire, betray all the secrets of our tumultuous relationship? Read out the inspired poems that I write by my fire at night? Try to find words for this wild woman I am learning to inhabit? Give them an interpretative dance demonstration? I have no idea. I'm apprehensive about the whole thing.

"Hey, look what I found," says Nikki, plucking the small green fruit of the styphelia, the ballerina flower that I've been watching the spinebills beak-deep in.

"Oh, wow, I didn't know you could eat them," I say, popping one in my mouth. "Yum."

"My latest discovery is this," I say, directing Nikki to a nondescript rainforest tree. "Native guava."

"Really?" she says, surprised. It's unusual for me to know a plant that Nikki doesn't. Breaking off a leaf, I crush it in my fingers and hold it to my nose, committing it to memory before the flowers fall.

"Where to next?" I ask, Nikki flicking through the bush-food book.

"Well, it says that tubers would have been the main carbohydrate around here."

"Not anymore," I say grimly. "Well, there are fringe lilies, but we're hardly going to dig those up."

"Same with orchids," Nik adds. "And if we knew how to prepare cycads we could make bread."

"I'd prefer not to poison everyone, if possible."

"Oh, well, we'll just have to do our best with what we do know," says Nikki optimistically.

By day's end, our cumulative knowledge turns out to be rather impressive.

Our baskets brim with forest berries: the last of the sour currants, the sweet bite of the red-bearded heath, devil's twine, molucca bramble, yellow wombat berries, lilly pillies, hordes of geebung and my favourite – dianella. Beach berries are also plentiful: native scaevola, the coastal bearded heath, and the bush-food strawberries of the pigface fruit. The salad basket overflows with native hibiscus leaves, warrigal greens, native sarsaparilla, lomandra tips, scrambling lily shoots, native spinach and nettle from the creek, and a collection of edible weeds: dandelion, dock, wood sorrel, purslane, chickweed and plantain.

We collect bulrush rhizomes and stem bases to roast on the coals, a couple of tree-fern fiddleheads, as well as the macadamia and bunya nuts we were gifted. For a cordial, we plan to steep banksia and grevillea flowers picked while nectar-laden in the early morning.

"At least it's the best time of year for bush food," I say to Dan, who is sitting cross-legged next to me as I pound the red bead-like seeds of saw-sedge. "Here, go wild," I say, handing him wattle seed to grind.

"Birdseed breakfast?" Dan asks, teasing, even though he knows I plan to mix it with flour for ash cakes.

"You sound like Shaun," I smile back. I heard from Kate last week that Shaun had left the army. He should be here.

"Hey, taste this," Dan says, getting up to fetch me a roasted kurrajong seed from the sack of pods he collected from the trees in the Bunnings carpark.

"Now *that* is good bush tucker," I say. There are upsides to Dan's love of town. "Hey, we could make warrigal-green kurrajong pesto!" I say excitedly.

"Okay, your turn to be a guinea pig," I add, handing him the pandanus seed that took about half an hour to extract from its shell.

Chewing with his mouth open, Dan stands legs wide, in Crocodile Dundee pose. "Well, you can eat it, but it tastes like shit."

"Now you just need to pull out the baked-bean tin from behind your back," I laugh.

"Look what I've found," calls Nik, running towards us, unfurling her palm to reveal two ripe mauve roly-polies.

"Oh my God, I've been watching that vine ever since Mark raved about them," I say.

"Well, there's no point sharing these amongst fifty people," says Dan, with a mischievous grin.

Nik slices one into four pieces. I savour mine on my tongue. The flavour is a cross between blueberry and white grape, but much more subdued, like a delicately fragrant wine. No wonder we're all such sugar addicts. This is about the sweetest wild fruit I've encountered.

"I'm glad you're going to be here for this," I say to Dan, watching him grind the stone in circles.

"Yeah, well, why wouldn't I be?" he says with slight irritation. The grinding stops.

"Claire, I was never going to do it the same as you," he says, holding the rock in his upturned palms, as if deliberating on its weight. "It was big enough for me just getting out of the city. I got what I needed," he says, wiggling his tattooed foot. "In my own way."

Of course it was. Reaching out, I draw him into a tight hug.

"Thanks, Dan."

"What for?"

"For being you."

He looks back at me with one eyebrow raised, and a mocking shake of his head. I laugh and wipe the corner of my eye with the back of my hand.

*

The bush telegraph has been busy. Ute loads of visitors from the local farming community roll up, along with a photographer from *Australian Geographic*. I lead a rowdy group to my shelter.

Up front are Ted and May, our ninety-year-old neighbours, who moved to the area as newlyweds in their early twenties.

"So this is where all my grass has been goin'," Ted says, pointing his walking stick up at my roof. "If I knew you were that hard up, I'd a given youse some tin!" He grins, obviously impressed.

I smooth a seat on my swag for them to sit down on. One by one, the crowd hushes as they duck under my door, as if entering a church. The last in is a young guy in cowboy hat and boots. Stuffing his hands deep in his pockets, his mouth gapes as he stares up at the chimney. My firestick bag is passed around.

"Didja make this?" he asks.

I nod.

Outside, he approaches me. "Man, I've always wanted to do this. I thought you were a bunch of hippies but this is seriously cool."

A flush creeps into my cheeks. "Yeah, I guess so," I answer. It's just daily life now, and I'm always seeing ways it could have been better (I never did get around to more pottery). I'd forgotten that I have done exactly what I set out to do: I lived in the bush for a year – without matches!

"You could do it, too," I say lightly, as the young guy looks wistfully at my shelter, knowing as soon as I say it that there's plenty of reasons why he can't, or won't. While the few thousand dollars and the luxury of unattached time mightn't seem like much, it's more than most people have. And that's the easy part. Hardest is the belief that it's possible, that you can do the thing you've always wanted to do, the one thing that calls to you more than anything. The thing you'll only regret in its absence.

*

MY YEAR WITHOUT MATCHES

Mud is the grand leveller. All the able-bodied visitors are given a quick camouflage demo before being let loose on buckets of mud and clay and leaves. Divided into teams of six, they are given their stealth mission – to stalk the wild chocolate bar, unseen by other teams or scouts like me on the prowl. I'm amazed by how little encouragement is needed. With a brief instruction on sensory awareness, the teams sink and fade into the brush. I pretend not to notice as the first team belly-crawls from behind a tree towards where I protect the prize. From the corner of my eye, they look like a family of giant lizards, eyes bright beneath mud-encrusted eyebrows.

Ryan's mum and sister stand back, in a bit of a daze, part heat-induced, and part culture shock after leaving small-town middle America a couple of days ago. His mum sprays clouds of insect repellent around their heads. Despite their obvious discomfort, they maintain a buoyant cheeriness. I can see Ryan is a bit on edge, trying to marry the different parts of himself that have collided with meteorite suddenness. I'm glad only a few of my friends were spontaneous enough to turn up at late notice. Nikki's hordes are making up for it.

Sam has kidnapped Ryan's dad, and it's a different man who pulls up to the Gunyah a few hours later, waving a stiff hat out the ute window.

"Fell off the back of a truck," he says, looking decidedly pleased with himself as he helps unload a roo from the back.

"Way to go, Dad!" says Ryan.

"Thanks, son. Now you can show me a real Aussie barbie."

"You're on," says Ryan, grabbing a shovel to start digging a ground oven.

With the roo baking underground, Kate and Sam usher everyone together. I'm nervous, still having no idea what I'm going to talk about. I'm relieved when Ryan offers to go first.

"Well, it started with one bundle of grass, and ended three thousand later. End of story," says Ryan, pretending to get up and leave. A chuckle ripples through the audience. The round face of our local guide, Mark, appears in the back row. Ryan nods to him in acknowledgment.

"Yeah, it's ... ah," he laughs awkwardly, "it's been a bit of a big one, I guess you could say.

"I was planning on telling you about my shelter," he says, holding up his notes, "how I designed it, built it without power tools, what I learnt about heat and ticks and grass and primitive windows and tinea. But I'm not going to.

"I could instead tell you about how to tan a hide with brains, how to make fire in the rain and without a knife, how to skin a shark, trap a wallaby or spear a stingray, how it feels to walk blindfolded through a rainforest at night or get so absorbed in a trail of horse tracks that a day passes in what feels like an hour. But that would also be like telling you about the frame and not the painting." Ryan clears his throat, as the fire crackles.

"I come from a family of ranchers: my grandfather, great-grandfather," he says, glancing sideways to where his dad sits, arms folded.

"They all lived life in the open air, knew how to do things, you know, real things. I've always felt like I was letting the team down, not following in their footsteps. I think I came here to try and be that person ... prove myself, I guess.

"Truth is, most of the time I was beating myself up for not being that person, for wanting to just hang out, well ... often just with one person in particular," he says looking over at Nikki. Ryan's mother smiles and nods in the front.

"It took me most of the year to be okay with that. And to be okay with knowing that my passion is for yoga and meditation. And, really, to be okay with just being me." Ryan's voice cracks. He steals a look at his dad, whose hat is cocked low, obscuring his face.

The remaining three of us pick up where Ryan leaves off. These are not tales of heroism or grandeur, of skill mastery or amassing repositories of knowledge. They are not neat, pretty or sugared up, but gritty, raw and real. While the journeys we describe are different, the destination is the same. We speak of what we came searching for and what we were shown instead: the path to our hearts.

At first I'm worried that I'm rambling, but as my words spill out I can sense them taking shape, assembling themselves like paragraphs on a page, knitting together into a narrative. I feel the story lifting above me, merging with the communal pot of stories bubbling away on the fire, becoming part of the broth of everyone's story. That's why this is important, I realise. Kept to ourselves, a story is too fragile, liable to wither or blow away. The story is not truly lived until told. It's only through the telling that the story can mature, can ripen and claim a life larger than its own – a gift for others.

The crowd claps as the four of us gather with our arms around one another, an arm extended at either end in memory of Shaun and Chloe.

"Okay, enough talk. Time to eat!" Dan announces, everyone dispersing in a clatter of dinner preparations.

I watch as Ryan approaches his family, stopping a few feet short of where his dad stands, poker-faced and unmoving. Ryan steps closer. Suddenly his dad reaches out, drawing Ryan to him in a back-slapping man hug.

A cloud of lemon-myrtle scented steam rises, as Dan peels back the sweating paperbark and the bushels of green leaves from the ground oven. In the bottom of the pit, the skinless roo is curled like preserved remains. The flesh is deep pink, falling off the bone. The smell drips throughout camp. Nikki lays out the bush-food buffet, while I throw the chopped roots and stems of water lily in a wok on the fire with some garlic. Plates pile high with berries and leaves, shoots and roots; cups overflow with banksia cordial.

"Sure this isn't spiked?" grins Ted, looking around at the glowing faces.

The roo circulates on a paperbark platter, more than enough for everyone. When bellies are full, guitars, drums and percussion strike up around the fire.

I wander to the back of the Gunyah, where photos of the year are tacked onto cardboard. "Ten More Bundles Shaun" captions the bushy head poking out the top of the treehouse. I sniff a laugh.

There are our shelters in stages of building, Ryan parading in a deer-hide loincloth, Nikki doing the hula in a blady grass skirt, Chloe and Dan pulling faces, me biting into a snotty ball of wattle sap. Look at us all down at the waterhole in the first week. Gosh, that seems like a lifetime ago. Babes in the woods. We've definitely weathered since then, but not hardened. We're more like well-worn leather, creased, broken in. Perhaps we're like plants, flowering best after a hard season.

A wave of affection for my tribe washes over me. While solitude was something I needed, I couldn't have done it alone. In fact, it was only *because* of them that I was able to be alone in the way I wanted to. They were the safe container that allowed me to thrash around within. I could wander far from home because there was a home to wander back to, someone to hear the story and tend the cuts and bruises. Being alone was a choice I made day to day. It was the very existence of an alternative that gave me the freedom to keep diving deeper into it. The irony is exquisite. Tribe *is* sacred survival. Despite my sometimes wishing for different members, who else but this particular configuration would have shown up my judgments and blind spots in such neon brightness over and over? Who else would have accepted me back unconditionally? It was perfect, for all of us.

My blood family might not be here but another one is. I curl up within the campfire circle as the music plays on.

8.

can barely bring myself to pull on the same festy pair of
ripped cargo cut-offs, now stiff with dirt and mould. It hardly
matters. Ryan and Nikki are on a family holiday somewhere
between the Big Banana and the Big Prawn, and Dan has
moved to Byron. All gone. The teary goodbyes said and done. Just
me again. And ten thousand hungry mosquitoes.

I sit on the damp log outside my shelter. It's definitely changed
shape. The patch job that Dad and I did on the cracked sapling
has finally given way under the stress of weeks' worth of sodden
grass. The whole shelter stoops in a hunchback, and with every
storm its incontinence is worsening. Termites have invaded a
number of the runners and are fast eating their way through the
base of my clothes basket. I can feel entropy tugging hard on its
skirt hems, hardly bothering to wait until I'm gone before it runs
amok. And I won't be here to defend my shelter, to dry it out with
my smoke and keep it buoyant with my presence. I can't bear the
thought of leaving it, the stone hearth cold night after night. It'll
be like abandoning a child. If mould doesn't claim it, loneliness
soon will. I sigh and get up to straighten some of its storm-tousled
hair. There is a gracefulness to its aging, though, a quiet acceptance of the natural order of things, that it is right to reach for the
earth, to long for rest.

*A few more weeks, just keep those arms up for a few more weeks,
darling.* The shelter groans. *I know, I know, it's been a big year for
both of us.*

Yawning, I pick up a half-made basket, spin it around in my hands and toss it back down. My mind drifts to thoughts of cafes with friends, movies, washing my hair. Catching a bus or browsing online. I yawn again, holding the binos up to watch a restless flycatcher, my interest tiring before my arms do. I'm the restless flycatcher around here, I think, waving off the mosquito hordes from my face. My God, I'm actually *bored*.

I just assumed I would stay three more weeks, until the twelve months is officially over, but now I'm not so sure. It feels like a long time. I've been walking loops around The Block like a lonely dog looking for its owner, past the tattered photos flapping at the back of the Gunyah, the broken macadamia shells in the communal firepit. Inside the empty shelters, I stand still and listen, thinking I hear voices coming down the trail. It's a ghost town. Everything has lost its sheen – the curtain has been drawn back, and I can see the mechanisms behind the magic. Even my sit spot is flat and lifeless, as if the land has shut up shop. Maybe our closing ceremony did exactly that. We did just tell our stories to a hundred people, join hands and send up our thanks in a giant group *whoosh*. Last night I dreamt of a petrol gauge on empty. I am tired. Maybe it is time to leave? But to where and to what? The questions hang in the humidity.

*

The day dawns blessedly cool. I've been dragging my swag outside at night to stargaze. It means I end up burning the candle at both ends, though. Venus had me up an hour or so before first light again this morning, shooting its arrow into my dream world and asking me those recurring questions – what will you do in this wild life? On this precious day?

Packing some lunch, I follow the creek south, leaving it to head uphill along the eastern saddle. By mid-afternoon I stand atop a rock platform, looking out to where the sea glimmers in the distance. Skirting along its edge is a long black snake in constant motion – the highway linking the country's north to south. The speed of the cars shocks me. That will be me soon. It won't be long until I'm no longer up here, traversing the ridges barefoot, but down there in the fast lane. I track one red car as it darts in and out of the lanes, trying to get ahead.

I'm suddenly panicky. What if I forget this? If I never again take my shoes off in the rain? Forget how to spin a fire into being? Get so caught up in the traffic that I lose the feel of words and images that arise with a wide horizon and unmetered time?

I sit and nestle myself between rock and sky, as if anchoring myself here, etching my shape into the stone. As I lean my head against the granite, the shadows of the lone tree next to me flicker over my face. The pattern is familiar, five leaves fanning out from a single point. I look more closely. A brush box, the first I've seen all year! It was a field of fallen brush box that I first saw with Daniel, when I stood upon a tabletop stump and my world crumbled. Small cream buds dot the spindly twigs. It's almost unrecognisable from the rainforest giants I'm used to . It could have been that but instead has ended up here, clinging like a limpet to a rock. We both have. Right now, I could be anywhere in the world, and yet I choose to be here, listening to the rustle of leaves, the croak of the friarbird. In a blip, though, I will be gone. The highway life is reaching in for me. I feel like a caterpillar newly emerged from its cocoon, wings damp and folded, the patterns not yet visible.

A stand of old-men grasstrees below me sway their heads in the breeze. What these old fellas must have seen on thousands of afternoons just like this one, with camps lit up like fireflies along the river, bands of travellers making their way up the valley from the coast.

Further south, denuded farmland gives way to a forest pock-marked by logging coupes. In one, the tracks left by the bulldozer have created the outline of a tree, the central trunk the main trail in, the canopy sketched out by the to and fro of the machine as it hauled out the logs. A few warm tears roll down my cheeks. No wonder I bulldoze through my life trying to do so much, when so much is at stake. But that is just as unsustainable, a similar kind of violence to the one eating up the Earth.

Tears splash onto the rock, the lichen turning a deeper green. What can I do with this life, while precious, wild lives are being extinguished around me? How can I know what to do when there is so much to do?

I imagine myself back in the office, the falling trees heavy on my shoulders, the dull ache behind my eyes from staring at a computer screen. I can't go back to that. It's important work, but it's the wrong direction for me. But what, then?

Wind whistles through the needles of the grasstrees.

Hollow bones, the needles whisper. *Be hollow bones.*

Far below, the sun glints off an open bulge in the creek before drawing in sharply at an elbow bend. The bank is the bone, directive and strong, the river hollow within. Together they pulse the current downstream, expanding and contracting in an ongoing dialogue.

Hollow bones. Be hollow bones.

The river carries, receives. Grasping nothing, judging nothing. It accepts both the push and pull of the tides, the fullness of flood and the emptiness of drought.

"To live from the place of the feminine is to follow where the energy is flowing," Malcolm said. "Don't question why, just surrender to where it pulls you."

I've been hollowing out my bones, clearing out the channels so that I can be a river for life to flow through, so that I can move and be moved simultaneously, animated by the pulsing of feeling and instinct.

It's like walking through life blindfolded – tuning my ears into the quieter sounds, treading with the lightness of paws. Rather than walking to a destination, I will weave my way towards it, each thorny thicket and sandy path another texture to be felt and navigated through. My bearing will be set not by some idea but by visceral contact with the world, nudged forward by experience's wisdom, by sensation and, sometimes, the inexplicable impulse that I will know not to argue with. My slow pace will be of little consequence; there is nowhere to get to but where I am. I'll know that it's right by the leap in my heart and the willingness in my walk. I'll know I've arrived not by what it looks like, but by the feel of it underfoot.

Standing to straddle two boulders, I feel the straddle of these two worlds – one whose slow dance I have been learning, and the fast ride I am soon returning to. I have the urge to take a giant step off the ridge and be down there, cruising along the highway, the wind teasing back my hair. Do I need to leave, or can I somehow live in both? The image of myself with a foot in both worlds lands with a thud of rightness in my chest. A bridge! That's exactly what I want to do, be a bridge between worlds, bringing the city to the wilds and the wilds to the city. I don't know what that means yet. My feet will guide me. I can trust them, just as a migratory bird trusts its wings to carry it back across oceans to the same valley, the same tree.

I followed my feet here to the shifting light of the forest; to the deep, cold chasms of water, where the river loops back on itself like a ribbon; to the spaces between bare feet falling on dew laden trails.

I followed mine to this place of absence; to the stripped-back rawness of sinew and bone, feather and stone; to the smell of sticks rubbing together moments before combustion; to the swelling of bark, the ripening of berry; to the softening scrape of my thumbnail down the backbone of a reed; to the awareness of blue flame leaching to white.

I followed mine to this nondescript ridge, to the company of this small tree. There is so much to do but it starts here, with this simple exchange of breath, this moment-to-moment offering of life to one another.

I reach out and pick a leaf, crush it between my fingers, and breathe it in, a long slow breath. It starts here with this, bearing witness to both the scars below and the humble beauty of this tree pregnant with flower. Breathing it in and breathing it out. Breathing and being breathed. We can't think our way out of this mess, we need to feel our way. Facts and figures won't move us, only hearts in love with this world will. Rewilding of our world needs be simultaneous with the rewilding of our hearts.

There is so much to do, but right now this is enough. The next step will come, will fill my hollow bones and urge me on, so long as I keep listening, keep one eye out for her tracks and an ear pricked for her song. So long as I continue to feel the beating of the wild heart within.

EPILOGUE

'm sitting inside a bustling cafe, my hair still wet from an early morning ocean dip. A steaming pot of chai arrives and I wrap my hands around it while the laptop boots up. It's easy to take for granted now; three and a half years have passed since I had to rub sticks together to earn my morning cuppa.

I was ready to leave by the end – craving human culture, flyscreens and occasions to wear a dress. Still, I found it surprisingly hard to return. I tried living in inner-city Sydney – impossible; I could hardly sleep for the stimulation overload. I lived for a time in a cabin on the outskirts of a small creative rural village. It was beautiful, but disconnection of another kind. There's been an underlying sense of dislocation wherever I am, as if I've been uprooted from my home country. Currently a beach house with friends in Newcastle seems to be striking a happy medium, the ocean's wide horizon nearby, a bush reserve not too much further, with cafes and yoga studios in between.

Last night I lay on a picnic rug in the backyard, staring up at the few visible stars. My family laughs at me when I unroll my swag on the floor next to the guest beds when I visit. I sleep better closer to the ground, I tell them, and it's true. I haven't got used to four walls. They continue to feel claustrophobic, blinkering me from the ever-changing world outside. Sometimes I imagine the walls vanishing, the neighbours looking around at each other from their couches for the first time, gathering together to build a circle of shelters, to cook over a fire at night and tell stories. How much more fun we'd have. How we'd come alive.

The Blady Bunch quickly scattered to the directions. I miss them, even wishing sometimes for the sound of Dan's van blaring Kylie Minogue up my driveway. Nikki flits between various bush properties in the Hunter Valley and runs bushcraft courses. Chloe still lives with Niko on the mid-north coast and is almost a psychologist. Ryan followed his long-held dream of living for a year in a Zen monastery in Upstate New York. He now lives in New York City and can be found riding his bike across the Brooklyn Bridge at dawn and dusk on his way to a Zen temple. Dan is homesteading in the Byron hills and has started his own gardening and landscape business. Shaun was shepherding tourists on horse rides for a while in the Victorian Snowies and up in the Daintree, and is now in Sydney, cashing up before he works out where he'll go next. We are generally all better friends than we were during the year – well, except for Nikki and Ryan, who aren't on speaking terms.

I have missed The Block even more, especially in that first year afterwards. The feeling would at times sweep over me strong as the ache of a lost lover. I missed my shelter, my fires, my sit spot, my birds, the silence. It felt wrong not to know whether or not the powerful owl still haunted the lowlands, the platypus the river. It was another layer of getting to know it; by what I yearned for, what memory revealed to me in thousands of snapshots throughout the days – the wisps of smoke rising through my fingers as I held them above a fire, the flinty black tails of the baby drongos. They would be bringing up their own young now. The ache was bittersweet. It told me how much I had fallen in love. How much I belonged.

A year or so ago I returned to The Block. After the birth of their second child, Kate and Sam decided to hold off on any more programs. It had been empty since we left. I parked down at the bridge and walked up the main trail. It was eerily quiet, only the friarbirds rebelling against the stillness. Dan, Shaun and Nikki's shelters had been razed by bushfire. Chloe's had fallen down,

Ryan's was as solid as ever. I left mine until last, approaching the trail with trepidation.

Ducking under the banksia umbrella I could already see the space where once was my shelter. It was pancake flat, bar one stubborn sapling refusing to give in, a bent elbow trying desperately to hold itself up off the ground. The lean-to had fared a bit better, and I crawled in under the sagging and frayed roof. Shards of pottery lay half buried in the sand, a basket swinging lopsidedly from a kitchen rafter, memories so thick on the ground I found it difficult to walk without tripping. The whole site was saturated with the presence of that young woman, all her hopes and dreams and joys and struggles. It was all still there, the emotions snap-frozen in the grains of sand she walked upon, in the timber of the trees she lived under. I wasn't expecting this. It catapulted me right back there again, into the intensity, the ecstasy. My knees buckled and I reached for the sitting log.

I was suddenly struck by the magnitude of that year, by an overwhelming love for the girl who had brought herself out here, her passion, her dogged determination. What a beautiful, crazy thing to do. It was nothing less than an initiation, a threshold she created to cross over into her power as a true adult, as a Wild Woman, as an integral part of the Earth's community. And she did it. She did it a bit tough sometimes, but she did it. She loved it.

The bush year cracked me open, and the years since then have been a process of learning how to live the lessons while back in the land of the busy, how to live in the material world and yet stay connected to the spirit that moves through all things, which permeates life in the forest so viscerally.

The commitment I made at the end of the year to be a bridge between the wilds and the city started with words on a page, which (gradually, painstakingly) took the shape of a book. It was (in hindsight) the perfect way to keep me from forgetting, the backtracking over the story embedding it deeper, allowing it to expand and touch all the sides. The writing life triggered similar struggles: for being, surrender, and trust in a process of uncertain end. The letting-go muscles have stretched longer and wider.

These days I'm taking the poet Rilke's advice and learning to live the questions themselves, with his promise that one day I may grow into the answers.

People ask me how I'm different. Friends tell me I'm softer, more present. In some fundamental way I feel stronger, like the foundations under me are more solid. I sense more of the subtleties of my experience, as if seeing life through wide-angle vision. It's a perspective that relies on regular immersions in wild nature. When life threatens to suck me into the whirlpool of endless "doings", I feel myself grow thin and brittle. It takes conscious effort (and often some initial resistance) to turn and swim in the opposite direction. I have discovered it doesn't need weeks or days. A regular afternoon or even an hour in the bush is enough to pick up the conversation and plump up the feathers. I've started a new basket, a kangaroo hide is salted under the house, and although I'm out of form, my palms maintain a rough scaly patch reserved for hand-drill. I'm studying plants more intently and my binoculars are never far from reach. As these last words are being written I can hear the wilds calling me out for a longer visit. I'm already spreading out the maps, planning the next adventure.

My intention is to keep building bridges: writing, and guiding others on their wild journeys.

The fire is still burning. I'm going to keep tending the coals, keep fanning the flames.

ACKNOWLEDGMENTS

The writing of this book was immersion in another kind of solitary wilderness, one that I almost certainly would have lost myself in were it not for the generous and loving support of my friends and family. Sometimes the thought of being able to thank you all was enough to keep me going.

Arian Bloodwood: there from the start, there at the end and every step of the way. Over twelve campfires you listened to my tale and reflected back to me a narrative that I couldn't have seen myself. Your insight, wisdom and indefatigable belief and encouragement not just in the book but in me infuse every page. It simply would not have happened without you. I am deeply grateful for your friendship.

To the wild women of the Bellingen Valley for preventing me from mouldering away at my desk: Olivia and Jude for consistently feeding me love and sauerkraut and letting me sprawl on your floors; Tori, Zeah and the girls for reminding me for whom I wrote; and Sam, Emilie, Sharma, Thea, Emma and the playback crew. You've shown me how to live with mountains and rivers flowing in your veins.

To the Byron crew. What welcome serendipity to find David Roland, a kindred spirit, walking a parallel path to mine. It has been a blessing to negotiate together the bumpy road of memoir. Anneli Knight's unfailing and buoyant enthusiasm for my writing was a burst of warmth at just the right times, as was the camaraderie of my colleagues Willa and Ali. The Northern Rivers Writers' Centre is a remarkable resource for regional writers and certainly helped midwife this book. Both the residential mentoring program under the excellent mentorship of Marele Day and the Byron Bay Writers' Festival's "Pitch Perfect" competition were invaluable stepping stones. Nestled in the Byron hinterland, Laurel Cohn provided astute editorial assistance that helped me build strong structural bones and a clear narrative arc. Her support and encouragement extended far beyond the job description and were chicken soup for this writer's soul.

Another fine writer's resource, Varuna, the Writers' House, gave me a two-week residency in the Blue Mountains, allowing me to write brave and fierce amidst its solid walls.

To the friends who diligently waded through my early drafts – Susie Russell, Loosie Craig, Robert Gordon, Carol Perry, Emma Brindal, Caiyloirch Marques, Bobbi Allan and Dorin Hart – my heartfelt thanks for seeing the potential and urging me onwards.

To Beth Emily Hill, Sunni Boulton and Terry Gaechter, whose inboxes were revolving doors for my chapters and my churnings, many thanks for being fabulous cheerleaders, sharp readers and great friends.

I am blessed with a circle of friends too numerous to mention here. To all of you who journeyed with me I am ever grateful. The particular assistance and leg-ups offered by Daniel Beaver, Jane Elworthy, Suzanne Atherton, Simon Etherington, Jarra Hicks and Jess Allan are much appreciated. To my beloveds Emma Pittaway and Amie Illfield, thank you for helping me stand with some grace in the fire. I am so lucky to have such wise women walking beside me. Zoe, you redefine the meaning of unconditional support. I'm so proud of us! You helped get this book over the finish line with me intact. Enormous love.

My family has been there alongside me for every hard-won page. Mum, Dad and Liv, your unflagging support for me and my crazy projects never ceases to amaze me. You are the rock that this book is built on. We did this together. Nige, Nick, Mike,

Harriet, Leah, Dwayne and all the kiddies, thank you for being a wonderful familial nest to fly back to.

To the all crew at Black Inc: Jeanne Ryckmans for championing it from the beginning, Imogen Kandel and Elisabeth Young. To my fantastic editor, Nikola Lusk, for believing in the project and working tirelessly to make the book the best it could be, your guidance and insightful suggestions were the perfect fit for this book. Thank you for easing me through the final stages with such collaborative grace. Gratitude also to my agent, Gaby Naher, for being an ever enthusiastic ally, and to Anne Deveson for taking the time to consider my pages and share authorial wisdom over tea.

I am indebted to the wisdom of many teachers, some of whom I have had the good fortune to study with – Joanna Macy and Tom Brown Jr – and others whose work has deeply informed mine, including Bill Plotkin, Clarissa Pinkola Estés, Marion Woodman, Jon Young, Starhawk and Oriah Mountain Dreamer. Malcolm Ringwalt from the Earth-Heart Institute, my journey would not have run nearly as deep or wide without your visionary teachings and guidance. Many thanks. Vivian Revitt, thank you for seeing me and keeping me true to my muse. To Lou, the wildest and brightest heart I have ever known, I think you would have loved this book.

The year itself would not have been possible without the vision of Kate Rydge and Sam Robertson. May the ripples continue to flow from your generosity. Kate B and Carmel, you were fairy godmothers for us all that year. To all the instructors for your infectious passion and generous sharing of knowledge. To the Blady Bunch – my co-conspirators and warriors of the heart – I am blessed to have been able to share the adventure with every one of you. You truly are family. Thank you for giving this book your blessing. You all hold a book of that year inside you that I could not tell. They are your stories alone.

And finally, to the wild plants and animals who continue to be my greatest inspiration, and the indigenous people of this land, I offer my greetings and deepest gratitude. To all the "edgewalkers" and "bridgebuilders" who continue to plant green shoots amidst the concrete, I give my thanks and fall into step beside you.